Family Therapy

Complementary Frameworks of
Theory and Practice

Volume 2

Family Therapy

Complementary Frameworks of
Theory and Practice

Volume 2

edited by

Arnon Bentovim

Gill Gorell Barnes

Alan Cooklin

1982

published for

The Institute of Family Therapy (London)

43 New Cavendish St, London W1

by

ACADEMIC PRESS London Paris San Diego São Paulo Sydney Tokyo Toronto
GRUNE & STRATTON New York San Francisco

ACADEMIC PRESS INC. (LONDON) LTD.
24/28 Oval Road, London NW1 7DX

United States Edition published by
GRUNE & STRATTON INC.
111 Fifth Avenue, New York, New York, 10003

British Library Cataloguing in Publication Data

Family therapy.
Vol. 2
1. Family psychotherapy
I. Bentovim, A.   II. Gorell Barnes, G.
III. Cooklin, A.
616.89'156   RC488.5

ISBN (Academic Press) 0-12-790546-4
ISBN (Grune & Stratton) 0-8089-1480-4

Phototypeset in Great Britain by Dobbie Typesetting Service, Plymouth
Printed in Great Britain by T. J. Press (Padstow) Ltd.

Contributors

ARNON BENTOVIM *Department of Psychological Medicine, The Hospital for Sick Children, Department for Children and Parents, The Tavistock Clinic and The Institute of Family Therapy, London*

DORA BLACK *Edgware General Hospital and The Hospital for Sick Children and The Institute of Family Therapy, London*

TERRY BRUCE *St. Bartholomew's Hospital and The Institute of Family Therapy, London*

JOHN BYNG-HALL *Department for Children and Parents, The Tavistock Clinic and The Institute of Family Therapy, London*

DAVID CAMPBELL *Department for Children and Parents, The Tavistock Clinic, Uxbridge Child Guidance Clinic and The Institute of Family Therapy, London*

ALAN COOKLIN *Marlborough Hospital and The Institute of Family Therapy, London*

MICHAEL CROWE *Children's Department, Bethlem Royal and Maudsley Hospitals and The Institute of Family Therapy, London*

CHRISTOPHER DARE *Children's Department, Bethlem Royal and Maudsley Hospitals and The Institute of Family Therapy, London*

ANNE ELTON *Department of Psychological Medicine, The Hospital for Sick Children and The Institute of Family Therapy, London*

GILL GORELL BARNES *Department for Children and Parents, The Tavistock Clinic and The Institute of Family Therapy, London*

BRYAN LASK *Department of Psychological Medicine, The Hospital for Sick Children and The Institute of Family Therapy, London*

STUART LIEBERMAN *St. George's Hospital Medical School and The Institute of Family Therapy, London*

WINIFRED ROBERTS *Marlborough Hospital and The Institute of Family Therapy, London*

MARGARET ROBINSON *Chelsea College and The Institute of Family Therapy, London*

ROBIN SKYNNER *Institute of Psychiatry and The Institute of Family Therapy, London*

Acknowledgements

We would like to thank the many colleagues including secretaries and librarians from our institutions whose assistance has played such an important part in the writing and preparations of the contributions for this book. We would also like to thank Sylvia Donald and Linda Collins of the Institute of Family Therapy for their assistance in the final production.

Preface

The year 1982 sees seven years development of a professional association for Family Therapy in Britain (AFT), a flourishing journal, and signs of accelerating interest in the field. Practitioners, theories and practices abound. The aim of this book is to try and place some of these developments in context and to examine the relationship between some of these apparently diverse ideas and approaches. As editors, we have been privileged to have a ready-made group of authors who have shared some basic assumptions, and some common professional history, while representing specific points of view in their own right. This group is the Institute of Family Therapy (London), and the authors are its members. We hope this work will provide a useful milestone in the rapid development of the field, as its production has been in the development of the Institute.

The group was conceived in 1973 when Robin Skynner convened teachers to run the one year Family and Marital course under the auspices of the Institute of Group Analysis. Thus began what he has called an "open systems" method of training in Family Therapy. One of its great strengths was that it brought together teachers of different disciplines and orientations who were prepared to unlearn some aspects of their old allegiances — sufficient to create something new as a group. After three years, the group of teachers felt that there was a need for a setting from which the work could develop further, and in 1977 the Institute of Family Therapy was established with the aims of furthering teaching, practice and research in Family Therapy. The open systems nature of Robin Skynner's original concept has in many respects continued. This is reflected both in the variety of disciplines, settings and theoretical views held by the contributors to these volumes, as well as the fact that they hang together as a whole.

Our title indicates that we are concerned with a variety of complementary frameworks to view the theory and practice of Family Therapy. We are not concerned with the exposition of one "right" way of conceptualizing the work or practicing it, but of trying to present a set of usable frameworks for practitioners. A set of models has been described which are helpful in thinking about families, in the practice of Family Therapy, and in particular for the application of such notions to the wide variety of settings where Family Therapy can be, and is, now practised. Throughout, the emphasis is on the encounter between the therapist and the family, and we have asked contributors where possible to bring their own experience, their own case material and, if possible, the blow-by-blow account of work which can convey more than description alone. Thus we have aimed the work at the beginning practitioner who needs a compass on a new and uncharted sea, as well as the experienced old salts who have taken and steered a particular course. We hope that the work will provide a helpful background for the development of the ideas of this latter group.

The Contents contains a complete list of chapters in Volume 1.

Beginning Volume II, Part IV is concerned with a framework which is present implicitly through those already described. This book might have been called "Overlapping Frameworks of Theory and Practice" rather than "Complementary", and inevitably similar phenomena occur and are described from a variety of different points of view. The "Context of the Life-Cycle of the Family", is an essential one for the therapist to grasp if he is able to work with families at many different stages of their own development. We start with Stuart Lieberman's chapter on "Forging a Marital Bond" (Chapter 14). He examines the elements of the marital bond, such as their physical components, issues of dependence and independence, self-esteem and companionship, and the way that these come together in marital choice and can give rise to marital disharmony. He describes the way in which marital choice becomes so much a part of the systems-over-time framework of the family's, and the way that such issues show themselves through marital dysfunction, and has to be met therapeutically.

Anne Elton in the next chapter, Chapter 15, describes "The Birth of the Baby and the Pre-School Years". She outlines the complementary psychoanalytic and systems interactional frames for viewing this period of development both for the infant, pre-school child and the family. She describes factors which impair bonding and the tasks which the families have to negotiate for successful development during this period, such as the transition from the dyad of the marital pair to the triad of mother, father and infant. She describes the way that such transitions are affected through relationships with grandparents, the growth of parenting roles, and what facilitates or prevents such moves. The issue of control, particularly as it relates to working with families with very young children, is highlighted in this chapter.

In Chapter 16, we move to what Christopher Dare has called "Family Systems and the School-Going Child". He regards this phase as a key to understanding the growing complexity of the family unit, through transactions that the individual child has with the world outside the family, and then returns to the family to enrich and enlarge its structure. This framework is then used to examine the pattern of disorders during this phase, and some modes of therapy and securing that are needed to strengthen generational boundaries and develop co-parenting skills.

David Campbell (Chapter 17) examines adolescence as a phenomenon in its own right and "Adolescence as a 'Family' Process". As Anne Elton was in relation to the pre-school years, so he is concerned with the struggle for control and, in particular, how the early childhood structures need to be destroyed if the adolescent is to be able to make the move towards adult status. He examines the particular issues of Family Therapy with adolescent families, and takes two important frameworks for a closer look; what he describes as *persuasion*, an approach where the family system is directly led towards new patterns of behaviour, and the use of a *paradoxical approach* which neutralizes the family's systems resistance to change, thus freeing the creative potential of the system to find its own adaptive solutions. He describes the application of these ideas in a detailed case study, which further illustrates the theme of complementary frameworks presented in this book.

Christopher Dare examines the next stage of the life-cycle by focussing on

"The Empty Nest": families with older adolescents and models of Family Therapy (Chapter 18). He describes the biological bases for the detachment processes in families with older adolescents, and considers the growth of sexuality identity formation and family influences of loyalty and belonging which influence the speed of the process. He relates dysfunction and therapeutic interventions in this phase to the capacity of the parental couple to manage the transition to the "empty nest" without needing a third person in it.

The final stage of the life-cycle is completed in John Byng-Hall's chapter (Chapter 19), when he describes "Family Therapy and a concern with Grandparents, Other Relatives . . ." (he also extends these considerations to "Pets"). He shows the way in which such family members can be seen as of major importance often after the initial work is done, and brings up the issues of how and when family members outside the nuclear family should be considered as part of the therapeutic work. He re-introduces the notion that to complete Family Therapy, the adults in the family have to meet and work through some of the conflicts which are still held with grandparents and members of the extended family. He describes pets as sources of information, and the way that family reunions and visiting families can play an important part in Family Therapy. He stresses the necessity of linking up experiences which such events can achieve.

Although Part V is also concerned with the life-cycle, it is considered from the point of view of intrusions and disruptions in the natural process arising from major life-events. In Chapter 20 by Stuart Lieberman and Dora Black, loss, mourning and grief are explored. They consider both individual and family responses to loss and the particular patterns within the system which can occur in response to such events. They focus on both adult and children's conceptions of loss, how the children conceive of and handle loss of parents, and how parents conceive of and handle loss of children. Although this chapter takes loss through death as its main focus, it applies similar thinking to loss through separations, divorce or abandonment of children.

In Chapter 21, Margaret Robinson follows this theme in the context of "Reconstituted Families, their implications for the Family Therapist". She points out that currently, one in ten children are brought up in single-parent families, and that the proportion of reconstituted families will inevitably increase. She makes the point that this is not only due to divorce and remarriage, but is also stimulated by the concern that children should grow up in families rather than institutions. Margaret Robinson categorizes reconstituted families: adoptive, fostering and step-families. She applies the systems framework specifically to the reconstituted family, whereas implicitly in some other chapters, the framework for the systems model seems to be based on the intact family. She also reiterates the importance of the framework of the social context and the interface between the family and the professional. The *rights* of children and the way that social agencies do or do not become involved in various situations is examined here. She further examines the issues of loss in other situations including adoptive and foster families, as well as stepfamilies, particularly in relation to the child's capacity for attachment and re-attachment.

She points to some nodal times when intervention using a family frame can be applied to a variety of situations where this would not at first seem appropriate, such as in adoption, fostering and access, as well as stepfamilies.

In Chapter 22, "Intrusions in the Life-Cycle", Dora Black describes the specific "Effects of Handicap on the Family" and the role of Family Therapy in working with such families. She describes some basic assumptions about handicap, the impact of the handicapped child on the family, society and the community. She describes the particular crisis periods and, again, emphasizing the relationship between the natural crisis in the life of the family and artificial intrusions. She describes specific handicap problems, and finally illustrates the Family Therapy approach to all these issues through a number of case examples.

Bryan Lask, in the final chapter of this part (Chapter 23), examines the "Impact of Physical Illness in the Family", both organic illness *per se* and psychosomatic disorders. Psychosomatic disorders have played an important part in the development of Family Therapy techniques, especially from the refining of the structural approach by Minuchin and others in Philadelphia. Bryan Lask not only attends to these issues, but also what Weakland has called "Family Somatics: A Neglected Edge". He feels that the relationship between a family interactional viewpoint and illness and disease has received some consideration, but deserves a far more extensive examination and research effort. He reviews the literature on interactional research and object loss in physical and psychosomatic illness, and in particular the relationship of marital and family interaction to the manifestations and attitudes to illness. He critically reviews Minuchin's approaches to psychosomatic problems, and describes a variety of other frameworks. He is also concerned with the effectiveness of intervention, and describes his own conceptual model and framework for viewing the interaction between illness and the family.

The final part of the book is concerned with the "Settings in which Family Therapy is Practised". Each setting has its own particular set of problems, and requires a different set of principles. Bryan Lask continues the theme of physical illness in the family by examining the "Practice of Family Therapy in Paediatric Settings". He stresses the value of multidisciplinary work and the complementary roles of the paediatric team and the Family Therapy team. He describes principles which facilitate a Family Therapy approach, such as the "bridging", and use of the paediatric/family therapist/co-therapy team. He lists indications for Family Therapy, and examines the pitfalls of Family Therapy in paediatric settings as well as the advantages. The themes are illustrated with a detailed case study.

In Chapter 25, Dora Black looks at the issues of "Practising Family Therapy in Child Guidance Clinics". Child guidance has been one of the settings in which Family Therapy has flourished most in the United Kingdom. She describes the patterns of organizations of child guidance, the child guidance team and its work, and the way that a Family Therapy practice can revolutionize the work to meet the needs of the community more effectively. She challenges Haley's classic paper which showed why Family Therapy should not be practised in child guidance. She critically examines the advantages and disadvantages of work in that setting, and considers indications and contra-indications.

Terry Bruce, in Chapter 26, describes the unique experience of "Introducing Family Work to a 'Secure' Unit". This unit is designed to contain some of the most uncontainable and disturbed children between 13 and 19. They are admitted from a variety of other institutions, usually because of severe violence. Through a number of moving case examples, he demonstrates how focussing on connecting the "here-and-now" behaviour of an individual with the major disruptions and painful events of the family over time a different pattern of behaviour can emerge from the child, providing that he is being satisfactorily parented in a new "family" in the unit itself. In the course of this work, he uses structured meetings between child and family, geneograms to fill in the missing links. He examines the important issue of the way in which staff can themselves feel, and can be treated as if they were the custodial parent in a divorce, while the actual parent feels like the rejected spouse with very limited access, but demands a loyalty which expects disruptive behaviour. Terry Bruce describes the gradual re-editing of past events so that the young person is free to use his new "family" to be able to both grow and move into the world.

In Chapter 27, Stuart Lieberman and Alan Cooklin have touched on a number of the salient issues which have to be faced when "Family Therapy is introduced into General Psychiatric Practice". They introduce the framework of the inter-actional research on schizophrenics and their families, which although so far has remained limited in terms of application, has been seminal in the generation of many of the ideas which are found throughout this book. They then consider the implications for institutions if such notions were applied more widely.

The final chapter in Volume 2 (Chapter 28) by Arnon Bentovim describes a "Family Therapy Approach to Making Decisions in Child Care Cases". This is an important and often neglected area of work, and can play an important part in preventing the need for admission to special secure units of the kind described by Terry Bruce. There are 120 000 children in Local Authority care, 50 000 being there for three years or more, and three out of four being in care until 18. Arnon Bentovim argues that a vigorous assessment needs to be made of the family's capacity to provide the child with a sufficiently parental context. That assessment needs to include the possibility of making the painful decision that separation is necessary, and a "new family" needs to be found. He describes two complementary frameworks within which this assessment is made; the child's need for secure continuing parenting from whatever source, and the need for a family with a continuity of history and a patterning of interaction which gives meaning to the events that have been experienced. He describes specific ways to assess "parenting skills" and infant and child responses to facilitate decision making. He finally illustrates the multiple levels in terms of child, family and social context that have to be considered if necessary changes are to occur for that child to live in a family in which he can thrive.

Although many frameworks are described in this volume as well as in Volume 1 (Chapters 1–14) including theoretical frameworks for viewing healthy and unhealthy families, frameworks of practical techniques and procedures to work with, engage and motivate families to work, frameworks of the family as having a history reflected in its life-cycle, and frameworks for considering intrusions in this cycle, there will inevitably be omissions and repetitions. Our aim has *not* been to present two totally comprehensive volumes, but to weave together some common threads which have originated in and been applied to different contexts. We hope, therefore, that the frameworks described in these volumes and the way in which they can be seen to be integrated into a set of operational notions from which specific actions can follow, will help the practitioner to think about the frameworks with which he or she finds himself or herself working. He may be able to identify through the therapists who have written chapters in this book and get some ideas about settings where he has to find his own way because none have trodden in that direction before.

London   Arnon Bentovim
March 1982   Gill Gorell Barnes
                                                                   Alan Cooklin

Contents of Volume 2

xiii

PART VI—FAMILY THERAPY AND THE SETTING

Contents of Volume 1

Part IV

Context of the Life-Cycle

Chapter 14

Forging a Marital Bond

S. Lieberman

I. INTRODUCTION

In this chapter I hope to provide an understanding of the way which marital choice is made, and the subsequent work required by the two people who come together to forge a marital bond. Many complex strands of conscious and unconscious choice govern the selection of marriage partner, and I have focussed here on the less conscious aspects of choice as they are influenced by both internal and familial factors.

Dick (1967) working from object-relations theory, developed an integrated and a general view of marital choice and pathology based on concepts of ego development. Dick's theoretical model for a complete marriage was one in which a "full and undisturbed flow of two-way communication between the conscious and unconscious parts of two people" was possible. Each partner was able to identify with and tolerate the regressive or infantile needs of the other when necessary providing powerful and perpetually satisfying marital bonds. He describes the collusive marriage as one in which mutual idealization contains the ambivalence of the partners, an ambivalence based on the conflict between conscious expectations and deeper needs. Scapegoating and projective identification are the mechanisms through which ego-splitting can operate to destroy the shared marital world and idealization of the partners, fracturing the marital bond.

II. COMPONENTS OF THE MARITAL BOND

Marital bonds are created out of the individual needs of each spouse, and the transgenerational influences which are brought into play. A marital relationship has unique properties of its own, above and beyond the characteristics of the individuals who make up that relationship. But the forging of that bond which creates the relationship must take individual characteristics into account.

As individuals develop so do needs, which create pressures seeking fulfilment in a long-lasting relationship with a member of the opposite sex. Skynner (1976) emphasizes that

> normal healthy development is characterised by a progressive capacity to relinquish the original relationship of egocentricity, total dependency and expectation of gratification without returns in favour of a more mutual relationship.

The impetus to pair is a result of the body's sexual and physical development coupled with an increasing struggle on the part of the adolescent to

seek gratification of his or her needs outside the familiar parental relationships.

A.   Physical Components

Physical needs of a sexual and non-sexual nature are part of this drive to find a
partner. Although the division is to some extent artificial, non-sexual physical
contact has been shown to be a vital need arising in infancy. Bowlby (1971) has
argued the evidence for the importance of attachment behaviour, increasing our
awareness of this essential aspect of human life. The physical need for contact
diminishes in urgency throughout early childhood into adolescence and
adulthood, but remains present as a distinct element in its own right. Cuddling,
grooming, touching, hugging, holding hands and other forms of physical
conduct including the social kiss are all part of the need we feel to be in actual
physical contact with another person. As in any other trait, there is a great deal of
individual variation. In the early pairing of pre-adolescents and adolescents, non-
sexual cuddling, kissing, touching and holding are common. Physical contact, to
be felt and feel others, to cuddle and groom, underlie the initial urge to seek out
the solace of a companion (who is socially acceptable). Passionate petting, genital
foreplay and sexual intercourse occur later, given impetus by the sexual feelings
brought on by physical sexual development. The initial gratification of non-
sexual physical contact leads perceptibly to the arousal of sexual feelings. These
needs are the biological substrate upon which the psychological needs come into
play.

B.   From Dependence Towards Independence

The dependence of infancy and childhood is replaced by adolescence with an
intense ambivalence towards the inner feelings of dependence. Wanting to be
cared for is felt as a threatening albeit pleasant regressive pull away from the
burgeoning creation of an independent identity. An individual's growth into
adulthood is marked by a progressive increase in independence. The original
helplessness of the infant, whose life depends on his or her caretakers, must alter
with time into the competence and capacity to become a parent. This transformation is exacting emotionally and psychologically, and it reaches a peak in
adolescence and early adulthood. However the need to be cared for remains as an
integral part of us all, and one feature of the attraction of a marital relationship is
the fulfilment of this individual need in an adult form.

   The failure of an individual to achieve a minimal level of emotional independence prior to marriage, however, is stated to be a leading cause of marital
breakdown (Dominian, 1968). Intense emotional dependence in an individual
creates within them the need to find a person to prevent their dread of loneliness,
and to take responsibility for them. If in turn they are unable to give reciprocal
support, such marriages are unlikely to last. Emotional dependence may be
hidden beneath a facade of competence which is initially difficult to unmask, a
sort of pseudo self or false self (Bowen, 1966; Winnicott, 1965). In developing a

psychoanalytic framework for a systemic approach to family therapy, Cooklin (1979) believes that some individuals develop a depleted image of themselves which, in adolescence, seeks fulfilment in the prospect of reinstatement of lost relationships. The existence of such a relationship in one's spouse, though complementary at first, may auger ill for the relationship as trust leads to loosening of repression and the return of repressed parts of the self.

C. Deception and Self-esteem

Sullivan (1970) defined self-esteem as self-regard. Our regard for ourselves is incorporated into our identity during our growth from infancy. A child's ability to feel satisfied with his self-worth and contributions to family and community depends initially on the regard which his parents feel and show towards him. This regard is internalized, and becomes a bedrock of security for each of us. Its importance to the choice of a marital partner is highlighted by Satir (1967) who considers self-esteem a crucial concept. She feels that individuals with a low self-esteem remain at the stage prior to internalization in which self-worth is dependent upon what others think of them. Dependence on others for one's self-esteem cripples individuality and autonomy. If a marriage partner is chosen because that partner's interest and affection boosts one's own self-esteem, then the couple are storing up trouble for the future. This is especially true if both partners misread an initial self-confident façade and marry because of the boost to their esteem from the other.

Dominian (1968) expands this theme further. Bad feelings about one's self are traced to developmental stages in early life which have left an individual with exaggerated feelings of inadequacy, hostility or destructiveness. A marital partner is chosen for their imagined ability to "make them good". There is an unconscious powerful expectation to remove bad feelings and replace missing childhood affection. Four patterns emerge. The first is the relentless hunt for a partner who will melt the bad feeling away. The second pattern is an abnormal selfish preoccupation in the context of a marital relationship. This pattern can be inverted when an individual copes with low self-esteem by entering upon a career of insatiable service to others. Finally, low self-esteem may result in the idealization of a parent so that the spouse is pursued only insofar as the attainment of that ideal is fantasized.

Since none of us can develop a perfect regard for ourselves, it is safe to assume that to some extent we all gain from the fact that another person could love us enough to agree to spend their life with us. The danger lies in the circumstance in which both partners possess a low self-esteem, each one being boosted by their partner's feelings. They will find it difficult during the coming years when a cooler, more realistic appraisal by their partners reduces the boost to their self-esteem.

D. Companionship

One individual need which has recently become more critical to a marriage is that of companionship. Recent marital trends have shown there is an increasing expectation that marital partners not only must fulfil their traditional roles as bread-winner or housewife, but that they provide companionship and like each other as friends (H.M.S.O., 1979). Skynner (1976) emphasizes that the partners in a marriage will be most fulfilled when they can provide the type of relationship in which they can grow emotionally and attain their separate identity, seeing a place for competition and mutual activities. Certainly, as potential spouses age, the initial impetus of sexual passion and compatibility gives way to a cooler, more considered look at the partner as a potential companion.

One final individual need involves the psychological requirement to perpetuate family line and identity. A growing awareness of self in adolescence brings recognition of human frailty, ageing and death as well as the regenerative potentials which are now in the adolescent's possession. Marriage is the beginning of a new family and new children who will carry on family lines and traditions.

III. MARITAL CHOICE

The choice of a marital partner is not a random occurrence. In western cultures where the choice is left to the primary participants in the relationship, many factors exist to narrow the field of marital choice. Social, religious, ethnic and geographic considerations form a background for the psychological and emotional factors. There is strong evidence (Roff, 1950) of the tendency for like to choose like in regard to social class, religion, ethnic and racial backgrounds. There is also a tendency for persons living in close geographic proximity to marry. Incest taboos, age and physical appearance also tend to limit the field of eligibility of spouse choice. But within this field, the choice is influenced by less tangible factors.

In discussing these intangible factors I wish to concentrate on familial influences. The process of moulding a child, which occurs from infancy through to puberty, incorporates a seminal model of marital relationships based on the child's parents. The intimate details of the interactions between parents, and to a lesser extent, grandparents, aunts and uncles and other extended family couples, provide early and lasting models for spouse choice and marital expectations. It is not surprising that individuals have consciously or unconsciously chosen spouses whose traits are similar to their parents or other close family members.

I define the parental image as those physical, personality or emotional traits which an individual consciously or unconsciously associates with a parent. Parental image influences marital choice in a variety of ways. Consciously, a choice may be made based on the parent of the opposite sex (as would be consistent with the resolution of the Oedipal complex). Alternatively, a spouse may be chosen because of their similarity to a parent of the same sex (as would be consistent with identification). The choice may be due to physical resemblance, i.e. "he looked just like my father's photographs when he was young". It could be based on temperamental similarities, i.e. "he went into the most terrible rages, the same as my dad", or the choice could be based on personality traits "she was always clean, neat and tidy and very houseproud, like my mother". Conversely, parental images may provide a standard against which an opposite choice is made, "he was nothing like my father", or "I made certain that she would be completely different from my mother in every way". This mechanism partly accounts for the choice of spouse from other races, cultures or religions. Finally, parental images may be mixed and incorporated in the conscious choice of a spouse who "looks a great deal like my mother's side of the family, but is temperamentally much more like my father".

So far I have limited discussion to the conscious factors involved in the choice of a spouse. But the previously mentioned factors are often unconscious influences at the time of pairing off. Unconscious factors take precedence because they motivate and influence choice without being open to discrimination and working through. For example, one woman chose her husband originally because "he and I liked the same things dancing, music we just got on well together". Years later she realized how much like her mother he was in personality.

Love at first sight or irresistible attraction originates in the unconscious matching of internally held constructs or images. A sufficiently strong and lasting attraction will provide enough motivation for marriage before conscious deliberation has tempered initial feelings and impressions. The whirlwind courtship and impulsive marriage are subject to unconscious motivations to a large extent. Most marriages are constructed out of a tangle of conscious and unconscious motivating forces.

IV. STUDIES OF MARITAL DISHARMONY

Marital disharmony and dissension have been a subject of therapeutic interest in the past decades as divorce and its aftermath have grown alarmingly (H.M.S.O., 1979); but there has also been an interest in its influences on the causes and effects of mental illness. Many psychiatric studies have examined populations of mentally ill patients. Blacker (1958) surveyed 8000 married mental patients and found that the incidence of broken marriages was the same as occurred in the general population. But it was noted that personality disorders were three times as common among broken marriages as were psychiatric states. Serious conflict in marriages was found to be more common in the presence of personality disturbance in an early Marriage Council survey as well (Dominian, 1968). Kreitman (1962) found that the incidence of mental illness in the spouses of psychiatric patients was greater than that of the general population. His classic paper presented five hypotheses which might account for this finding:
(a) that both marital partners were subject to the same noxious environmental factor,
(b) that illness in one partner occurs as a reaction to breakdown of the other partner;
(c) that pathological interactions exert a cumulative detrimental effect leading to breakdown,

(d) that psychiatric treatment is facilitated for the second spouse when the first
   to fall ill is already in contact with psychiatric services, and
(e) that there is a pre-existing assortative mating of the mentally ill.

In a subsequent study Kreitman (1969), disproved the theory of assortative
mating and concluded that the neurotic couple are increasingly involved with
each other (being socially isolated). They then tend to acquire each other's
characteristics, including those which lead to psychiatric disturbance. He also
found that wives were more likely than husbands to reflect the illness of their
spouses. That pathological interactions or "contagion" operates in marriages
received further confirmation from Buck and Ladd (1965). They found that the
longer couples were married, the more likely that both partners in a marriage
were to become psychoneurotic. These studies of the spouses of mental patients
have been complemented by other studies which have examined marriages in the
general population. Pond et al. (1963) reporting on the marital adjustment and
history of parents of working class families found that family influences in
childhood played an important role in determining the occurrence of neurosis.
They conclude that the adult interactional relationship of marriage both reflects
the childhood experience of the couple and may also play an independent role in
the production of neurosis.

Using the Ryle Marital Patterns test, Ineichen (1976) studied a population of
normal couples and matched them with a population of young married couples
whose wives were considered neurotic by their General Practitioners. He found
that the neurotic wives and their husbands gave and received less affection than
the normal couple.

Other studies have examined the spouses of patients having specific diagnoses.
Marital tension was found to be the most significant causal factor in suicide
attempts (Greer et al., 1966), yet no clear personality factors have been found in
the spouses of those who attempt suicide which account for the suicidal attempts
(Bhagat, 1976). In their studies of the "Melancholy Marriage", Hooper et al.
(1977) examined the communicative and interactive spheres of depression. They
based some of their methods on general system theory and concluded that
interactional and communicative elements in the marriages of depressed patients
(both male and female), differed substantially from the interactions in some
normal marriages, especially in areas such as emotional expressivity and ability
to confront and disagree.

Both Fry (1962) and Hafner (1977) studying agoraphobia in women felt that
the symptoms of agoraphobia were in some instances a manifestation of a
pathological homeostasis between husbands and wives. One study looking
in detail at 33 multiproblem families (Tonge et al., 1975) reported that
50% of the children were reared in a situation of serious parental conflict.
Over half of the families had gross marital disharmony, and in these
families, children with serious psychiatric disorder were more frequent. They
state that although not much is known of the effects of being reared in a
parental battleground, in all probability the influence of such tension is as
important as overcrowding or poverty. In another study, Philp (1963) reported
that difficulties arose from the marital relationship in 57% of his problem

families. These conclusions have been confirmed by the work of Rutter *et al.* (1977).

Distilling the meaning from these studies, I conclude that they confirm the central importance of the marital bond to the well-being of the individuals involved, and the well-being of their families. A clinical study of 30 marital couples referred for family therapy (Lieberman and Hyde, 1980) lends further support to this view.

V.   A TRANSGENERATIONAL VIEW OF SPOUSE CHOICE

A.   General Principles

Parental image is one of several transgenerational determinants of marital choice. We are born and raised into families which are complicated systems composed of three or four generations of extended family members. Marital choice may just as easily be based on grandparental introjects or the incorporated image of a favourite uncle, aunt or cousin. A potential spouse might be attractive because he or she rekindles feelings which were once reserved for a deceased relative. Choice based on internalized representations of extended family are more often unconsciously determined than those based on parental images. For example, a man who met his future wife 2 days after his grandmother's funeral refused to see any connection between them. Only after pointing out the coincidental similarities of temperament, name and ethnic origin, was he able to connect his buried feelings at the time of meeting her with his feelings for his grandmother.

As in the above example, transgenerational influences can catalyse the timing of marital choice. Marriage occurs as part of the normal family life-cycle. It is a nodal event since it presages the birth of a new nuclear family with potential for expansion into a large extended family. Many marriages occur as part of the smooth transition from childhood to adulthood. But other marriages occur as a family replacement function: the need felt by individual family members to regain or recapture a previous relationship with a dead relative. This (mostly unconscious) triggering of marriage is a common occurrence and may be, but is not necessarily, pathological. The death of a parent, grandparent or other relative stimulates such feelings of grief and loss within a family and its individual members, that rather than suffer the full brunt of the grieving process, much of the feeling becomes reattached to another person. For example, one woman who had lost both her parents as a young teenager fled her home town 2 days after her favourite sister's funeral. She then flew abroad and on the day of her arrival, in a state of numbness and despair, met her future husband. She became calm, her desperation left her, and she failed to mourn her sister's death. Thus her new attachment had preempted the resolution of her loss, and possibly interfered with her capacity to manage future losses.

Transgenerational influences are most clearly displayed in the family collision. I refer here to the inevitable differences in the family cultures of the two individuals whose marriage is also a joining together of two extended kinship networks.

Marital choice is heavily influenced by parental and family desires and pressures. Although marriages often occur between individuals because their respective families are compatible, it is also common to find that family disapproval and opposition drive two people together in rebellion against their respective families. The first visit to the family home by a prospective bride or bridegroom highlights the family cultural differences. The results of such a visit may be pleasant and rewarding or humiliating and catastrophic. One woman from a working-class background was snubbed by her fiance's influential parents. The marriage had been partly motivated by his desperate efforts to escape from his parents' influence. Following the marriage however, she had made several serious suicide attempts. When the context of these attempts was examined, it could be seen that both their families had in fact completely ostracized them.

I refer more extensively to the family collision (Lieberman, 1980), when discussing its effect upon child-rearing practices. The major point I wish to make is that both the transgenerational influences which have become introjected within an individual and those still in existence in the immediate environment play a major part in the determination of marital choice.

Once a marital bond is begun, a choice is made, the marriage contract is entered into and the honeymoon ends, the marital couple are left alone with each other as they are, not as they were imagined to be. The forging of a strong and lasting marital bond involves a great deal of hard work within the emotional cauldron of the marital relationship. Much of the previous discussion details the internal and external levels of influence on marital choice.

The psychology of the choice therefore is based on fantasy, internalized and reprojected models, family replacement pressures and interactional dilemmas. Skynner (1976) discusses an interesting phasic process for the work which takes place during the forging of a marital bond. The "falling in love" stage is marked by admiration, enthusiasm, a sense of fulfilment, of belonging, of losing oneself as a part of something greater. During this stage, the real and imagined strengths of the spouse are borrowed but not yet internalized as part of oneself.

The second stage is marked by disappointment and a feeling of loss of the previously idealized attachment as the cold reality of the spouse's smelly feet, snoring in bed, body odours, angry outbursts or irritating laughter break through the fantasies of perfection. The final stage offers the autonomy of a new partnership in which the marital couple have incorporated within them those skills which their spouse has to offer and accepted their spouse's less admirable qualities. Throughout this process, a commitment to each other and trust in each other's commitment is a necessary pre-condition. If a spouse has been chosen partly because of unconscious factors much of the work involved in creating a lasting marriage involves acceptance by each spouse that their partner does not possess the projected imaginary qualities which went into making the original choice as well as accepting the traits which were originally ignored or denied.

Not only must adolescents and young adults transfer their love, energies, commitments and loyalties from their family of origin, i.e. their parents (their original attachments), but the couple must afterwards reconcile the differences between the transferred images and the reality of their new marital partnership. If pre-marriage expectations are too high and little psychological and emotional work is done to readjust to the new partnership, then disastrous matches will occur. Marital tension and disharmony result and the consequences can be tragic to the couple, their children and their extended families.

B.   An Illustrative Marital Case: The A's

(1)   Background
Mr and Mrs A met in London on a street corner in 1969. Mrs A had just flown in from Nebraska the day after her sister Ginny's funeral. She fell in love with Jim immediately and spent ten passionate days with him. He proposed to her but then found that one of his previous girlfriends was pregnant by him so that he felt obliged to marry her instead. Mrs A returned to the United States with a curious feeling of disbelief. Five years later, Mr A telephoned her from England and asked her to come over as he was divorcing his wife. She immediately dropped her life in Nebraska and set up home with him in England. When Mrs A became pregnant with her first child they decided to marry. After their child's birth they began to argue about his upbringing, sexual matters and money. They were referred for treatment after Mrs A threatened to leave with her son for Nebraska.

(2)   Analysis of Marital Choice
The following is an analysis based on information from sessions involving the construction of geneograms (see Fig. 1), from letters written to their parents and from their own understanding of the way in which their relationship was forged.

Mrs A fled Nebraska in 1969 following her elder sister's death. Her sister had been her only close family contact since the death of her mother and father in 1965 from cancer. Her sister was legally blind at the time of their parents' death so that they were separated and fostered into various homes. She idealized her relationship with Ginny, insisting that it was her one "perfect" relationship. The funeral so angered her because of the hypocrisy of her other relatives that she felt she had to escape. Jim replaced the "perfect" relationship she had had with Ginny. Jim's choice of Cathy was less straightforward. In 1969, his mother's mother had died. He became involved in a frenetic social life in an attempt to find a replacement for this "selfish but caring, kind and generous teacher". Cathy (a kind, generous teacher) came along at that time and their relationship instantly fulfilled their individual needs. His subsequent marriage to a woman he did not love was doomed to failure. Jim also had a distant relationship with his father which he felt a need to improve. His father related to him in a demanding way: "he was close and special but often away in my early life; he was not overtly warm or social. We argued a great deal". Part of Cathy's replacement function was to be like his father (see Fig. 2).

The replacement which each partner served for the other was present partly as a conscious recognition and partly unconscious. When Mrs A was asked why she

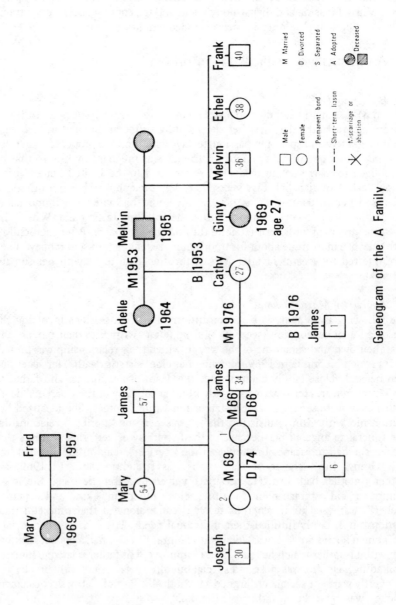

Geneogram of the A Family

Fig. 1

had chosen her husband she replied that it was love at first sight. Mr A emphatically agreed. She fell in love with his gentleness, awareness of feelings, caring and uninhibited tenderness. When asked about her relationship with Ginny, she described it as one of tenderness, caring, gentleness and awareness of inner feelings. Mr A chose her for her generosity, tenderness and caring, although he recognized at the same time that she was, on occasions, distant, cold and selfish.

Fig. 2

After the birth of their child, Mr A began to argue frequently with his wife. She became upset, anxious and saddened by his unexpected behaviour. She had chosen her husband as a person who seemed to fit naturally into her life. He was unaware that she would be upset by arguments. Both their marital choices were based on the unconscious recognition of similarities between their spouse and close relatives from their past. The need to work together to rear a child brought their differing cultural backgrounds into conflict.

Therapeutic work was aimed at dispelling the idealizations, working with the unresolved grief and allowing the couple to negotiate realistic compromises. The therapeutic tasks involved conjoint marital sessions of a reflective nature, task-setting, and individual forced mourning with Mrs A. Communication with extended family members for information and support helped to change relationships within the extended family.

The final outcome of this case remains to be evaluated, but it is illustrative of the need to thoroughly understand the marital sub-system. Scientific studies confirm the pivotal importance of the marital relationships to family life. A family therapist's work is not completed if the marital sub-system remains a mystery. Understanding of the marital sub-system requires awareness of the intrapsychic and environmental influences which led to spouse choice and the progress of the subsequent process of the marital relationship.

REFERENCES

Bhagat, M. (1976). The Spouses of Attempted Suicides: A Personality Study. *Brit. J. Psych.* **128**, 44-46.

Blacker, C. P. (1958). Disruption of Marriage. *Lancet*, **i**, 578.

Bowen, M. (1966). The Use of Family Therapy in Clinical Practice. *Comprehensive Psychiatry*, **7**, 345-374.

Bowlby, J. (1971). "Attachment", Penguin, Harmondsworth, Middx.

Buck, C. W. and Ladd, K. L. (1965). Psychoneurosis in Marital Partners. *Brit. J. Psych.* **3**, 587-590.

Cooklin, A. (1979). A Psychoanalytic Framework for a Systematic Approach to Family Therapy. *Journal of Family Therapy*, **1**, 153-167.

Dick, H. V.(1967). "Marital Tensions". Routledge and Kegan Paul, London.

Dominian, J. (1968). "Marital Breakdown", Penguin Books, London.

Fry, W. (1962). The Marital Context of an Anxiety Syndrome, *Family Process*, **1**, 245-252.

Greer, S., Gunn, J. and Keller, K. M. (1966). Aetiological Factors in Attempted Suicide. *British Medical Journal*, **ii**, 1352-1355.

H.M.S.O. (1979). "Marriage Matters".

Hafner, R. J. (1977). The Husbands of Agoraphobic Women: Assortative Mating or Pathogenic Interaction. *Brit. J. Psych.* **130**, p.233-239.

Hinchcliffe, M., Vaughan, P., Hooper, D. and Roberts, J. (1977). The Melancholy Marriage. *Brit. J. Med. Psychol.* **50**, 125-142.

Ineichen, B. (1976). Marriage and Neurosis in a Modern Residential Suburb. *Brit. J. Psych.*, **129**, 248-251.

Kreitman, N. (1962). Marital Disorder in Married Couples, *Brit. J. Psych.*, **108**, 438-446.

Kreitman, N. (1964). The Patient's Spouse. *Brit. J. Psych.* **110**, 159-170.

Lieberman, S. (1980). "Transgenerational Family Therapy", Croom Helm, London.

Lieberman, S. and Hyde, K. (1980). Interactions between Predisposition to Marital Conflict, Marital Dissatisfaction and Neurotic Symptoms (unpublished).

Philp, A. F. (1963). "Family Failure", Faber and Faber, London.

Pond, D. A., Ryle, A. and Hamilton, M. (1963). Marriage and Neurosis in a Working Class Population, *Brit. J. Psych.*, **109**, 592-598.

Roff, M. (1950). Interfamilial Resemblances in Personality Characteristics. *Journal of Psychology*, **30**, 199-227.

Rutter, M. (1977). Other family influences. *In* "Child Psychiatry: Modern Approaches", (M. Rutter and L. Herson, eds), Blackwell, Oxford.

Satir, V. (1967). "Conjoint Family Therapy", Science and Behaviour Books, Palo Alto, California.

Skynner, A. C. R. (1976). "One Flesh, Separate Persons", Constable, London.

Sullivan, H. S. (1970). "The Psychiatric Interview", Norton, New York.

Tonge, W., Jones, D. and Hillam, S. (1975). "Families without Hope", Headley Brothers, London.

Winnicott, D. (1965). "The Family and Individual Development", Tavistock, London.

Chapter 15

The Birth of a Baby and the Pre-School Years

A. Elton

I. INTRODUCTION

The period in a family life-cycle from the birth of the first child to the time when the youngest starts school spans on average eight years. While this is a relatively short proportion of any individual's life, it is emotionally a highly intense one for all the persons intimately involved. During this time, the family experiences continual rapid change and the sense of loss that must accompany change goes with it. The often heard comment made about small children: "How quickly they grow up!", reflects the constant reminder of ageing as well as loss of the pleasure and pain in the infant and toddler stages. Greater lack of inhibition of feelings and more general sharing seems to be a feature of this period. This may be a mirroring of the infant's intense and uninhibited expression of his feelings, or a real sharing in the never-ending wonder of birth and the growing of new personalities, or a combination of both. Certainly society appears to take a keener interest in forthcoming and new babies than in other stages of family life. Recently I observed a young man who had obviously moved from the area, come excitedly into a shop to tell of his new baby. The cashier congratulated him and asked about sex and size; the shopkeeper commiserated on broken nights; typical responses; but how often would parents go into a shop to tell of an older child's prowess?

While sharing of the anxiety and even of the fury aroused by small children can often be done socially, so can sharing of their curiosity, their often embarrassing outspokenness and comical confusions in sorting out their environment. Of course this precise openness and lack of inhibition may present one of the most difficult challenges of adaptation, to parents who are themselves naturally reticent. It may be a problem for all parents at times, either within the family or outside.

II. THEORETICAL APPROACHES TO CHILD DEVELOPMENT

Much has been written about the period of infancy and the pre-school years.

A. Psychoanalytic Approaches

Psychoanalytic writings have concentrated on individual personality development, and in particular on the emotional ways in which any individual learns to relate. From Freud onwards, the importance of early experience has been stressed with particular emphasis on the child-rearing practices of the parents, although Klein (1963) also refers to the importance of temperamental differences in the infants. Other analysts, like Erikson (1950) drew heavily on anthropological studies to point out the differences in personality type associated with varying patterns of child care. Bowlby (1969), while emphasizing the importance of a constant figure in order to facilitate the development of attachment and so of the capacity to relate, has also discussed attachment behaviour from a biological viewpoint. He postulates that attachment behaviour is designed to maintain proximity to the mother, and that this closeness provides safety from predators.

Winnicott (1956) has concentrated more on the quality of the mother-baby relationship. He describes what he calls "primary maternal preoccupation", a phenomenon occurring sometimes, although by no means always, during the first few weeks of an infant's life. He sees this as a state of enormously heightened sensitivity to the baby's feelings in such a way as to enable the mother to anticipate his needs. In Winnicott's opinion, the basic need of the infant is for some one person to be sensitive to his feelings enough in advance, to save him from fears of annihilation, and in so doing to give him a basis on which to build the idea of a person. After a few weeks, the infant is secure enough to begin to exist as a developing individual. The state of primary maternal preoccupation, of almost symbiotic absorption in the infant, ceases and the mother's psychic energy is again available for other interests. From this time on through the baby's growing up, his need is for a mother who not only satisfies wishes, but who also periodically "fails" him, and so provides a graduated experience of frustration. Winnicott's (1958) discussion of good enough mothering is of inestimable value since he emphasizes that there is enormous range and variation in what constitutes adequate, indeed good, parenting. Considered in family systems terms, primary maternal preoccupation breaches the generation boundary in a major way. Indeed the description is of a relationship which might seem enmeshed. But this is an enmeshment which is normal, transitory and above all, functional. Winnicott himself describes the state as a "normal" illness which a psychologically healthy mother can experience and recover from. The father has an important role in this, that of supporting his wife during it.

B.   Interaction Studies

More recently, much work has been done studying the determinants of infant development in an interactional context. The studies are based on detailed observations of the reciprocal moves of baby and care-giver (usually mother). They stress the initiative of the infant equally with that of the parent. The emphasis of these works is twofold. The first is to study bonding, the ways in which attachments are made and the emotional qualities of the relationships. Secondly, the infant's development in terms of acquisition of skills is followed.

In an effort to examine whether satisfactory bonding may be positively encouraged Kennell et al. (1972, 1975) have studied mother-child interaction from the moment of birth. They suggest that there are indications that the immediate post-partum period is of particular significance and that mothers, given their babies at this moment, may bond more closely and quickly. Macfarlane (1977) quotes evidence suggesting that if fathers were allowed greater participation not only during labour but also in the first few days after birth, they subsequently spent more time with their infants.

In discussing the comforting aspects of mothering, Dunn (1977) emphasized the importance of taking into account both the temperamental irritability of the baby (as indicated by his crying and fretfulness) and the response of the mother to it. What the baby will learn is how his mother comforts him (or perhaps fails to), and in this process he begins to develop some awareness of her as a person and some understanding of how to communicate with her. Mothers too are affected by their infants, and Dunn quotes research showing that very lively and communicative babies called out more responsiveness in their mothers.

Observations of the detailed interactional pattern, "the dance" between mother and child have been described by Stern (1977). This work examines the playing time enjoyed by the couple. Again this is seen as a most important factor both in the development of attachment and in the stimulation of skills, both motor and verbal. Stern comments on possible areas of difficulty. Lack of sensitivity to the infant's moves may lead to a frequent missing of cues and so to frustration. Alternatively, the mother may from anxiety or other reasons, intrude on the infant, demanding responses in a way that is overstimulating and controlling. For its part, the baby may be either very unresponsive and lethargic, or very actively demanding, and so disappoint or exhaust the parent. In all these studies, the reciprocity between infant and care-giver is seen as fundamental. The observations show how communication patterns as well as relationships are built up, or perhaps to be more exact, how the communication style is a function of each relationship the baby makes. Family therapists who work directly on communications will find themselves very much at home with such theories of development.

As mothers still do most of the early caretaking of infants in our society, the studies mentioned above have all concentrated on mother–infant relationships. However all have recognized the importance of father, both in direct relationship to the child and as supportive of the mother. Schaffer (1977) remarks on the number of specific attachment the infants he observed had formed. While consistency of attachment figures is generally recognized as very important, this does not mean exclusivity. While little work has been done yet on sibling attachments, these are obviously also very meaningful; Heinicke and Westheimer (1965) found that of the separated children whom they studied, those who were with siblings were less distressed. Stern (1977) comments on the way in which quite young children can respond to babies in the specific modes which are comfortable for babies. While one may regard this behaviour as instinctual, it also means that the family as a system has ways of integrating new members, although some of these will in themselves create stress (Dunn, 1977).

III. POSSIBLE IMPEDIMENTS TO SATISFACTORY BONDING

A. Separation Factors

Various factors can seriously impair the early bonding and the appropriate development of the child and so of relationships within the family. Most obviously actual separation of mother and infant at birth for a prolonged period can interfere. Such separations can occur either because of maternal illness, or more commonly because of the illness or prematurity of the baby. Spitz (1945) in his studies of hospitalized neonates pointed out their impoverished psychological development and their depressed mourning state. If a separation has occurred at this time, bonding may be more difficult to achieve once the baby is home. The parents may have distanced especially if they were aware that their baby might not live. Baldwin (1977) found that there was a significantly higher incidence of prematurity in abused children than in the population generally, although there are other serious problems in these children's families. In their study of brief separations Heinicke and Westheimer (1965) found that even with an older age group, the mothers as well as the children often seemed to withdraw from the relationship during the separation, and so found it harder to re-establish it subsequently.

B. Factors in Parents

Maternal or puerperal depression is of course another factor militating against satisfactory attachment. Depression is likely to dull sensitivity and empathic capacity. This can result in the infant being both uncontained in the emotional sense and inadequately stimulated by play. In such situations, the child lacks the opportunity to attach intensely enough with the result that he may then be unable to separate happily and appropriately. While fathers, or other family members could certainly fulfil the mothering role during a severe maternal illness, it seems that what is most common is a mild but chronic depression which does not incapacitate the mother but is most insidious in its effects. Richman's survey (1978) of three-year-olds showed that a very high proportion of their mothers were depressed. They were more likely to be so if the fathers were unsupportive, and if there were adverse material circumstances.

C. Factors in the Infant

Finally the infant may have specific attributes which make it more difficult for good bonding to take place. These may be temperamental characteristics such as high activity or passivity or very great irritability. More obviously, he may be born with some handicap: either with a sensory handicap such as blindness or deafness which obviously affects communication, or with others which may necessitate early or repeated hospitalizations and additionally may make it alarming or distressing for his parents to handle him.

IV. THE FAMILY'S TASK IN DEVELOPMENT

I would like to discuss this period in terms of the crisis of adaptation required along three paradigms:

A. Relationships between spouses,
B. New relationships with the extended family and
C. Parenting requirements and stresses.

Throughout, I will be writing of an indigenous British population and not of other ethnic groups.

A. Relationship between Spouses

(1) Dyads to Triads

From the time that a pregnancy is known, the relationship between the spouses begins to alter. In the case of a first child, the need for adaptation is likely to be greatest since the couple have to give up their intimate dyadic relationship to make space for this third person. During the pregnancy, the baby is not only physically present *in utero*, but also vividly occupies the parents' fantasies. Although this period can help the couple prepare for the necessary changes they are still essentially operating as a twosome who can give each other attention without interrupting demands from another family member. However as soon as the baby is born, the dyadic relationship immediately vanishes. The special privacy and intimacy of the marital relationship can seem intolerably threatened by the arrival of a third person whose existence demands sharing. The primary maternal preoccupation described by Winnicott may present a real challenge to the father whose role is to support his wife while unable really to share in it. Although he can have the compensations of also getting to know his baby, the new bond between mother and infant brings what Mahler (1954) describes as "homeostatic equilibrium" between this pair which is certainly very different from the previous spouse equilibrium. Both parents may fear that their own individual needs will not now be met because of the paramount demands of the baby.

(2) Necessary Adaptations

Considerable changes in everyday life style are necessary. These may comprehend not only major and anticipated adaptations such as the mother giving up outside work for a period, but also seemingly trivial differences. The whole fabric of daily living alters. Its pace has to be dependent on the infant's needs and his cycle. Parents are no longer free to plan the timing of their activities, either domestic chores or pleasures, according to their own individual adult capacity. How often does one hear parents of young babies say "I (we) can't seem to get anything done"? In particular parents may no longer be able to sleep as much as they need or are accustomed to. The physical exhaustion of caring for a tiny baby may not have been adequately anticipated by the couple before the birth. If this burden is borne mostly by one parent rather than shared, the other may not appreciate its weight. Both may feel neglected as a result. The adaptation demanded and need to follow the infant's pace rather than the adults', is of course greatest in the early months; but it is at this precise period that the couple are also having to learn to become a threesome.

Fortunately most couples surmount the crisis of adaptation called for by the arrival of a baby successfully. Their shared and individual pleasure in their infant and delight in getting to know him are more than adequate compensation for the sleepless nights, and the temporary foregoing of adult activities. However this stage is a very demanding one, and if the couple feel that their own needs cannot now be met, this can cause marital friction and dissatisfaction. If both spouses feel a lack of sympathetic support from the other, they may turn elsewhere to find it. Such moves may lead to further dissatisfaction and so a vicious spiral of distancing may occur.

(3) Case Example: Belinda's Family

An example of this occurred in Belinda's family. Belinda was the first child of a young couple. At the time of her birth, father had a job which took him away from home quite frequently. Belinda was ill as a small baby and Mother turned to her own parents for support. When Belinda was two, Mother brought her to the clinic complaining that she was clinging and overdependent. In discussion, it quickly emerged that mother was unable to allow her husband share in the parenting, saying that she did not trust him to manage Belinda as he had no experience of her, quite unlike maternal grandmother. This situation was obviously causing considerable marital pain, as well as affecting Belinda's behaviour.

It seemed clear that in this family, the wife's turning to her mother for support in her husband's absence had led to a distancing from him. This pattern had become so well established that even when the husband got a job which allowed him to be more at home, he was still not included in the parenting/child system, and so in fact he tended to increase his work hours. There was considerable rivalry between the husband and his mother-in-law, and this rivalry added to the original distancing between the spouses to further decrease their intimacy. Belinda's very over-close relationship with mother was probably originally a response to this decreased intimacy, but by the time of referral was also contributing to it.

The therapist suggested that the father regularly arranged an activity with his daughter which would necessitate them both leaving the mother. This could meet both the father's wish to have a closer relationship with his child and the mother's that "he should see how difficult Belinda could be for himself". Doing this it could bring them together as parents, a situation they had not truly experienced, and if this happened they might regain their marital closeness. Belinda could find an actively involved father. The father suggested taking Belinda out with him when he went to buy his daily paper. Mother expressed anxiety about this saying she was afraid that father would forget Belinda's existence and lose her. This comment was the turning point; the excuse was so patently ludicrous, the father so evidently caring that the mother, laughing ruefully at herself was forced to recognize something of what she was doing and shamed herself into allowing the change.

Natural jealousy can cause initial difficulty in sharing. Pincus and Dare (1978) instance some examples of this in their recent book, "Secrets in the Family". More pernicious, because more embedded in the system is the kind of jealousy and fear of being undermined that is seen in families where perverse triangles as described by Haley (1967) are the mode. This occurs when a spouse has been used secretly as ally by one of his parents against the other in a perverse cross-generational way. Incestuous families provide a strikingly concrete example of this kind of cross-generational coalition, but it is more commonly manifested in subtler ways, as part of a continuing warfare between the grandparents. The result is to make the individuals concerned feel both that they cannot have a strong positive identification with their parent of the same sex, and that this is the model of marriage they are familiar with. With the birth of his own child, the spouse may fear a repetition of the pattern. Rather than risk being the parent outside the coalition, he may ally with his child against his partner. So the cycle is repeated inevitably. As Haley (and Lieberman in Chapter 14) have shown, this kind of alliance is so powerful that it does get transmitted down the generations.

B.   Relationships between Spouses and the Family Task

(1) Typical Patterns

Marriages may be based on some kind of specific collusion such as a shared acting out of rebellion, or on a very complementary relationship such as nurse/patient. Dicks (1967), using object relations theory, discusses this kind of marriage most thoroughly in his book "Marital Tensions". The theory is that both partners as children, identified not only with the good parts of their parents, but also with the "bad". In order to maintain a relationship with the "good parent" (or object), the feelings relating to the "bad parent" had to be split off and repressed. To quote Dicks

> What is essential about this way of looking at mental life is that it is not feelings, not impulses as such, but affective relationships between self and some figure outside the self which are repressed.

This repression or splitting off means that feelings are not available to the self for the making of future relationships. In marrying, the spouses hope to rediscover lost aspects of their primary relationships, and so the marital relationship is idealized. However, parts of the repressed relationships are likely to return and challenge the idealization. Since each spouse cannot bear to acknowledge the existence of such repressed qualities in their relating, the partner has to be scape-goated and seen as carrying all those parts. It is not uncommon for such marriages to struggle to maintain the fiction that the marital relationship is ideal; in such situations a child then becomes the scapegoat, and symptom-bearer.

(2) Case Example: Stephen's Parents

An example of this kind of collusion was that of Stephen's parents. They presented with concerns about Stephen, a very intelligent 10-year-old who was failing academically at school and who was presenting considerable behaviour problems there and at home. Both parents criticized everything Stephen did, but also failed to set him any clear boundaries and let him do as he chose; if either parent did impose any demand, the other immediately undermined it. The therapist was able to show them this and help them parent Stephen more unitedly and effectively, at which point the underlying tensions in the marriage became much more open and painful. In the subsequent work with the marriage, the couple's undermining of each other continued; the overt system was that the wife was the hard-working and responsible one both at home and outside, whereas the husband was seen by both as rather irresponsible at home and while working, doing so in a job which allowed for considerable freedom of routine and demanded quite a lot of semi-social meetings. This situation provided a fruitful base for continual nagging and friction. When the therapist explored the families of origin of the couple, some striking similarities emerged. Both spouses felt absent to their parent of the opposite sex. Both had mothers who had seemed to bear the burden of keeping their families together emotionally. In the wife's case, her father had supported the family materially but had had many extra-marital affairs, which meant that he was not emotionally available either to his wife or to his daughter. In the husband's family the situation was somewhat different in that as he saw it, his mother had kept her emotional energy free for her hard-working and distanced husband, and had not had enough for her children.

The wife's split was of an attractive, admired father and a negligent wife-demeaning one; in her identification with her mother, she perceived the woman's role in marriage to be responsible and unsupported, so leading to carping criticism of the husband. The husband's split was of a loving attentive mother, and a neglected submissive one; he identified with a father who belittled claims of family, being allowed to do so by a permissive subservient wife. In their idealization of the marital relationship, they had each hoped to find the attractive admiring father and loving attentive mother each totally absorbed in the other. Any failure to live up to this ideal called up both the repressed relationships and the behaviour which was identified with their parent of the same sex. The most overt scapegoating was of father labelled as irresponsible; from their past experiences, both could collusively share in this kind of image.

In marriages based on such collusive complentarity, there often is the risk that one partner will apparently carry most of the burden of bringing up the children, while the other appears as less responsible. Genuine sharing of parenting tasks is likely to be very difficult and to lead to considerable friction, and subtle undermining. Stephen's parents were able to recognize how much they had triangled Stephen into their relationship; but once they were able to parent effectively, Stephen was no longer a possible scapegoat, and they then had to face the underlying feelings in their own relationship. Only in doing this could they keep Stephen free of the conflicts. That involved either recognizing and living with the tensions or working to resolve them.

Whatever the marital system and relationship, there is no doubt that the couple always have to work at adapting from dyad to triad or more as further children arrive. The grandparents' responses are often active, and can contribute to making the task either easier or more difficult.

C. Changed Relationship with Grandparents

(1) Becoming a Grandparent

Becoming a grandparent, especially for the first time, is often a longed for event, albeit tinged with some ambivalence in that it marks the arrival of yet another stage in the life-cycle. The birth of a new generation brings actively to mind the inevitable death of an older one. Grandparents who take some real pleasure in their grandchildren can nonetheless be heard to say such things as "Children do spoil family life, don't they?"; or following a family visit "Of course it was very nice seeing the *parents*." The constant activity of small children may be very exhausting physically for elderly or even middle-aged grandparents; in their recognition of their tiredness, they may become all too uncomfortably aware of their age.

Nonetheless many grandparents look forward to having some of the fun and less of the responsibility of having children; in a way to a more relaxed and also more distant kind of parenting. Many achieve it, and in families with good relationships, the bond between grandparent and grandchild may often be warm and caring, while bonds between grandparents and parents become even closer. At first the care will be from the grandparent to the child, but even quite young children can give caring to elderly grandparents who may more obviously need it than their own parents. It is perhaps essentially less threatening to be asked to pick up a scarf because of granny's stiff legs than to be asked to be quiet because mummy has a headache.

(2) Changing Relationships with Grandparents

At the point when the first baby is born, the parent couple have to learn to negotiate a new sharing relationship with their parents at a time when they are already having to cope with sharing each other. Grandparents, especially grandmothers, may have a tendency to move into residence; if not actually, at least metaphorically. Such help is often received with some gratitude and certain relief around the birth. However, at this time the grandparents are often still parenting their own child, but as they have not yet learnt the new role of being grandparents, they may also tend to parent the baby and spouse. A common source of tension at this period, even of conflict, is ownership of the new baby. This is most marked where the parents are young and anxious, and the grand-parents protective (Belinda's family described above came into this category).

As the young couple have hitherto known their parents best in that capacity, they will tend to turn back to them in familiar ways; but may then feel trapped into a kind of regression into childhood and so react against it by contradicting the grandparental advice. If there are good enough relationships in the extended families, the couple will each be able to identify enough with their own parents' advice and role modelling to feel free to reject some help without guilt.

There are however likely to be two sets of grandparents to be related to and listened to, and this can cause confusion and throw further stress on the marital relationship. The couple may even have to negotiate between pairs of grandparents who are in conflict and rivalry with each other over whose advice is followed, and who can spend most time with the baby. Alternatively the couple may find themselves facing a phalanx of grandparents presenting an unexpectedly and unprecedently united front on child-rearing methods. Obviously the picture of rival sets of grandparents fighting over access to baby and parents is a dramatic exaggeration. But, whether they are present in the flesh or only in feelings, the parents have to face within themselves a very real reviewing of their relationship with the grandparents, and in so doing discover new truths about themselves. This can often be very startling. The cry, "Mum said and I never believed her till" is often heard; it contains the pain and guilt of having arrogantly discounted the grandparent's feeling or opinion as just part of their personality, their particular kink. Now the new mother finds that she too, as an individual, can experience exactly the same thing. On the other hand, there is the realization of unexpected difference: "I always thought that it would be like that because it was for my parents, but it isn't". In becoming parents themselves, all couples necessarily undergo such surprising discoveries. They find that they are more like their parents in some ways and more unlike or separate in others; above all they find that they are not exactly the personalities they thought they were before they had a child. Such discoveries can change the relationship with the grandparents. Some remaining layers of idealization of them may drop away, but a more significant appreciation may emerge. The grandparents may in their turn respond to their new role by greater openness. Sometimes the birth of a child will free grandparents to reveal hopes and disappointments they had experienced over their own children but had not been able to discuss before. Family bonds and understanding may then grow still closer.

Most people on becoming parents have a deep primitive wish for their own parents' support and approval. Lack of it can be very painful, and can certainly make it harder for the new parent to integrate successfully the surprising discoveries about themselves and their relationships. They are at this time very vulnerable in their fear of not managing their new responsibility well enough.

D. The Absence of Grandparents

If the grandparents are no longer surviving, the parent couple may have to work harder at facing new aspects of themselves. The possibility of reparation or open admission of misunderstanding to the grandparents no longer exists. However if the relationship was good enough, the parents are likely to manage this integration better than those with distanced relationships. The couple also have to miss any actual experience of shared pleasure between grandparent and grandchild, and they cannot receive approval and support themselves. Parents often express sorrow that a grandparent did not live to see a certain child, or relief that he/she just did survive long enough as if voicing a real feeling that the older generation can appreciate the knowledge of the continuity of life, even on their own deathbeds. And of course, given the great warmth and joy mutually gained in many grandparent/grandchild relationships, there is likely to be considerable loss to the new generation if it has not an active grandparenting.

Finally grandparents may become seriously ill around this stage. The new parents then not only have to deal with mourning and possible loss at a time when they are also enabling a new life to begin. They can also find that they suddenly have two generations dependent on them when up till then they had had none. If this happens, the marital relationship has to be very strong and supportive to weather the double life crisis.

V. TAKING ON PARENTING ROLES

In becoming parents, young couples are taking on a new role. Although many may have helped to look after children, it is rare for new parents to have had the experience of having to meet the total dependence of a baby, and then adapt to his growing individuality. I would like to discuss how they manage this task and the possible difficulties which may arise around two aspects, dependency and control.

A. Dependency

In the early months of a baby's life the greatest demand on the parents is the need to meet this dependency. In the previous paragraphs I have already outlined something of the context in which this can be done well. Both the psychoanalytic and the interactional studies referred to above make it clear that the intensity of relationship needed to promote good bonding of the baby to parent is considerable. Given a good mutually supporting marital relationship the spouses can help each other learn to relate and attend to the baby without undue jealousy or rivalry, and can continue to remember each other's needs. An absence of serious external stress, and the presence of a healthy baby all contribute to making this bonding and meeting of dependency go more easily. It is however important to remember how many families successfully overcome very major crises, such as severe illness in baby or parent, and emerge with close relationships and well functioning families.

Some of the factors which can seriously inhibit adequate meeting of the infant's dependency needs have already been referred to. Prolonged separation can make it very difficult to establish bonding. Maternal depression by reducing sensitivity can lead to a less intense attachment; which may often result in over-dependency later in the baby's life. Jealousy for attention between the spouses may distract from caring empathically enough for the baby, while distrust and distancing may mean that one is pushed out of enough direct contact thus impoverishing the baby by reducing the relationships it is possible for him to make (see Belinda's family). More external factors, both material stresses and crises such as illness in spouse, grandparent or of course older child, may all absorb significant amounts of parental attention.

I would like to discuss two factors which have not already been touched on, which can make the dependency harder for parents to respond to fully.

B. Quality of Relationship with Own Parents

(1) General Factors

The parent grandparent relationship has already been touched on. If parents have strongly negative feelings towards the grandparents, this can make identification for them as parents very difficult; logically since the adult must fear that the pattern will be repeated and their child dislike them. More ordinarily, as writers in the field since Freud have observed, there is a normal tendency to try and avoid making the "mistakes" of the grandparents. This carries a risk of over-compensating in the other direction; yet at the same time, positive identification with the grandparents will lead to copying them. Such positive identifications do not necessarily need to be consciously felt; as Boszormenyi-Nagy and Spark (1973) have demonstrated, family loyalty plays a crucial part in the repetition and recreation of the family systems and relationships occurring in previous generations.

Nowhere perhaps is this more evident than in the area of meeting dependency needs. It may be because at this stage, the infant is dependent not only on the adult's capacity to respond to him, but to do so with pleasure which provokes play. A vital ingredient would be lost if the playing were less intense, let alone absent, since the development of a good attachment hopefully demands the mutual giving and receiving of pleasure. Families may fall into a cycle of failing to find pleasure in this period of dependency, despite the real caring.

(2) Case Example: Rose's Family

Rose's family was like this. She was brought to the clinic when she was 18 months old because the parents were concerned about her temper and negativism. Rose herself was a delightful outgoing active baby, who certainly had moments of temper when actively frustrated, but these always seemed very normal for a child her age. The most striking feature of the family was the parents' inability to enjoy Rose and recognize real positive attributes to her. Mother was particularly unresponsive to many of Rose's bids for attention and to her play. There was an older daughter in the family, an 8-year-old Melanie, who was reported to have been a very quiet undemanding baby, and who was now a rather over-anxious clinging little girl. The parents were both quite over-anxious themselves about any stress Melanie might have to meet, e.g. at school; they themselves enjoyed a great many rather adult activities with her.

Father described coming from a family which was rather cold, with very distanced relationships and considerable emphasis on academic achievement. It was noticeable that he found it very difficult to convey any graphic picture of his family, other than distance. Mother on the other hand was very attached to her parents. However when she described her early childhood in more detail, it emerged that maternal grandfather had been away fighting in the war, during her first few years, that maternal grandmother had been working, and it was an aunt that mother remembered with most affection from that time.

Part of the treatment plan involved trying to help mother play with Rose. This only met with partial success; it was not that mother was depressed, but rather that she genuinely seemed unable to believe that she could enjoy her lively baby. However about nine months later, in response to Rose's growing ability to talk and her increasing independence, Mother did begin to take pleasure in the child. Her anxiety diminished considerably, her confidence increased, and she was able to plan activities which she recognized Rose would enjoy.

Rose's family highlights several of the factors which can contribute to making it hard to meet the infant's dependency needs. Father appeared to have a predominantly negative identification with his parents insofar as he recollected little overt warmth and little fun. As a parent, he seemed to be trying to "be the opposite"; he was rather over-warm, somewhat seductively so to Melanie, and he certainly arranged many treats and outings for her, although they did mostly have a somewhat "intellectual" basis. In this he was positively identifying with his own family of origin's valuing of learning. He was in fact less worried about Rose's activity than his wife was. Mother seemed quite unable to believe that it was possible to enjoy her children's infancy positively; in her mind it was a stage to be endured before the real business of living and relating began. From her history it appeared that the maternal grandparents had also not been able to enjoy this period in her life for a variety of reasons. Although it was possible that some other relative had taken pleasure actively in mother as an infant, her unconscious loyalty to her own parents and her lack of experiencing such delight from them made it very hard for her to find it in her own children.

The two children in the family had very different temperaments. Melanie was a passive undemanding baby, who caused the parents less anxiety because she made fewer moves. However at 8, she did present as a rather clinging little girl who had not been able to form an intense and secure enough attachment perhaps because mother had not been sensitive to her more subtle demands. By contrast, Rose was a very lively active baby who was able to complain more vociferously if her needs were not met and who did demand a more active playing attention from her parents. She also asked for it and received it from her sister.

Finally the marital system in this family appeared to be one which put a high value on shared adult entertainment such as concert- and theatre-going and travel. The needs of an infant inevitably clashed with this, and both parents shared some anxiety (and so were rivalrous with Rose) about missing out themselves. At the period when Melanie had been a baby, the family had been living abroad in circumstances which were personally more satisfying to the parents.

C. Effects of Deprivation on Parenting

So far I have discussed relative inadequacies and negative identifications in the relationship between parent and grandparent. There do exist however families where the parents were actually seriously deprived of maternal or parental care in their own early childhoods. Such parents may always be searching for someone to meet their unmet dependency needs. They may hope to find it in their marriage; in object relations theory part of their split idealized partner being an ever-caring spouse. That hope is unlikely to be fulfilled, so when a child is born the parent may turn to the baby demanding that he fill the gap and look after them instead of vice versa. Such a reversal can only lead to increasing frustration on both sides. The parent is unable to follow the infant's pace and respond sensitively since his or her own need for attention or peace is felt to be predominant. It is in such situations that children are most at risk of abuse by their parents. A child's need for attention, whether he shows it by crying, by following the parent around, or simply by needing to be fed or changed, can feel intolerable to the parent who needs someone to care for her/him. Delay in responding to the infant may lead to the infant either becoming apathetic and so unresponsive, or more likely to his being constantly fretful. Such fretfulness can be exhausting for the most stable parents; for deprived ones, it can trigger off active abuse.

The many studies of child abuse highlight the existence of such factors. Baldwin (1977) found a high incidence of neglect, multiple caretaking and actual abuse in the families of the parents; and in the abusing families in his sample, there were only 12% with both natural parents in the home. This indicates the unlikelihood of the parent having his or her dependency needs met at all in the marriage.

Martin (1976) while confirming some of these findings about parental background also identified many factors indicating that the baby who was abused failed to come up to parental expectations from the very outset. He found that there were more abnormal pregnancies, difficult deliveries, separations after birth and subsequently difficult to care for babies in his sample. Such gross discrepancies between the pleasure the parent hoped for and what they actually had to meet could be too great a burden for parents whose basic lack of confidence demanded as anxiety-free a start to their relationship with their child as possible. For parents whose own experiences led them to expect that diffi- culties are followed by disasters such unfortunate beginnings inevitably started a spiral of failures and disappointments.

D.   Child's Place in the Family

(1)   Identification with Sibling Place

The place which a child occupies in the sibship may be a factor making it harder for one or other parent to bond positively. This situation can arise when the parent identifies that place either with a sibling of their own with whom they had a particularly negative relationship, or when they identify the child with them- selves in some very negative way. On the other hand, the parent may fear the jealousy of an older child and so feel unable to relate as lovingly as they might to the newcomer. This is probably most likely to occur if that parent still has a particularly jealous relationship themself with a sibling. Pincus and Dare (1978) quote examples of this kind of situation. The sex of the child in question may contribute to his being associated negatively with another family member, but it is not uncommon to find such identifications made in a cross-sexed way. Names given for other family members might bring an unexpected weight of association. One mother of twin girls who were respectively called after the two grandmothers, both by then dead, admitted to instinctively feeling closer to the daughter named after her mother than to the one after her mother-in-law. This kind of instinctive closeness is normal and does not last. However, links making for negative association and labelling may be more harmful in their impact if they contribute to impairing straightforward bonding and acceptance of the infant as a separate individual.

(2) Case Example: John's Family

This situation was seen in John's family. He was the second of three boys being 3 years younger than his elder brother. Mother was the eldest of three sisters. His mother felt very detached from him, and was even rather hostile to him, whereas she had a very positive relationship with her older son. John had not been an easy baby, being born with severe eczema which was later attributed to marked milk allergy. Originally the therapist had thought that much of the difficult parent-child relationship resulted from having had a worrying start. But later mother confessed, with very strong feelings, to an intense jealousy of her next younger sister. This had existed for as long as she could remember and was maintained to the present time. She felt that her sister had always been the grandparents' favourite, and as such received the most attention. The mother herself associated John with this sister and found it extremely difficult not to ignore him in revenge, although then of course she felt guilty and worried about him. When she had a third son, she had no problem relating to him as she got on well with her youngest sister whom she also saw as relatively neglected.

(3) Case Example: Charlotte's Family

In Charlotte's family the identification made by the parent was with herself and the maternal grandmother. Charlotte's mother was the younger of two siblings, having an older brother. She had spent much of her childhood in care, and had a very ambivalent relationship with maternal grandmother whom she always felt was "irritated" by her untalkativeness and passivity. Charlotte herself was a much wanted baby, the parents already having an older son. When Charlotte was born, mother did not experience the immediate overwhelming sense of adoration she had felt for her son. As a result of this, she believed that she had failed Charlotte who like the grandmother was "irritated and deprived" by her passivity. At the same time she was afraid that if she was a failure as a mother, Charlotte would suffer the same painful separations as she had herself. She became depressed, and had considerable difficulty in feeling bonded with Charlotte.

E.   Taking Control as a Parental Function

(1)   The Need to Take Control
The need to introduce a gradual failure of immediate satisfaction is closely linked
to the increasing need for parents to help their children acquire control of their
instincts. Obviously by the time a child reaches school age, his control of his
emotions is still very partial, although he is certainly expected to have gained
considerable physical control over his body functions, and to be reasonably
responsive to requests for socially acceptable behaviour. All this demands that
the child can forgo immediate gratification without flinging a temper tantrum,
that he can share play and attention with other adults and children, and that
hopefully he has some empathy with other people. In order to reach this stage,
the parents will have had to be able to frustrate the child, caringly but
deliberately.

This area of control is where parents of young children most often fall into
difficulties requiring outside help. Parents who have not been able to meet the
dependency needs satisfactorily almost inevitably fail at this second stage. (John
was referred at 2½ and Charlotte at 3½ both because of temper tantrums, and
Rose's parents in a sense already saw her at this stage at 18 months.)

The guilt of not having been able to parent as well as they would have wished
militates against their being confident enough to frustrate consistently and
lovingly. Many other parents who have coped well with the dependency find
control much more painful. There are of course also parents who find this
second toddler stage easier, and many who find it particularly rewarding and
enchanting. This may reflect some uneasiness about extreme dependency
especially at a non-verbal level, as well as indicating pleasure in the lively
development and curiosity of 2 to 4-year-olds.

(2)   Problems with Assuming Control
Control can be difficult for various reasons. In the last two decades, there have
been certain schools of thought which advocated very permissive parenting: "Let
the child develop at his own pace". It seems likely that such theories arose
largely as overcompensatory reactions to some of the very rigid ones of the
previous decades. On an individual basis, similar reactions can occur either
because the parents have had rather strict upbringings, or because they feel that
they had. Social changes also contribute. The Newsons (1963) in their study of
infant care, report many parents seeing themselves able to allow more freedom to
their children because of improved economic conditions and in recognizing this,
understanding the grandparental strictness as arising from hard necessity. On the
other hand, the majority of parents in that study had no hesitation about
asserting control over their one-year-olds, and frustrating them either for their
own good, or for parental or family comfort.

In working with parents of young children, it often emerges that the parents can
remember vividly their own childish anger and resentment at being frustrated,
and are reluctant to arouse the same feelings in their own children. At the same

time these parents do want their children to restrict certain activities. Their difficulty in making definite demands can lead to all kinds of inconsistencies and confusions. A common ruse is the tall or frightening story, well documented in history as well as in clinical practice. In the early nineteenth century, children were frightened into good behaviour by being told that "Boney will come and get you". Nowadays it is more likely to be the police or the welfare, or of course any kind of fantasy witch-like figure. In such ways, parents try to evade the responsibility of being the unkind one who is making the demand. One mother I saw provided a good example of this in its most ordinary way. She had to bring her two-year-old (not the identified patient) to interviews with her, and one day suddenly said in passing, "I notice that when he goes to the plants you tell him not to pull them as they may fall and break; I would tell him there was a spider there. My husband does as you do." This particular mother had no problem with this child, perhaps partly because father was more straightforward, but she did have acknowledged resentment to her own parents for their past control of her. But such manoeuvres can only serve first to frighten the child needlessly and then, especially if used a lot, lead him to distrust the parent's word. In this latter situation control is unlikely to be achieved successfully. In systems terms, the parent is blurring and confusing what is, or should be a clear boundary; his wishes both as an individual and a parent are different from the child's, and that difference needs to be openly recognized for control to be achieved.

(3) Confusion with Parents' Own Control
The parents, other than those who have failed at the dependency stage, who find control of their toddlers most difficult are those who are rebelling violently against their own families. The kind of marriage which is based on rebellion or violence is likely to contain quite an overt element of quarrelling in the marital relationship, and to some extent lack of control, even fighting may be the family style. Not surprisingly, the children may follow this model. Frequently parents in a quarrelsome marriage fail to provide constant discipline; the inconsistency can exist both between the couple and from each individually. Stephen's family described above showed this pattern.

Marriages may be based on collusive reaction, near rebellion without including violence; in such marriages, the rebellion may be against any discipline at all. One may hear parents voice the disbelief that "the children must have what they want at all costs"; in such cases, the parents themselves are carrying unusually intense anger against restrictions which they felt coming from their own families of origin. Clearly such parents have considerable problems in helping their children achieve any control, although the lack of it may be manifested more by failure to achieve control over body functions than by tempers, since active fighting is not the family pattern, and the children are not positively frustrated.

(4) External factors Provoking Difficulties in Control
External factors can provoke especial difficulties in this area. Very cramped and unprivate living conditions such as house-sharing can push parents into being more pacifying with their children for longer than is appropriate; and then when

it comes, the battle to establish control is harder and may feel too cruel to the parents. Similarly, children who have had or have serious illnesses and hospital-izations may really require some spoiling, but this can all too easily become unduly prolonged. Chronic serious illness carries particular risks since parents often feel very understandably, that their child has to suffer so many restrictions that ordinary behaviour controls can be dispensed with to some extent (Lask, 1979; Elton, 1980).

Finally control of small children is difficult because of the infectiousness of their extremes of emotion. Parents who may have put much energy into gaining what is felt to be appropriate social control of their own emotions are in this period face to face with small beings who experience all those same emotions loudly, violently and openly. On the positive side, this allows parents to share in the intense curiosity, fun and zest for life; although the continual questioning can be exhausting, and drives many parents to the answer they had vowed never to give "because it is like that". On the negative side, it means being faced with tears and stormy rages several times a day, and if a parent is even mildly depressed, this can be a provocative event. It is all too easy for rage to provoke fury rather than patient understanding or appropriate anger, and many, if not most, parents can experience murderous feelings to their children and so can fear their own loss of control (Gorell Barnes, 1979).

VI. SYMPTOMS AND THEIR PRODUCTION

Since young children are extremely vulnerable both physically and emotionally, it is often the child in the family who is symptom-bearer. If difficulties only become manifest in a family after the birth of a child or children, it is very likely that those difficulties will be projected on to the child as scapegoat rather than on to an adult or the marriage. Although maternal depression is so common, it may often go unrecognized and untreated (Richman, 1978) and as has been discussed above, does in any case have serious implications for the healthy development of the child. Children have their own instinctual and individual difficulties to deal with which cause problems in their own right; their extreme vulnerability as receivers of projections (from all family members) can only compound the risk of their developing symptoms.

A. How Agencies Become Involved

(1) Patterns of Symptoms
In the first year to eighteen months, children are likely to produce symptoms in a physical manner. Eating and sleeping problems predominate although towards the end of the period problems such as head-banging occur. From about eighteen months onwards, symptoms are increasingly presented in a variety of ways; behaviourally by tempers and aggressive or negativistic behaviour around acquiring demanded habits (frequently around toilet-training), emotionally in

the development of phobias and separation difficulties, physically through continued feeding and sleeping problems, and also in psychosomatic illness and developmentally by delays in various areas. Of course babies may also well be suffering from painful feelings. Babies who are failing to thrive are typically often unhappy-looking, listless or negativistic. But the predominant presentation in this age group will be through physical problems.

Families may of course present directly in their own right. Couples may seek help for marital difficulties. Depressed mothers may approach their general practitioners, although it is likely that many do not, and fewer still reach adult psychiatric services. Families where children are abused or at risk may often be known to social service departments even before an incident. The immediate implication of this is that many services are likely to be involved in some way with families of young children under stress, and the proportion of such families known to any service designed to meet malfunctioning as opposed to normal functioning is small. Apart from G.P.s, the worker most likely to meet families with babies is the Health Visitor, and then other staff in the well-baby clinic. These workers provide a caring service, although one which is sadly increasingly stretched, and are in a very good position to identify serious stress. This applies particularly to families who are unable through guilt, fear, ignorance or depression to ask for help directly at any specialist agency.

(2) Diagnosing Problems

Consultation and support to staff of well-baby clinics, especially to health visitors, can help them assess more accurately the problems where further referral is advisable, and may in addition help them deal with their own fears about "psychiatric" agencies for small children, or with the often strained relationships with social service teams. Perhaps their greatest weakness is that they are so often seen by their clients as a service for mothers and babies only, and often tend to perceive themselves this way, despite attempts to alter. Given Richman's (1978) findings of the significant association between a poor marital relationship and lack of paternal support and the high incidence of maternal depression, this is unfortunate.

Since small children are extremely likely to present disturbance in physical ways, the most common specialist agency for their families to reach is a paediatric clinic. Many paediatricians are very skilled at assessing and treating family and child disturbance; they are also now usually aware of the kind of "at risk" presentations, that is parents bringing children who are not really ill. Again paediatric services can benefit from easy consultation with and referral to more specialist family or psychiatric services for the more severely disturbed of their patients.

(3) Preventative Services

Many families with pre-school children in difficulties do not approach any helping agency directly, and the children's problems are not picked up until they start attending playgroup or some other pre-school provision. While it might be desirable for such facilities to have easy access to some consultation, this is hardly possible since such groups are organized in a great variety of ways. Day nurseries are linked with other services, particularly to social workers and community health workers. Many children in day nurseries are likely to be showing difficulties, since the usual criterion for admission is family or maternal stress. Over the last few years, a number of parent and child nursery groups or day centres have been set up intended to help with family interaction and problems at this stage in the life-cycle. It may be that such provision has a positive future, at least in helping contain some of the most disturbed and deprived parents, and hopefully in intervening in certain behaviour problems in young children before they become too rigidified. However, as with most other services specifically designed for families with children under school age, there are real difficulties in reaching the fathers. Day centres for mothers and children have in some instances been set up in adult psychiatric settings. This is a welcome development, both because direct concern for the children of adult patients is long overdue, and also because the parent may be able to accept help with parenting without exaggerated fears of their child being similarly "ill". It is also easier for some husbands to get involved in such centres that they can see as everyday care than it is for them to accept child psychiatric settings.

VII. FAMILY THERAPY IN FAMILIES WITH CHILDREN UNDER FIVE

A. The Role of Agencies Providing Family Therapy

Family therapy for families with children under five is most likely to be provided in child guidance and child psychiatric settings and in social service departments. For families who are showing stress arising primarily from the need to adapt to this stage in the life-cycle, a whole family approach often proves very effective and can be fairly brief. However, many families who show difficulties in this period have parents who themselves have suffered significant deprivation and poor bonding and so may require more prolonged help. So far little work has been done with the three-generational family, although it might often be appropriate. Whole family therapy may be practised in both short-term and long-term situations, although in the latter group, there may also be need for additional help for either parent individually or for the marriage. There may also need to be considerable emphasis on work with the subsystem of mother (occasionally father) and child or children. When babies under verbal age are referred, the work is naturally directed most at the parents but the presence of the infant is often of inestimable importance. Much of the focus may be on helping parents pick up and respond to their children's cues, in particular to the hitherto unobserved ones. In some ways, this may allow them to have an experience of positive reciprocity which may not have occurred or may have been distorted in the early months.

B.   Case Examples

One couple who had a non-thriving 14-month-old daughter who had been abused, were amazed and enormously relieved when it was pointed out to them that their child responded very much more warmly to them when they arrived than she did to staff-members. Following this observation, they themselves were able to look at her far more intently and so noticed other positive cues. They were so relieved at this evidence of their baby's forgiveness for the neglect and the demonstration of her continued attachment, that they were able to continue working on their relationship with her. Charlotte, described previously, was seen by workers as desperately trying to stimulate her depressed mother into positive activity; not surprisingly these attempts often spiralled into tears and screaming and they so often failed. Once the interactional pattern was recognized, the mother could be helped to respond and games were devised to help both find calmer and more balanced ways of communicating with each other (this was in a Day Centre setting). It was only at the point when this was recognized and discussed with the mother that she was finally able to reveal her own despair about her previous feelings of inadequate attachment.

Parents can also be helped to respond to more obviously negative cues, both by discussion of what at that moment may be triggering off their child's tantrum and also by support in managing it.

C.   Young Children in Family Therapy

(1)   Principles of Practice
Where young children are involved in family therapy, the worker has to be able to adapt his practice in certain ways. First he must be able to tolerate rather more noise than is normal in interviewing. Although parents may certainly be asked to establish control over really loud play, and although the worker may select toys which are intrinsically less noisy (plastic as opposed to metal or wooden cars) little children can erupt into noisy moments, and of course babies may cry. It is essential to have toys since small children who may hardly be verbal cannot be expected to talk or listen concentratedly. The worker may instead have to learn to use the child's non-verbal communication and his play.

(2)   Case Example: Antony and his Family
Antony aged 4½ provided a good example of this. He was attending with his family parents and baby brother of 18 months because of his negative and withholding behaviour, which included constipation. The parents were both very anxious, self-deprecating and passive, and had always felt that Antony was "strange". Antony was an intelligent articulate child who looked very sad, and the baby Gerald was aggressive and loudly demanding. It had been difficult to engage the family because of the parental way of denying their right to help, but they themselves returned spontaneously after a gap of some months although they still found it hard to engage in work. In the second session, the parents were

talking of their doubts as to whether they should commit themselves to any work; during this time, Antony was trying to draw round a toy car and was getting into difficulties. It became apparent to the worker that Antony was trying to do the impossible, namely draw his car from all angles at once showing both inside and outside simultaneously. When this comment was made (and agreed to by Antony) mother suddenly responded in a more lively tone than she had ever hitherto used, and began to talk of her own perfectionist streak. Antony was then able to let Father help with his drawing. From this point, the therapy really took off and the whole family became positively lively and interested. It was noticeable that for a few subsequent sessions Antony always opened with a topic, often a complaint or worry about something, and that this reflected a worry of the parents. When they were able to understand why both of them found it hard to move into a decision-making role because of identifications with their own extended family, they were able to release Antony from the painful position of having to be too responsible. In examining their shared perfectionism, they came to realize that parents may have to work at understanding their children and could not expect to have such knowledge effortlessly and be able to do it "all at once".

It is not always necessary to use the content of the children's play; indeed it may well not be possible since in large busy families it is very difficult or indeed impossible for the therapist to attend to everything which is going on. Some children seem to use the play materials almost as a backdrop themselves, leaving their activities periodically to come and tell the therapist or parents something. But it is important to be aware in a general way of what the children are engaged in, both the kind of activity, and the interaction between siblings, and whether there are any indications of tension. If children do create anything, drawings, models or whatever, it does seem important to acknowledge it.

(3) Case Example: Roger and his Family

Roger's family was one where the content of the children's play was never directly referred to, although the interaction between the brothers was. In this family, the mother was helped to manage the symptom during the session. Roger was seen because of head-banging, and presented as a rather detached unhappy and aggressive 18-month-old. His older brother Charles, aged 6, was on the contrary a winning articulate little boy, ostensibly presenting no problem. The parents had found it very difficult to adjust to the very different personality of their second child, who was much more obviously determined and demanding than either Charles or themselves. However, it quickly emerged that there was in fact a control problem with Charles too. He had never slept in his own room, but was still in the parental bedroom, although Roger was sometimes in another room. This issue became the focus of the first interview, and parents were encouraged to deal with control of the elder child before they even attempted to do so with the younger. A fortnight later, the family returned reporting that Charles was now sleeping in his own room, that this had not been at all difficult to achieve, and that Roger's symptoms had markedly decreased. However the therapist observed that whenever Roger made a move during the session both the parents and Charles reacted anxiously as if he might create havoc in some way; although many of these moves seemed to the therapist exploratory rather than angry. This tendency to label Roger as a monster was discussed and the parents' feeling of being distanced from him understood; although it was not at all clear why this label should have been attributed to Roger.

At a third session 5 weeks later, the mother (who came with both boys) described that the head banging and tempers had almost disappeared during the intervening period, although there had been a slight recurrence in the previous week. During this session, Roger did begin to get angry and distressed at one point (possibly because he was being rather ignored). The therapist asked the mother "Can you help Roger?", and mother rather half-heartedly said that she would try. "But I don't expect so, he never listens to me." The mother then went and picked up the baby and brought him to sit on her lap; within moments she was cuddling and stroking him and he was responding by stroking her. During this time the therapist attended to Charles who had become interested in the moving camera. The therapist then said to the mother "So you could settle Roger very nicely, and it looks as if you both know how", and the mother then launched into a series of possible explanations for his temper, none of which labelled him as monstrous or even particularly aggressive, and all of which indicated her empathy with his possible feeling state (maybe he's left out, or tired or may be sickening for mumps which his brother has just had). Following this she was able to suggest possible reasons for the slight increase in Roger's tempers the previous week. It was obvious to the therapist during the control and comforting sequence that this mother and baby did in fact have a well tried and familiar pattern of comfort giving and receiving moves; but it did seem that the mother was too anxious when the baby became angry either to use them, or to "know" that she had done so. It seemed that the experience of doing it in front of the therapist could affirm her belief in her own capacity as mother to this particular child, and that she was then free to empathize with him and speculate about possible causes of distress. In doing this, she could see for herself that Roger's negative cue of anger was associated with other less objectionable feelings. When he again got upset later in the session, she could spontaneously move to comforting, and Charles then gave his brother a toy.

VIII. CONCLUSION

The period in the family life-cycle covering the birth of the children and the pre-school years is an immensely important one. It is formative not only of the individual children, but also of the subsequent relationships and "system" in this new nuclear family. The parents have the opportunity to repeat or attempt to reverse experiences and ways of relating which obtained in their own families or origin. In so doing, they can discover unexpected aspects in themselves and develop closer bonds of understanding with the grandparents. While many families can successfully overcome considerable stresses in this period, problems which arise during it as a result of pathological relationships and expectations within the family are likely to be far more resistant to spontaneous change; the new relationships may be bonded on a distorted basis. Intensity and disinhibition of emotions is a striking feature of this stage, and this in itself can create stress. So can the continual awareness of rapid change and growth, which brings both pleasure and loss. Of all periods, this is perhaps the least static in a family's life.

Although severe problems may arise at this time, and if untreated, these problems are likely to lead to increasing difficulties later, there may also be a better opportunity for positive professional intervention and prevention than at later stages. The wish to succeed and the hope of doing so are often strongest in the family at this time, and the openness and fluidity of the family system may be greatest. As family members are constantly learning about themselves, their relationships and the outside world they may be more willing and more able to accept help. Society also goes some way towards acknowledging and tolerating the stresses and problems of this stage. Most importantly, families themselves may not yet have the despairing feeling which can come from experiencing years of "failed" or unsatisfactory relationships.

REFERENCES

Baldwin, J. A. (1977). Child Abuse: epideiology and prevention. In "Epidemiological Approaches in Child Psychiatry" (Graham, ed.), Academic Press, London and New York.

Boszormenyi-Nagy, I. and Spark, G. (1973). "Invisible Loyalties", Harper & Row, Maryland.

Bowlby, J. (1969). "Attachment and Loss", 1, Hogarth Press, London.

Dicks, H. (1967). "Marital Tensions", Routledge & Kegan Paul, London.

Dunn, J. (1977). "Distress and Comfort", Fontana, London.

Elton, A. (1980). Work with pre-school children: system or subsystem. Journal of Family Therapy, 2, 131-148.

Erikson, E. (1950). "Childhood and Society", Penguin Books, London. 1967.

Gorell Barnes, G. (1979). Infant needs and angry responses: a look at violence in the family. In "Family and Marital Psychotherapy", (S. Walrond-Skinner, ed.), Routledge & Kegan Paul, London.

Haley, J. (1967). Towards a theory of pathological systems. In "Family Therapy and Disturbed Families", (G. Zuk and I. Boszormenyi-Nagy, eds), Science and Behaviour Books, Palo Alto.

Heinicke, C. and Westheimer, I. (1965). "Brief Separations", Longman, London.

Kennel, J. H., Trause, M. A. and Klaus, M. H., (1975). Evidence for a sensitive period in the human mother. In "Parent-Infant Interaction", Ciba. Symposium 33, London.

Klaus, M. H., Jerauld, R., Kreger, N., McAlpine, W., Steffa, M. and Kennell, J. (1972). Maternal attachment: the importance of the first post-partum days. New England Journal of Medicine, 286, 460-463.

Klein, M. (1963). "Our Adult World and its Roots in Infancy", Heinemann, London.

Lask, B. and Kirk, M. (1979). Childhood asthma; Family therapy as an adjunct to routine management. Journal of Family Therapy, 1, 33-49.

Macfarlane, A. (1977). "The Psychology of Childbirth", Fontana, London.

Mahler, M. (1954). Problems of infantile neurosis. *In* "The Psycho-analytic study of the child", Vol. **9**. Imago, London.

Martin, H. (1976). "The Abused Child", Ballinger, Cambridge, Mass.

Newson, J. and E. (1963). "Patterns of Infant Care in an urban community", Allen and Unwin, London.

Pincus, L. and Dare, C. (1978). "Secrets in the Family", Faber, London.

Richman, N. (1976). Depression in mothers of pre-school children. *Journal of Child Psychology and Psychiatry,* **17**, 75-78.

Richman, N. (1978). The Depression in mother of young children. *Journal of the Royal Society of Medicine,* **77**, 489-493.

Schaffer, R. (1977). "Mothering", Fontana, London.

Spitz, R. A. (1945). Hospitalisation. *In* "The Psycho-analytic study of the child", Vol. 1. p. 53. International University Press, New York.

Stern, D. (1977). The First Relationship; "Infant and Mother", Fontana, London.

Winnicott, D. W. (1949). "The Child and the Family", Tavistock, London.

Winnicott, D. W. (1958). "Collected Papers", Tavistock, London.

Chapter 16

What do They Learn at School?:
Family Systems and the
School-going Child

C. Dare

I. INTRODUCTION: THE FRAMEWORK

Bowen (1980) suggests that the family life-cycle is a useful teaching tool in the introduction of systems theory to family therapists. In so doing, he draws attention to a major feature of biological systems which is that they are capable of change over time.

The dominant innovations in psychological thinking distinguishing family therapy from most preceding schools of psychotherapy, has been the whole hearted application of interactional and transactional models. In order to establish this distinction, Minuchin and his co-workers (1974; 1981) and Haley, in certain phases (1963), have treated family systems cross-sectionally, by occluding changes over time and across generations. This is not to say that Minuchin denies inter-generational inputs, or life-cycle changes in families. For his purposes of changing the paradigms of conceptualization of the family, the inter-current transactional pattern of the family is taken as the exemplar, *par excellence*, of the family as a system. The structure of the family system is taken to be its interactional structure as revealed in the here-and-now transactional patterns. Similarly, Haley (1976), in his emphasis on the observation of repeated, sequential transactions, draws most attention to the current, cross sectional structure of the family system. In one work, Haley (1973) nonetheless demonstrates in the most magical and convincing way that the aims, at least, of family therapy, are intimately linked to the facilitation of life-cycle transitions.

For the present author, however, the overall impact of Haley's work has been to establish that the pre-eminent task of the family therapist is to see the structure of the family system as an over-riding pattern created in the present, with a potential for change in the future.

Even Hoffman (1980) in her beautiful analysis of the process of life-cycle transitions, suggests that there is a basic, or underlying, unchanging structure to the family system.

All this seems to miss an essential feature of fundamental importance in the application of general systems theory in its illumination of the therapist's understanding of families. General systems theory is necessary for the comprehension of biological processes whereby systems can be goal-seeking, adaptational, self-regulating and can increase and sustain the complexity of their own organization over long periods of time. General systems theory grew out of a critique of the major conceptual models underpinning nineteenth century physics and chemistry. Such models, if applied to living organisms, as indeed they were, are incapable of predicting the apparently teleological features of biological systems. Above all, they would seem to predict a diminution of organizational complexity in time. This latter aspect led Freud (1920) for example, to assume that the general course of psychological life would show the imprint of a longing for death. Other psychologists of apparently contradictory viewpoints, notably Clark Hull (1943), influential in the establishment of behaviourism, postulated drive reduction principles, on the assumption that biological systems would tend to reduce their level of stimulation, that is to say that they would tend to diminish their informational input.

Diverse observations such as that of biological evolution, the developments of human society and motivation by curiosity in non-human animals, show that in general, as individuals and as groups, biological organisms tend towards an increase in their organizational structure. This increase is achieved by receiving and assimilating information (cf. Bateson, 1979). As Katz and Kahn (1966) pointed out, inputs to biological systems can be energic (material) or symbolic (information). Open systems are characterized by their assimilation of inputs to outputs described by the transport equation (Von Bertalanffy, 1950).

Family therapists need complex models whereby families are perceived to be both consistent and continuous in some aspects, and changing and discontinuous in others. Even without consideration of transitions imposed by crises such as illness, migration, war or unpredictable losses and additions, families change and develop, over time, through transitions in the life-cycle. Such transitions require adaptations in family functioning and organization. The family therapist must be able to observe the direction and potential of the functional and organizational adaptations of the family while also being able to perceive features and patterns which are unchanging. In this way, the family therapist can apply general systems theory to the family, treated as an open system.

The input to the family is threefold:

(1) Information brought into the family, by the individual family members from their contacts within the world outside the family.

(2) Materials introduced and worked upon by the family members in accord with the family rules.

(3) As the individual family members change in time, and even though some of that change is in directions precisely controlled by the family system, their change also introduces fresh inputs into the family as a system.

The output of the family is also threefold, comprising:

(1) Materials (goods or services) produced by the family members in their economic activities.

(2) Social information propelled outwards from the family, acting as a contribution (that is as input) into the wider social system which is the family's context.

(3) People leaving the family, who, eventually, become creators of new families.

II. THE NOMENCLATURE OF THE FAMILY LIFE-CYCLE

There is no agreed terminology by which family therapists label phases in the family life-cycle. There is a major conceptual problem of finding words which indicate the phase of the family in family-orientated rather than individually orientated words. Phrases, such as courtship, pre-parenting and post-parenting are useful and acceptable, but our vocabulary is incomplete in its designations for the phases of the parenting stage.

A. The Parenting Time of Family Life

The present author suggests a breakdown of the parenting time of family life, that is, the time when the parents live with children, into three. These phases, correspond

(1) to the time when there are babies and pre-school children,

(2) to the time when the children are school going, and

(3) to the time when the children are adolescent and are preparing to leave home.

Unfortunately, these labels are unsatisfactory, first because they designate the family by qualities of the individuals of one generation, and secondly because families commonly contain children whose differing ages consign them to differing phases in the individual life-cycle.

The author (Dare, 1979) has suggested that the location of the family on the life-cycle can be identified by tracking the transitions through which the different family members are passing. This method is effective in identifying the stresses that a family system is enduring, for the greater the number of individuals moving through such transitions, the more demands there are upon the family to make adaptations and to evolve. The multiplicity of potential transitions is increased with the number of family members, and in general, families containing one or more adolescents preparing to leave home, can be seen to be likely to have adults in mid-life transitions parallelling offspring in pre-adolescent or adolescent *passage*. (This will be taken up, extensively, in Chapter 18 in this volume.)

There are no simple words to label the phases of the parenting time, but consideration of the family as an open biological system (1) with an input and output and (2) structures presiding over the transformations of one to the other, are important conceptualizations of the life-cycle during parenting phases.

III. INPUT TO THE FAMILY SYSTEM CONTAINING CHILDREN ATTENDING SCHOOL ("SCHOOL-GOING CHILDREN")

A. The Issue of Latency

The phrase "school-going children" is incomplete, partisan and misleading. It is used here to cover the time that, in psychoanalytic developmental psychology, is labelled by an equally partial and partisan word, that of "latency" (Freud, 1905). Freud considered this time in the life of the child to be one in which the manifestations of the sexual drives (the libido) to have been quietened as an outcome of the processes terminating the oedipal phase. Latency is considered to last until the upsurge of sexual drives in adolescence. As family therapists, we may find the concept of latency quaint, but at about the time when, or more commonly shortly after the child enters school, and up to adolescence (or, better, "preadolescence"), there is a clear diminution in turbulence in those families unaffected by the less predictable life crises. But Freud's designation, although relevant to this aspect of family life, does not make reference to the positive quality of family system changes engendered by the entry to school of the children of the family. Abatement of the intense exploration by the child of the jealousies, rivalries and conflicts of the three-person, parent–child triad, when the five to six-year-old child "enters latency", certainly brings a certain peace and relief to many families. The parents may find themselves freed to explore their own relationship. Departure to school may give the predominant child care-taker (usually the mother) opportunity to extend her or his out-of-home life. These processes may stress the family, but will function as additional inputs for integration and assimilation, through negotiation and possible conflict, by the whole family. Older children of the family respond to these parental and interparental changes and, themselves, are pushed into fresh roles in relation to the child entering school. They may find themselves as conductors, counsellors or informants to the younger child crossing the physical and psychological boundaries of the family.

B. The Capacity to Work

Anna Freud (1966) identifies an important "developmental line" in latency whereby the child develops a capacity to work out of the capacity to play. She also emphasizes the structuralization of the psychological processes of the child, especially on the basis of the internalization of the parental ideals and rules ("Superego" formation). The ability of the school child in school and out of the home, and to bring such information back to the home, constitutes a crucial input into the family.

This input is especially dramatic in immigrant families, (cf. Spiegel, 1957) where the school child may be the main source of acculturating information for the whole family, even across three generations. But all school children perform a comparable function, exposing the family to inputs which are often quite foreign to the parents. The child can demand notice, interest and adaptational response. The child will say "my teacher said . . ."; "my friend's mummy and daddy don't do that"; "surely you know what symmetry is".

C. Culture and the Transfer of Rules

The internalization processes that Anna Freud (1966) emphasizes, is relevant to the systemic patterns of families containing school going children. Children, as they absorb the rules of the family culture and contrast them with the rules of the outer culture, also, audibly, play back to the family, their version of the family rules, requiring the family to hear them afresh and to re-assess the relevance and acceptability of the rules.

The role of school-going children as vehicles of social input to the family accord well with Erikson's (1950) view of latency as a time when the child's ego attitudes to the instinctual drives* show the impact of the wider society as mediated by school or comparable institutions. He also suggests that children in the latency time begin to be able to form assessments of themselves, their abilities and qualities, in relation to their peers. At this time, therefore, children bring some of the judgements that they make of themselves back into the family. The parents begin to have reflections of the outside world's views and possible judgements upon them, as the child forms opinions with increasingly socialized and experienced minds and eyes.

D. Finding a Place in the World

Above all, perhaps, children at this time of life begin to identify their location in the outside world. Peer friendships become increasingly important, which in turn attracts and attaches the child to the outside world, which can stimulate feelings of loss, pride and uncertainty in the parents, announcing with a stridency that increases with time, that the child is a person in his or her own right. The ultimate move of the child towards adulthood and increased separation and independence of their family, the child's affiliation to teachers, peers and the outer culture of society, procures respite, re-assessment and corresponding anxieties in the family. Winnicott (1957) contributes to the psychoanalytic understanding of latency, the concept of the capacity to be alone. The corollary of the development of this capacity in the school going child is that the parents are exposed to the possibility that they can enjoy or suffer the implications for change in their own lives.

IV.   CHANGES IN THE STRUCTURE OF THE FAMILY SYSTEM DURING THE PHASE OF SCHOOL GOING CHILDREN

A. Output of the Family System

Characterizing that time in which it contains school going children, the output of the family system can be considered under the three headings:

(1) First, the *economic output of the family will be increasing.* Parental earning power can be increasing, as care of infants and toddlers diminishes, enlarging the psychological and physical freedom of the parents to gain from their

---

*This phrase is derived from the closed system concepts of psychoanalytic thinking which does not, of course, accord with the conceptual framework espoused here.

wage-earning occupations. There is often a general augmentation of the parents earning skills and resources at this phase, and this will largely be taken up by the increased expenditure that the growing children require.

(2) Secondly, as the *material and economic output from the parents is increased* and the parents become more experienced and senior members of their external social networks, the family with school-going children has more established and absorbing links and, hence, informational output to society. The families of origin tend to become less crucial as material and support resources as grandparents age. The grandparents may become less well off, financially, and may begin to become more dependent upon their established adult offspring. Parents' professional and leisure networks become correspondingly more important, and the family will tend to have a more substantial and influential social presence, enhancing outputs in that direction.

(3) Thirdly, the *children themselves will be in the process of becoming personages* in school and leisure networks, and in some ways may be "representing" their family in the outer world. This is especially striking if the children have precocious gifts artistically or athletically. The structuralization of a family containing, for example, a young musical prodigy provides an instance by extreme.

B. The Enrichment of Intra-familial Systemic Structure

The establishment, by its outputs, of the families presence in the wider networks, is parallelled by a corresponding enrichment and clarification of the intra-familial systemic structure.

The communication system is expanded and made more complicated by the factual, cultural and network enhanced inpute that this time can provide for the whole family membership. Stability and success gives confidence to the parents' ability to identify their own characteristics and to delineate them from those, on the one hand, of their families of origin, and on the other hand, from their children. The clarity of the intergenerational boundary forming structures of the family system can be enhanced by these changes. For families finding difficulties in making the transition into this phase, the communication systems of the family will be used to oppose the external affiliations of the school-going children. Intergenerational boundaries will be made more permeable, to attach the children to the parents, in order to diminish the establishment of the child's presence out of the home. Parents may call upon intergenerational confusions of role in their families of origin, and remain attached to grandparents of their children, rather than to become established in work or leisure networks. This may be reflected in the intergenerational boundary confusion and permeability in the family of creation. This ties the adults to the children and to the tasks of parenting and the offspring are handicapped in making full use of school.

C. The Development of Control Systems

The feedback loops that enhance or oppose the changes of family outputs in this phase of family life can be discerned in the above examples. They can also be seen in the structure of the control systems of the family. In general, as the parents become more skilled and confident of themselves, on account of the length of time and stability that they have experienced in their work and leisure activities, their comfort in expressing appropriate and effective controls is facilitated. Likewise, latency children, freed from the intensities of the pre-school family, and experienced and practised in accepting or otherwise accommodating the control of school teachers and peers, will become able to be responsive and flexible within the control systems of the family. This maturation of the control systems enables more complex command situations and structures to be used. The family becomes able to engage in increasingly complex, joint leisure and holiday activities. Larger amounts of physical space can be penetrated and ordered by the family in their home, outdoors or in a boarding house or campsite. The increased space and flexibility and complexity of family control increases the complexity and multiplicity of locations within which the family can function as a group. For example, the family can comfortably occupy seats in a cinema or restaurant or can organize long journeys on public or private transport. If on the other hand, the structure of the control systems does not develop in these directions, the family will not make the moves, or to put it the other way round, in order not to make these developments, the control systems may not evolve in this way.

A family operating under rules whereby the outside world is defined as hostile, dangerous and unreliable will not need to evolve a control system encompassing a wide range of locations. The family members will thereby not become accustomed to adapting to new environments, and, feeling uncomfortable and poorly controlled away from home, they can safely believe the world to be hostile, difficult and best avoided.

These examples of differing aspects of the system changes are very incomplete, but indicate the way that structure cannot be defined *in toto*, but can only be referred to by considering various elements of the family systemic structure.

V. DISORDERS OF FAMILIES CONTAINING SCHOOL-GOING CHILDREN

Disturbances in families can, by Haley's (1973) paradigm, be evaluated as showing withdrawal from the whole-hearted negotiations needed for entry into the ages appropriate phases of the life-cycle. The preceding section has demonstrated that evolution of the structure of the family to encompass the transition will be shown, for example, in systems around intra-familial and extra-familial boundaries, around rule and control-establishing systems, and around systems to allow separation and individuation. Resistance to change in each system will be linked to changes in most other family systems. The communication system will evolve to define and enhance resistance to take on the tasks and skills of the changes.

A. Failure to enter the School System

At the time of school entry, the most obvious mode of a family presenting its disability in grappling the tasks required of the new phase, is for the child to fail to manage to get to school. Somatic symptoms may be developed by the child which the parents might accept as a code request for the child to be allowed to stay at home. This can produce an intense focus on the anxious child, enabling the family to avoid the issues of re-assessing their own life-styles and their marital relationship.

B. Case Example: Steven and his Family

For example, a mother, Mrs S, used the time that her only child, Steven, went to primary school, to seek work. At the shop where she found employment, she realized that the manager offered a more exciting and dominating love ideal and she began to have an affair with him. Her husband, who had always jealously guarded his pretty young wife, and who had hoped that she would want another child when Steven began school, seemed to Mrs S to become pale and anxious. Five-year-old Steven became frightened about walking down stairs. They lived on a third floor flat, and so Steven began to be delayed in getting to school in the mornings. Soon, he would not allow himself to get to school at all on Mondays and Tuesdays. Mrs S had to let down her manager at work in order to look after Steven. She began to be anxious and unhappy at not being able to see her lover. She also felt relieved of the guilt she experienced when she had been so excited by their lunch-time love-making. She told her husband that she was frightened to go out, but she did not confess the whole story. Mr S was worried about his wife, and he knew that she had always been nervous herself about going to school. He insisted that she went with him to the family doctor. The G.P. diagnosed depression, and advised a spell off work. Mrs S decided that she would give up her job, accepted the family doctor's advice, and remained at home. Mr S began to do the bulk of the family shopping. He had a row with Mrs S's mother over his care of his wife, and she withdrew her services as an occasional baby-sitter for Steven. Steven's school attendance became much more regular, but he often looked pale and unwell in the mornings. Mr S became more and more the only one of the household to go out, apart from Steven in school hours. Mrs S seemed very angry and miserable for much of the time. Eventually, she was admitted to a psychiatric ward with a diagnosis of "depression and agoraphobia". Mr S re-established good relations with his mother-in-law as she began to care for Steven during Mrs S's admission.

The response of this family to the possibilities for change that school-going provided is especially clear. Both mother and son had a potential for sympto-matology, and it is possible that it was the actions of the helping agencies that facilitated an agreement that Mrs S was the problem. This example is drawn from a patient-orientated psychiatric service for adults. Family therapy was not offered to the family for some years, and then became possible when the child was referred for an overdose in the early teens. Mother had been in and out of hospital on several occasions in the meantime. Another example of presentation in a school-going child is given in the following section.

VI. MODES OF THERAPY IN FAMILIES CONTAINING SCHOOL-GOING CHILDREN

A. Intervention Strategies

The type of family therapy interventions appropriate for families containing school-going children is determined by two considerations:

(1) First, the features of the essential crises of the developmental phase shapes the interventive strategy.

(2) Secondly, the therapy can be seen to be effected by the creative constraints of the communicational issues with families of children who, although verbal, are dominated by non-adult modes of cognition.

B. Characteristic Crises

The crises characteristic of the families tackling entry and transition through this phase have been described extensively in the preceding sections but can be summarized as twofold:

(1) The insertion into, and the influence upon the outside world by the whole family membership, and at the same time, the intrusion of the outside world into the family with the accompanying possibilities of enlargement and enhancement of the intra-familial system.

(2) The freedoms given to the couple to take up a more externally orientated life-style, and for the boundary between the outside world and the family to become more permeable.

C. Technical Implication

Both these crises present specific technical implications. The reorganization of the extra-familial boundary to facilitate the two-way permeability will usually require therapeutic attention in families in this phase of the life-cycle, whether they present with a child or an adult in distress. Interventions appropriate to address this aspect of families with school-going children are likely to be those resembling structural interventions whereby the therapist actively conducts the family in the practice of new family organization. This is likely to include a very clear element of the encouragement of skills development.

(1) Boundary-strengthening Manoeuvres
The therapist is likely to establish him- or herself as potent, confident and skilful. From this position, structural moves to enhance the intergenerational boundary are likely to be useful, because permeability across the inter-generational boundary is a means of fixing or rigidifying the boundary between

the family and the outside world. For example, children not settling at night, coming down to the parents, getting headaches, asthma or nightmares, cause difficulties for baby-sitters. The parents therefore do not go out, and so do not have the activities in their networks, and do not enlarge and enhance their network links. The therapist, by insisting on firm controls from the parents in unison, enforcing clearer space for themselves as individuals and as a couple, within the family, will be opposing infringements of the intergenerational boundaries. At the same time, their own freedom across the extra-familial boundary will be increased. Similarly, dealing with school refusal by requiring the parents to ignore the child's anxieties and protests, and to achieve school attendance forcibly, will free the mother in the daytime for her own extra-familial development.

Such structural moves will tend to produce opposition by the family to protect the parents from their fears concerning their ability to feel safe in the outside world. Their uncertainties as to the quality of their non-parenting marital relationship, may cause them to feel unsure that they can sustain themselves as a couple.

(2) Strengthening Co-parental Skills

On the whole, a therapist is well advised to be "slow" in perceiving and working with these worries of the parents. The author advises against any interpretation or confrontation of these fears, certainly until the co-parenting skills have been augmented by suggestions and practice sessions in and out of the treatment context. Once a couple find that their skills as parents have enabled them to develop more effective control over their children's symptomatic activities such as anxieties or misbehaviours, they may well move quite naturally into an improved self-confidence about their marriage and their contacts with the outside world. The following example demonstrates the way symptoms can be presented by different family members sequentially.

(3) Case Example: Charles and his Family

The family of four contained an 8-year-old son, a 6-year-old mentally retarded son, and their two parents. The referral letter stressed the 8-year-old Charles' stealing as the problem. The therapist observed, to himself, that the 6-year-old Sean had been successfully placed at a day centre (a school for the severely mentally handicapped), and that this had signalled the possibility of entering upon a critical transition. The parents had long been afraid that their handicapped child was too disturbed for the available schools. Skilled team work in the local services had been very effective, and in principle, the couple were delighted. Charles began to steal sweets from local shops. He distributed the stolen goods to his peers at school, and when found out, said that he had to do it because otherwise no one would like him. He said he was teased because he had a mad brother.

The therapist chose to encourage the parents to develop a very strict regime with Charles. Under active direction, they suggested and implemented the following plan: they warned all the local shopkeepers about Charles, and they asked the school staff to keep a close eye upon his largesse. Charles, who had seemed a pathetically anxious and distressed young boy, rapidly became much happier and stopped stealing. The couple soon began to say that Charles was not the real problem, but that it was his father. He had lost all interest and ambition in his job as an accounts clerk in a London theatre. He was preoccupied with thoughts of suicide.

After five sessions over three months, it was quite clear that Charles' problems had been mastered. The therapist would not agree to see the couple alone despite such pressure from them for such an opportunity. They declared their view that the depression was not to do with the children, but was the outcome of the marriage. The therapist pressed the family to go on looking at ways of increasing the fun in their lives, as a family. He emphasized going swimming, dancing, having barbecues, and suggested that they buy a sun lamp in preparation for a holiday in Spain. He encouraged discussion of these projects, utilizing sensually worded details and rhythmic elements (he suspected a sexual distance between the parents). After a further six sessions over three months, the family declared themselves better, terminated therapy, and went off on holiday.

D. Cognitive Styles

Finally, the implications of the particular qualities and cognitive styles of young school children can only be mentioned. The author believes that in work with families and this age-group, therapy should be adapted to allow children to communicate in ways other than that of speech although not, of course, excluding speech. This topic has been addressed elsewhere (Dare and Lindsay, 1979). Play materials such as plasticene, drawing paper and crayons and a doll's house with dolls and family puppets, allow children to communicate in play and fantasy. By this means, the children are able to use symbolic expressions of their views of the family processes and systemic structure.

REFERENCES

Bateson, G. (1979). "Mind and Nature", Wildwood, London.

Von Bertalanffy, E. (1950). The Theory of open systems in physics and biology. *In* "Systems Thinking", (E. E. Emery, ed.), Penguin, Harmondsworth.

Bowen, M. (1980). Forward to "The Family Life Cycle", (E. A. Carter and M. McGoldrick, eds), Gardner Press, New York.

Dare, C. (1979). Psychoanalysis and systems in family therapy. *Journal of Family Therapy*, **1**, 137-152.

Dare, C. and Lindsey, C. (1979). Children in family therapy. *Journal of Family Therapy*, **1**, 253-270.

Erikson, E. H. (1950). "Childhood and Society", Norton, New York.

Freud, A. (1966). "Normality and Pathology in Childhood", Hogarth Press, London.

Freud, S. (1905). "Three Essays on Sexuality", Standard Edition, VII, Hogarth Press, London.

Freud, S. (1920). "Beyond The Pleasure Principle", Standard Edition. XVIII, Hogarth Press, London.

Haley, J. (1963). "Strategies of Psychotherapy", Grune and Stratton, New York.

Haley, J. (1973). "Uncommon Therapies", Norton, New York.

Haley, J. (1976). "Problem Solving Therapy", Jossey Bass, San Francisco.

Hoffman, L. (1980). The life cycle and discontinuous change. *In* "The Family Life Cycle", (E. A. Carter and M. McGoldrick, eds), Gardner Press, New York.

Hull, C. (1943). "Principles of Behaviour", Norton, New York.

Katz, D. and Kahn, R. L. (1966). Common characteristics of open systems. *In* "Systems Thinking", (E. E. Emery, ed.), Penguin, Harmondsworth.

Minuchin, S. (1974). "Families and Family Therapy", Harvard University Press, Cambridge, Mass.

Minuchin, S. and Fishman, H. C. (1981). "Family Therapy Techniques", Harvard University Press, Cambridge, Mass.

Spiegel, (1957). The resolution of role conflict within the family. *In* "The Family", (N. W. Bell and E. F. Vogel, eds), Free Press, New York, 1968.

Winnicott, D. W. (1957). "The Child in the Family", Tavistock Publications, London.

Chapter 17

Adolescence in Families

D. Campbell

I. INTRODUCTION

I want to begin by sharing with the reader the opinions, or theoretical biases which will frame this chapter. First, I believe adolescence is a psycho-social stage of development for which the primary task is identity formation; second, that this process of identity formation is an interactional process which takes place in a social context. The social context in this case is the family.

The focus of the chapter is not upon the adolescent as an individual, but rather the impact which *adolescence* has upon the family system, and the interaction between that system and the individual. I am interested in examining the way family systems accommodate the specific changes which are demanded by adolescence.

II. TAKING ADOLESCENCE INTO THE FAMILY

A. Adolescence as a Phenomenon

The phenomenon of "adolescence" tends to arouse strong feelings: excitement, confusion, sadness or elation, and consequently, there is no lack of interest in it as a phenomenon. Parents are distraught by their adolescent children, teachers strive to motivate them, police battle to control them, and pop stars arouse them. Traditionally, the focus of interest has been on the adolescent as an individual, and the professional worker can turn to illuminating work by such people as Anna Freud (1958) and Blos (1962) to understand the internal workings of the adolescent mind.

Within this body of literature, various writers suggest that the adolescent phase of development depends on recognition or feedback from outside sources for successful resolution. Erikson (1968), a major contributor to the thinking about adolescence, described the adolescent's search for identity, not as a solitary process, but as a process of recognition from the community. Interestingly, Erikson also commented on the interaction which exists between the individual and the community. The community recognizes the individual, and in turn "feels recognized by the individual who cares to ask for recognition; it can by the same token, feel deeply—and vengefully—rejected by the individual who does not seem to care". The adolescent's interaction with his outside world is only touched on in Erikson's work, yet this presages the tremendous energy and thought which have developed that view so fully in recent years.

B.   Family Therapy and Adolescence

Family therapists began to turn their attention to the specific problems of adolescence in the 1960s. The argument for family therapy for disturbed adolescents was advanced forcefully by Ackerman (1966), one of the founding fathers in the field.

> The adolescent's instability, his tenderness, his fluid ego, and the fragility of his personality have impelled psychoanalysts to give up the idea of therapy during this transitional phase . . . . Intervention at this [family] level can be extraordinarily effective if it is undertaken in an appropriate situational context.

Ackerman found that problems of "identity formation, conflict with parents, shifts in standards of conscience, problems of acting out—all respond well" to treatment of the whole family.

About this time, Minuchin began publishing the results of his work with disorganized, multi-problem families in New York. One paper (1964) clearly described the dynamic pattern of interaction between mothers and "acting-out" adolescents. The lack of reactivity from the parent creates a deficit in the child's awareness of his impingement on others, and then the child acts up to get a response, acting as though he had a right to anything because of his early deprivation.

From a few voices in the wilderness, the interest in adolescence and families has grown dramatically. A comprehensive review of the field of family therapy in adolescent psychiatry has been prepared by Bruggen and Davis (1977). Another review by Breunlin and Breunlin (1979) evaluates the findings of the major research being done with adolescents and their families.

This growth of interest and ideas has led the student of adolescence from a view of the individual to a view of the individual in context. I believe this represents a philosophical watershed in the field of psychological understanding of such proportions as the division between the physics of Newton and Einstein. Newtonian physics studied the characteristics of objects, and divided the world into mind and matter, but Einstein stated that it is not possible to view an object separate from time. The distinction between mind and matter has become meaningless. The analogy applies to family therapy in that the individual does not exist apart from his interactional context. The individual is, in fact, a collection of experiences of interaction. I believe we can only *know* the individual by experiencing him in the context of his interactions.

C.   New Perspectives on Adolescence and the Family

The frontier beckons the family therapist toward a new way of thinking about adolescence. The internal, emotional turmoil described so eloquently by clinicians recedes in importance, and is supplanted by the notion that in the context of the family, adolescence is a grand manoeuvre in the workings of the family system.

Family therapists are being asked to view reality with a new set of spectacles. These spectacles place individual behaviour at the service of behaviour of the family system. This is not to deny, for example, that the adolescent experiences confusion, sexual pangs, existential doubts and feelings of deep dependency; rather the new perspective defines these experiences in a social context. The new perspective says that when existential doubts become a social event, i.e. are shared with another person through word or action, they should be viewed as manoeuvres designed to elicit a reaction or pattern of reactions from another person or group. As Milton Erickson has said: "Symptoms are contracts between people".

The writing of Selvini-Palazzoli *et al.* (1978) elucidates this point. In their attempts to fathom the workings of disturbed family systems, they write:

> We came to understand that to understand the game, we had to force ourselves to observe all appearances in these families as merely the pragmatic effect of moves, each in their turn soliciting countermoves in the service of the game and its perpetuation (p. 41).

At this point, one must ask whether this extreme view of "all appearances . . . as merely the pragmatic effect of moves" applies to all families or only to families with a psychotic member. I maintain that this view or new perspective is particularly applicable to families of adolescents. What seems to be important is that the family therapist is able to step back, and view the adolescent as a family member. It is akin to ignoring the grace or power of a football forward and instead, seeing him as one part of a well-functioning (or not so well functioning) team. For example, his passes are viewed in terms of creating space on the pitch into which a team-mate may run and take the ball and score. Could the team-mate have scored without a good pass? When considering a goal scored, the pass and shot contribute equally to the final outcome. In this context, a shot does not exist without a pass and vice versa.

What is the nature of the game which adolescents and their families play? I agree with Erikson (1968) that one may describe adolescent behaviour as a quest for identity. In order to create or "find" such an identity, the adolescent must have some response to his behaviour. In order to have a consistent, supportive identity, the adolescent must have consistent responses or feedback from other people. The adolescent's aim is to gain some control over these feedback processes to ensure the creation of his or her identity. Finding a particular role or identity is not as important as having some control to ensure that an identity: *any* identity is created. In Selvini-Palazzoli's terms, the "moves" of an adolescent are attempts to gain control, or "define the relationship", and the adolescent gains control by acting in ways which force the system to accommodate his behaviour with new structures.

Adams (1975) has contributed interesting thoughts about the relationship between structure and control.

> Structures do not exist independently in nature but are made by man . . . structures require man's differentiation of their consistencies to constitute them . . . Structures are entirely relative to the operating unit for which they are structural.

In other words, that which is beyond our control is seen by us as structure. "What may be structural for a peasant may be well under control by landlords."

The relevance of these ideas for adolescence is this: each child experiences a unique set of structures, for example patterns of family transactions. The structures may have to do with the way people respond to him or to attitudes which limit his behaviour, and they may be seen to be beyond his control. However, as the child approaches adolescence, there are changes which occur in many areas of his life, and the *raison d'être* of adolescence is to somehow gather these changes into oneself and formulate an identity. As Erikson (1968) has stated, this identity formation is

> dependent on the process by which a society [and here *I* would say, family] identifies the young individual, recognizing him as somebody who had to become the way he is.

III. THE STRUGGLE FOR CONTROL

What is this process of interaction between adolescent and family by which an identity is "recognized" and formed? I think this process is a struggle for control.

A. The Destruction of Early Childhood Structures

The adolescent feels his growth constrained by structures from his childhood, and feels he must destroy these structures in order to be recognized by new ones appropriate to his adolescence. For example, if an adolescent has been regarded by the family as "mother's baby", he or she may challenge this structure by stealing a car and driving recklessly, as though to communicate that the adolescent is responsible now for his own "life or death". By now regarding this child as a dangerous risk to his own life, a new structure has been created by the adolescent. It is not that the adolescent gains control over the structures in his family, for there will always be structures which are beyond his control; rather he acquires greater ability to influence the *system* to create new structures.

This is a very important point: the great paradox of family life is that we have an illusion of control; each family member's behaviour is influenced by and in turn influences the other family members. Some adolescents struggle mightily to deny this reality and act in ways which attempt to establish a unilateral control over the family system. However, the system will always be beyond changing by any of its individual members.

When an adolescent injects new behaviour into a family system, he is adding "things that will have to find their place among the other elements and will permanently change the particular pre-existing arrangement" (Adams, 1975). However, the particular way in which these new things "find their place among the other elements" is beyond anyone's control, because it is determined by a process of interaction among parts of a total system. To borrow an example from

Bateson (1979), it is akin to the unpredictable pattern which is formed when a heavy object shatters a pane of glass.

B. What is Real?

One might say there are two realities: we are individuals and we are parts of a system. The adolescent's crisis is that he gets stuck between the two realities as though they are on different levels. He has strong feelings, wishes and thoughts which seem to occur inside his own skin and therefore must belong to him; yet he is also aware that the feelings, wishes and thoughts are about people or things beyond his skin. How can he get control over his *own* life when he gets so angry at his *parents*? Adolescence is a time of crisis simply because the adolescent is more aware of himself and the family is more aware of him. This throws the conflict of the two realities into sharp focus. From the family system point of view, the conflict between the two realities may threaten the status quo: a crisis under any circumstances!

The harder the adolescent fights to gain control over the family relationships which will validate his identity, the harder the system fights against him according to its governing principle: that all parts are interdependent. It's a stalemate; the pressure builds up; something has to give; and the family is suddenly sitting in front of you asking for help.

C. Other Views of Reality

The richness of the literature about adolescents and families comes from the various descriptions of the adolescent's struggle to untangle himself from the family system. Shapiro and Zinner (1976) describe shared unconscious fantasies which determine family members' behaviour. The parents may project certain parts of the family unconscious fantasy into the adolescent. The parents see the child in a distorted way, not as he is, and his identity is lost in the service of holding some part of the family unconscious fantasy. Byng-Hall and Miller (1975) refer to the unconscious fantasy as a family myth, such as "We are a close, loving family", which disguises a repudiated theme, such as "We are about to break apart because of anger in the family".

Stierlin (1975) developed ideas about "ownership". If, at the time of adolescent separation, a child is "over-owned" by being enlisted as a "delegate" for the family, he is unable to own himself. He states, "The capacity to own inner property is a function of how we are owned or disowned". The adolescent can only own his life if he is seen to own it by others in the family.

Boszormenyi-Nagy and Spark (1973) interpret adolescent "acting-out" behaviour as a manifestation of loyalty to the family. For example, a rebellious, drug-taking daughter may bring excitement and life to the parents' "dead" marriage; her behaviour may summon authorities who can be helpful to the family; she may be forcing parents to demonstrate their love and concern. Above all, her behaviour stimulates involvement and thereby renewed loyalty to the family system. The central task of the adolescent is to negotiate his release from the family. A child in a family becomes indebted to his parents for years of love and care. To repay his debt he offers loyalty to the family. The adolescent must be liberated from these loyalty obligations in order to free himself to start a life of his own.

IV. ADOLESCENCE AND FAMILY THERAPY

A. The Nature of Family Therapy in Adolescence

What of family therapy then? An integral member of the family system, despite protestations to the contrary, the adolescent can be liberated by changes in the rules which govern the kinds of relationships allowed in the family. When the rules are changed, the relationships change allowing different types of circular feedback to flourish among family members. For example, a child who had been seen as angry and threatening, may receive a different kind of feedback from others, allowing him to change his identity.

How does one know that a change will necessarily be beneficial? If one believes that family systems contain a powerful force for constructive growth (for the system and therefore its members), then systematically removing maladaptive rules allows adaptive rules to become established spontaneously. This may sound radical. It is based on a very positive view of human nature. There are two schools of thought concerning the most effective way to bring about change in the governing rules of a family system: one is *persuasion*; the other is *paradox*.

V. PERSUASION AS AN APPROACH

A family I saw recently illustrates the adolescent struggle for control, and the way this is closely linked with identity formation. This case also demonstrates some methods whereby a family system is directly led toward new patterns of behaviour.

A. The Brookline Family

Mrs Brookline was an attractive 45-year-old woman who had been divorced for 8 years and was bringing up her two children, Gail 14, and Michael 18, on her own. She referred her family for help because Gail was sullen, angry and uncommunicative towards the family, but mainly towards mother. I saw the three of them together for the first session; Michael was unable to come to the second, and as mother and Gail entered the therapy room mother said, "Take off your coat, Gail". Hearing this, I became interested in the family rule or structure whereby mother tells Gail what to do about her clothing. I was very keen to pursue this to see what kind of control battle may exist, and to see how I might help mother and daughter negotiate successfully. Gail, it turned out, was accustomed to asking her mother's advice about what she should wear.

B.   Extract of Session

The following conversation took place between Gail (G) and myself (T):

T: Gail, why do you ask your mother what to wear?

G: Sometimes, I would just like her to tell me . . . but if it's something I don't like and she suggested it, I won't wear it . . . if it's uncomfortable to wear for whatever I'm doing then I'll just say I don't want to wear *that*.

T: She doesn't really know enough about you then. She doesn't know which of your clothes are comfortable and which are uncomfortable.

G: Well, I don't really know.

T: What I'm trying to understand is that you invite her in to suggest some clothing you might wear, but she doesn't seem to know enough about you and your clothes to do a good enough job.

G: She *does* know, but sometimes she just chooses the wrong things.

T: *Why?* . . . and why should she choose the wrong things?

G: Well . . . if it's too hot for me to wear something.

T: Well why doesn't *she* think of that?

G: Well, it's not up to her to think of that.

T: Yes, it is, you've asked her to do your thinking for you. Why doesn't she consider the temperature and style, and where you're going, and what looks right with your colouring . . .?

G: She *does* consider it, but I suppose she likes me to do it for myself.

T: She wants you to do it, but you said you'd rather that she does it *for* you . . . I'd like the two of you to talk about that . . . about who's going to decide about the clothes.

Gail claimed that her mother wanted her to choose clothes for herself. If this was so, why couldn't Gail follow her mother's direction, be an independent teenager and all would be fine? My hunch is that she could not choose her own clothes for two reasons: (i) by having mother do it, she was serving a function for her mother and ultimately the family system, but (ii) by inviting her mother to choose clothes and then criticizing her choices, she kept the conflict alive and was in effect saying, "I can choose my clothes better than you". This "symptom" kept mother and Gail in the arena of conflict, and provided Gail the opportunity to be in control in an area, appearance, which was very important to mother.

C.   A Later Session

During a later session in the therapy, it became clear that although Michael had not been "referred", his own development and identity formation were being impaired. Michael and mother had apparently a very close, conflict-free relationship, and when I heard the first inkling of disagreement between them I asked Michael to pursue this with his mother:

Michael: Do you mind when we have disagreements?

Mother: Of course I mind. I mind very much. But to a certain extent we are able to sit down and discuss them.

Michael: Yes, which is what I said before. We don't have major disagreements.

Mother: Well, I wouldn't say that. Tuesday nights . . .

Michael: Yes, that's what I said before, we either have a very big blow-up or . . .

Therapist: The two of you are going to smooth this whole thing over. Aren't you? It's a conspiracy.

Mother: Against whom?

Therapist: Against me, I suppose. But I won't have it. See, Michael, you said before, "Disagreements separate us," and I said, "Can you talk to your mother about that?" and when you talked to her you said, "Do you mind?" . . . and it was a shift, really, from what you were thinking to what she was thinking . . . She must be a *very* powerful person . . . and *very* influential . . . Does she feel that way?

Michael: She *is* influential . . . She's influenced us from day one and what she is we are.

Therapist: And at "day 18 years" she still does.

Michael: I don't know whether I'd like to have it any other way . . . but . . . (long pause).

Therapist: But, what?

Michael: I've often thought, I don't know what she's . . . what I'm gonna do when she's gone.

I was discouraged when Michael said, "I don't know whether I'd like to have it any other way". But he followed that remark with a "but", and I thought that was my lever to prise off his façade of submission. I asked about his "but" because I wanted him to voice an objection to his mother's influence. In doing so, he made a slip of the tongue: "I don't know what [she's] . . . going to do . . ." which made me wonder about the sacrifice he was making for his mother.

It is interesting at this point how mother comes into the picture much more forcefully:

Michael: I know I'm thinking ahead, but I have thought, "What am I going to do when she's gone".

Mother: Don't you *ever* think you will have time to think about things on your own or make decisions for yourself?

Michael: Yes, but at the moment I'm thinking of, say, myself in so many years' time.

Mother: And you still think I would be making decisions for you in so many years' time?

Michael: I don't know . . . not necessarily decisions but a backup . . . to fall onto, I don't know.

Mother: That gives me an immense amount of power over you, though.

Michael: Maybe because you *have* got power over me.

Mother: Maybe because you're *making* me have power over you.

Michael: Well, I don't do it consciously.

Mother: But you *are* doing it consciously. You're perfectly aware of what you're doing.

Michael: Only now because I'm now thinking about it, but before I was thinking about it . . . .

Mother: What would happen to you if suddenly I wasn't here any more . . . now, not in years to come.

Michael: I don't know . . . I suppose I'd muddle myself out.

Mother: Does that go with the same comment you made when you turned 18 in November and said, "I don't really want to be 18 'cause I don't want to have to take responsibility . . . decisions for myself"?

Michael: Could be.

Mother: I don't really want to have that much power over you. I don't want to feel that I am pulling the strings.

Therapist: O.K., I'm going to come in here because I think, really, this is the challenge for your family, for all of you: how can the two of you have a relationship with each other which is not so powerful . . . in which you are not so powerful over Michael.

There seemed to be something "fishy" about mother's protestations, but I couldn't figure what it was about until after the session when I had a longer time to puzzle over that dialogue between Michael and his mother. I kept thinking about mother's comment, "You're making me have power over you," and I wondered if Michael's identity was bound up with the control he felt he could exert over his mother's dominating behaviour. He felt he could turn it on and off like a tap, but he was stimulated to do so by his mother's dominating behaviour. The interdependence of their behaviour became clear to me. No one had unilateral control.

D. Some Conclusions

This method of therapy encourages family members to discuss and face the struggles for control which are usually masked by ambiguous relationships and ambiguous hierarchies in a system. Haley (1980) actively explores family hierarchies because he believes unclear hierarchies lead to an organization (family) in confusion which leads to eccentric behaviour in the adolescent. What is particular about the persuasive approach as practised by Minuchin, Haley and others, is that family members are told what needs to be done or enlisted to actually enacting it in the session. Also the therapist selectively responds to certain types of behaviour and not others. Madanes (1980) describes her work in which she only responds to a definition of the parents as the ones in charge of the adolescent's eccentric behaviour.

VI. THE USE OF A PARADOXICAL APPROACH

The paradoxical approach to therapy aims to neutralize the family system's resistance to change, thereby freeing the creative potential of the system to find its own adaptive solutions. I have found this approach very effective with families in which the adolescent is showing more disturbed behaviour, such as anorexia. I recently saw an anorexic girl of 19 with her family for ten sessions of therapy. I would like to preface the therapy account with a discussion of symmetry and homeostasis.

A.   Symmetry and Homeostasis*

Bateson (1973) describes two types of relationships: complementary, in which behaviours of A and B are dissimilar but fit together such as voyeurism fits exhibitionism, and the second: symmetrical, in which behaviour of A stimulates more of the same behaviour in B. Disturbed families are locked in symmetrical relationships in which attempts of say, the adolescent, to define the relationship stimulate similar behaviour in others.

For a disturbed family, such as an anorexic one, this struggle becomes a *raison d'être*, and the virtual existence of the family system depends on the maintenance of this struggle by homeostatic mechanisms. Homeostasis, or the tendency of keeping things as they are, is a principle which characterizes all systems, and means that the system tends to behave in a constant way within a defined range. Homeostasis exists in a dynamic relationship with growth or change. Without change there is no homeostasis. A homeostatic family system is bombarded by the forces of change from both within and without, e.g. a husband loses his job, a teenager leaves home, a new baby arrives.

A well functioning homeostatic system will incorporate these changes with more or less distress without losing the basic structural parameters which define the range of behaviours which are acceptable within the system. However, a less well-functioning system cannot incorporate change because the boundaries which define homeostatic behaviour are more rigid, unable to bend under pressure. These families approach a therapist when the family system is under threat of change.

When families feel their homeostasis is threatened, they may remove the threat by putting it into the therapist, who is seen as the agent of change. With the therapist representing change, the family can close ranks behind their homeostasis to ward off this external threat. I think what families want from me is that I take away their pain without the threat of change; and that I simultaneously become a combatant in the struggle between homeostasis and change. A family is a very powerful system, and if I succumb and push for change, I will be rendered therapeutically impotent.

Instead, my initial task is to ally myself with the homeostasis in the family. I must, for example, learn to respect symptoms as the major manoeuvres for preserving status quo, and above all, I must believe that a symptom, however painful, serves the purpose of protecting the family against worse tragedies and therefore is cherished. I must not ask a family to give up a cherished symptom before they are ready.

---

*(See Chapters 1, 4 and 9)

B. Case Example: The Swanson Family

The Swanson family were referred to the Department for Children and Parents of the Tavistock Clinic for family therapy by their G.P. when Linda, aged 19, had a nervous breakdown in December 1979. She was attending college to study A levels, but began losing weight and feeling increasingly depressed with loss of self-confidence. This culminated in her dropping out of college and spending most of her time in her room at home crying, scratching her skin, and wishing she were dead.

(1) Family Structure
The family consisted of mother and stepfather, and 15-year-old Karen. Mother's first husband, the girls' natural father, was described as a manic depressive who committed suicide 8 years ago when the girls would have been 7 and 11. Brian, the stepfather, had known the family for many years. During father's illness, he became a friend and support for Mrs S and this had led to marriage two years prior to referral. The girls retained their father's family name. I was immediately struck by the physical appearance of the family. Mr and Mrs S were attractive, engaging and very neatly groomed and dressed. Karen was bright, talkative and friendly, slightly overweight, and Linda sat in stony silence. She seemed wary and drawn, like a cat waiting to pounce on anything I said or failed to say. She was thin but did not have the skeleton-like facial expression which characterizes the advanced anorexic state.

(2) The Early Stages of Family Therapy
The early stages of the therapy were spent exploring the family's background, the inevitable links between Linda's depression and her father's suicide, and the triangular relationship between Linda, her mother and her stepfather. As I saw it, Linda's powerful symptoms helped her avoid the loss of a very close relationship with her mother through the new marriage. Also she protected her parents from facing the natural disappointments of their relationship which was based solidly on support and prior mutual suffering. I was struck by the amount of anger and disqualification aroused in the family every time I suggested the symptoms might have some value to the entire family system. This alerted me to the need to maintain the status quo, and the need to preserve the myth that the family was suffering the effects of an evil force: anorexia, far removed from the reality of their own relationships.

Some interesting things happened around Easter. There was a three-week gap in the therapy. Linda had planned to spend a week living with a French family near Paris. She was looking forward to the trip; one of the French family was a doctor and they had also had an anorexic daughter. Linda felt she was well-understood by them. But during her trip and the fortnight back in England, she slowly lost weight. She weighed about six stone. I had urgent phone calls from the G.P. and the stepfather about the possibility of hospitalization. I understood this to mean that Linda's life outside the family represented a "threat of change" to the family system, and that her weight loss served the function of solidifying the necessary family homeostasis.

(3) A Later Session

In the first session after Easter, we discussed Linda's eating habits, and it became more and more clear that Linda and her mother were locked in a powerful symmetrical struggle. I was pursuing the idea of Linda and her mother having another break from each other, and discussing the hospitalization in those terms. I also wanted to bring stepfather more strongly into the picture, as though to step between the two women. (In this session, a colleague is observing behind the viewing screen.)

Therapist: There are two possibilities for you two to have a break. Either you [mother] could go off on a holiday, or you [Linda] can go into hospital.

Mother: [to therapist] Well if I just went off for a holiday and Linda's left to her own devices, do you feel she has the perspective to get it together?

Therapist: She's not left to her own devices, Brian would stay.

Linda: What's the point of that, Mum going off on her own. She wouldn't enjoy herself without Brian there. [Linda raises the first objection.]

Therapist: She might do it for you, for your benefit.

Linda: If she went on holiday, spent money to go on holiday, they'd both want to go together.

Therapist: I know, I'm sure they would, but I'm saying she might make that sacrifice for you.

Linda: I'd rather make the sacrifice for her . . . if I may . . . step in.

Therapist: How would you make a sacrifice?

Linda: To go to hospital . . . and they can save the money they would spend on a holiday . . .

Mother [Mother's face shows an exaggerated, "I don't believe this" expression.]

Father: Let's not think about the economics of it, let's just decide what's practical.

Linda: Well, no, but enjoyment as well.

Father: I know.

Therapist: [to Mother] What do you think?

Mother: [exasperated tone] Linda wanting to *sac*rifice . . .

Linda: No . . . I don't want to sacrifice, I'm just using your words . . . I don't see it as that.

Therapist: Mm hmm.

Linda: [Puts head in hand with anguished expression]

Mother: [here went on to say she was so worried about Linda's physical condition, that she feels she is not the best person to monitor Linda's eating but that she needs medical supervision.]

I was fascinated to hear Linda rush to criticize the plan and to reject my use of the word sacrifice. This section ends by mother "appearing" to relinquish the responsibility in favour of medical experts. This is a frequent manoeuvre: it serves to remove conflict from the system.

As we continue, when Linda is asked to comment on these plans, she supports the prevailing view.

Therapist: What if Brian was the one who fed you?

Linda: It creates too much tension in the family, and also they haven't got medical experience, and also they can't carry out a diet at home where I can put on weight first. I'm very frightened of putting on weight, I want to stay the same. They just maintain me. I don't know what you think [to therapist] but is staying at 6 stone a good thing or not? . . . [More discussion about Mother leaving and Father taking over the feeding. Linda asked me if I felt Brian had the knowledge to cure her and I said, "Yes".]

(4) Consultation and Result

I left the room to have a consultation with my colleague who suggested that the resistance to Mother leaving the system was too great. Linda seemed to redouble her efforts to protect her mother, and also to be the one who makes the sacrifice. Together we devised a plan whereby I would acknowledge I was pursuing the wrong path. This might have the effect of reducing the family's resistance to me. Then I could continue the discussion about alternative plans for feeding with greater chance of acceptance. We also felt it was crucial to set Linda up with a dietician (external to the family system) to help her plan her own diet. I returned to the family with the following message:

Therapist: My colleague does not agree with one of the points I've been pursuing; she feels this isn't the time for you [Mother] to go away. She feels it is better for you to stay until you can see that Linda is managing her diet better, and then that's the time to have a break. She thinks it would be too upsetting for you to be away at this particular time. My colleague agrees with your ideas about diet but also suggests you get a medical consultation to discuss the best way to bring about the ideas you have about your weight.

We continued discussing the practical arrangements of negotiating a diet with the dietician.

Therapist: It would be *your* diet, what she would do would be to tell you how much you need.

Linda: She would say you need "x" grams of protein. What form would you like it in. Would you prefer chicken? . . . Yes, well, obviously that's nicer than being presented with bubble and squeak that you think is disgusting . . . Yes, obviously . . . and I like cooking . . . but I just don't know if it would be too much for the family . . . and would it involve me staying at home every day? [I can feel Linda struggling with the family homeostasis.]

Therapist: Well, let's give it a try, and we'll see if it *is* too much for the family.

Linda: It would involve me staying at home, every day?

Therapist: I think, until you felt strong enough to leave . . .

Linda: I've got plans I'm hoping to put into motion; some holidays planned and so forth . . . [to Mother] Shall I go a little bit into that? . . . Shall I tell him about that? . . . .

Mother: It's up to you.

Linda: Well, [to Father] do you think it's relevant?

Father: [Gives affirmative motion with hand.]
Linda: What I'd like to do is be better . . . fit but not fat . . . by the end of
   May . . . etc.

And on she goes describing her plans for holidays, A-levels, and university,
which will occupy her life for the next year.

I asked stepfather to take complete charge of Linda's food intake. He was to
take her to the dietician, help her cook, and be the first line of support for Linda
in place of mother. Mother agreed. During the next fortnight before our next
session, Linda stuck to her diet, sharing the cooking with Brian and gradually
gained weight. When they came to see me, they wanted to talk about problems of
loneliness and boredom at home.

Following this meeting Mr Swanson rang to ask if he and his wife could see me
alone. I agreed and the meeting seemed to provide a good opportunity to
strengthen the marital dyad. I discussed the fact that now Linda was gaining
weight, there might be the excitement and also fear of their getting closer
together.

I think in this small excerpt one can see Linda's symmetrical struggle with her
mother: a struggle in which making a greater sacrifice is a means to being "one-
up". It is inevitable that a therapist is sucked into similar struggles with the
family members, and I certainly felt strong resistance during this session.
However one might speculate that I was involved in a symmetrical struggle with
Linda before the "break", and that when I came back in and admitted by error
or weakness, this freed Linda from having to defeat me with her symptom
and allowed her to use the suggestions about alternative plans for her weight
control.

(5)   Moving Gently Into the Future

As the struggle between Linda and her mother began to ease, Linda was able to
put herself into the future. She discussed extensive plans which covered the next
18 years of her life, and whether she follows them or not, I think this is a sign
that an adolescent is beginning to move beyond the symmetrical struggle with
the family and toward a life of her own.

I am reminded of some of the work of Milton Erickson (1973) who described
an overpassive mother who was unable to let her adolescent daughter separate
from her. He questioned the mother carefully about each of the "changing
steps of her daughter's pubertal growth and development, always emphasizing
how the daughter is a different person from herself." Erickson emphasized
how the daughter, as she developed, would become attractive to boys of 15,
then 16, then 17. In doing this, he reinforced the idea that the daughter is
young and developing whereas the mother is mature, of another generation,
and attractive to mature men like father. This technique helps to differentiate
mother from daughter, and to strengthen generational boundaries within the
family.

VII. INTO THE FUTURE

I would like to lead you, the reader, into the future by leaving you with some ideas which have been brought to life by an ancient American Indian culture.

A paper by Dell (1980) uses an analysis of the Hopi (American Indian) language to say western therapists are bound by the Aristotelian view that reality consists of "things", and that dualisms could be created between material and immaterial, real and unreal, or objective and subjective. The Hopi see reality in terms of "events", or more accurately "eventing". An "event" is a thing which breaks reality into bits and destroys process, but "eventing" is a verb which refers to an emerging process. The Hopi view concurs with Whitehead (1934) that "existence is activity ever merging into the future". Dell states, "Reality is not confined to what happens now, but also included what happened a few minutes ago as well as what will happen shortly."

To return to an earlier statement about the family therapist attempting to change the structure within the family system, if the view of a "person changing his behaviour" is interpreted in the light of Hopi thinking, as a structure or a way of thinking over which the western family have no control, then I assert that such a view of reality or such a "structure" can usefully be abandoned in work with families. Dell states, "If we try to change an object, we are then stuck with the idea that it is either changed or not changed". Consequently, any recurrence of the undesired behaviour is seen by the family as evidence that therapy is "not working", and a pessimistic mood prevents change. If, on the other hand, such a view of reality can be altered by both therapist and family, change can take place as an emergence into the future.

> The Hopi viewpoint is that one may prepare for future change via a specific, repetitive activity or behaviour . . . the more one does this the more future change is accumulated . . . . the more hopeful and confident he become of future change, despite the fact that none has occurred.

Finally he writes, "The accumulating invisible change is matched by a corresponding decrease in the intensity of the behaviour in question".

If the "Western" way of thinking about change can be dissolved as a structure in the minds of families and replaced by a new structure which makes "emergence" into a reality, then I believe the possibility for change within a family is increased enormously. I feel the application of this world view is particularly relevant to families engaged in the adolescent process of the emergence of a new identity.

REFERENCES

Ackerman, N. W. (1966). "Treating the Troubled Family", Basic Books, New York.
Adams, R. N. (1975). "Energy and Structure", University of Texas Press, Austin, Texas.
Bateson, G. (1973). "Steps to an Ecology of Mind", Paladin, St. Albans, Herts.

Bateson, G. (1979). "Mind and Nature", Wildwood House, London.

Blos, P. (1962). "On Adolescence", Free Press, New York.

Bruggen, P. and Davies, G. (1977). Family therapy in adolescent Psychiatry. *British Journal of Psychiatry,* **131**, 433-447.

Boszormenyi-Nagy, I. and Spark, G. (1973). "Invisible Loyalties", Harper and Row, New York.

Breunlin, C. and Breunlin, D. (1979). The family therapy approach to adolescent disturbance: A review of the literature. *Journal of Adolescence,* **2**, 153-169.

Byng-Hall, J. and Miller, M. (1975). Adolescence and the family. *In* "Adolescence: The Crisis of Adjustment", (S. Meyerson, ed.), Allen and Unwin, London.

Dell, P. (1980). The Hopi Family Therapist and the Aristotelian Parents. *Journal of Marital and Family Therapy,* **6**, 123-130.

Erikson, E. (1968). "Identity, Youth and Crisis", Faber and Faber, London.

Freud, A. (1958). "The Psychoanalytic Study of the Child", Vol. XIII, 255-278.

Haley, J. (1973). "Uncommon Therapy", Norton, New York.

Haley, J. (1980). "Leaving Home", McGraw-Hill, New York.

Madanes, C. (1980). Protection, paradox and pretending. *Family Process,* **19**, 179-191.

Minuchin, S., Auerswald, E., King, C. H. and Rabinowitz, C. (1964). The study and treatment of families who produce multiple acting-out boys. *American Journal of Orthopsychiatry,* **34**, 125-133.

Selvini-Palazzoli, M., Boscolo, L., Cecchin, G. and Prata, G. (1978). "Paradox and Counterparadox", Aronson, New York.

Shapiro, R. and Zinner, J. (1976). Family organization and adolescent development. *In* "Task and Organization", (E. Miller, ed.). Tavistock Publications, London.

Stierlin, H. (1975). The dynamics of owning and disowning: Psychoanalytic and family perspectives. *Family Process,* **15, 3,** 277-288.

Whitehead, A. N. (1977). "Nature and Life", Greenwood Press, New York.

Chapter 18

"The Empty Nest":
Families with Older Adolescents and Models of Family Therapy

C. Dare

I. INTRODUCTION: BIOLOGICAL SYSTEMS AND ADOLESCENT PROCESSES

The delivery of a fresh generation of adults is, as a minimum, a crucial biological function of the human family. This contrasts humans with many species which deliver eggs or imagos into the world: a fantasy for humans that George Bernard Shaw entertained for humans in *Back to Methuselah.* Late adolescents, or young adults, which are alternative terminologies exactly illustrating young people's role in the life-cycle as a biological system, are either the end-products of the family life-cycle, or are initiators of its first phase. The family life-cycle, having no real beginning or end, evolves continually through the generations, showing the fluidities and the fixities of complex biological systems.

As they move into the outside world, adolescents have to be the repositories of the adaptive qualities derived from their general culture and their specific genealogy, but must also have been prepared to be the agents of innovation that will carry their culture into a changing bio-social environment. It is not at all clear what the *biological* basis of these capabilities can be. General systems theory has been devised to account for these classes of capabilities (von Bertalanffy, 1950) as has been described in a preceding chapter in this volume (Dare, Chapter 16), but it must be emphasized that this theory is most appropriate when a subject is put into a biological context. It is for this reason that it is relevant for family-systems therapists to be interested in the biology of adolescence, not as a physiological process, but as part of the evolutionary adaptation of the species.

A. How do Adolescents Leave

The question is about how adolescents are enabled to leave their families of origins (and see Campbell, Chapter 17); it concerns the nature of the biological substrate whereby they move out into the world. Such questions are not commonly asked because it seems that the biological basis for the attachment of offspring to elders has attracted much more attention. Bowlby (1969, 1973 and 1980) for example, has sought to examine the psychological development of the individual as shaped by the needs for the infant to become attached to the care-taking mother. Bowlby (1969) evokes the social organization and milieu of the earliest human groups known to have existed by their fossil remains in East African savannah, and speculates as to what in-built behavioural patterns would be required to ensure the survival and safety of human infants. A strong propensity to link up with the care-taker and stay in close proximity to her would be of great importance. Bowlby has labelled these "attachment behaviours". He has suggested that there are probably also some forms of innate responsiveness from adults towards children that potentiate the effectiveness of the infants behaviours. Powerful tendencies to attachments between human infants and their care-takers is especially vital because of the enormous vulnerability of the human infants, and because of their extremely long growth and maturational time-span. Attachment behaviours are clearly part of the building blocks for family life, and Heard (1982) has shown that attachment theory can be a practical tool for the family therapist.

B. Detachment Mechanisms

Fewer questions have been asked concerning the biological, instinctual systems that may lie at the root of the detachment process, and yet the intensity and duration of the relationship of the immature offspring to parents probably needs built-in terminating mechanisms. Primate studies (e.g. Dolhinow, 1972) attest to the fact that the family groups of higher primates (e.g. gorillas, chimpanzees and baboons) all have resources of vigorous expulsion to eliminate adolescent youngsters from the family. What patterns of happenings precipitate physical expulsion are uncertain, but the presence of a sibling is usually one feature. The forcible, physically reinforced exclusion of adolescent primates from their family group is accompanied by clear distress on the part of the youngsters, especially at night time.

It is striking how human separation of adults and their adolescent offspring is rarely described in terms of an expulsion, although the reverse description, of the adult fighting against the increasing independence of their children is often portrayed. The mythology of most cultures presents the young having to wrest "freedom" from the older generation, not the elders having to expel the young.

C. The Role of Incest Prohibitions

A major feature of many human mythologies and forms of social organization is that they show traces or heavy markings of incest prohibitions, and it is possible that these prohibitions form part of the innate patterns of behaviour that facilitate the separation of adolescents from the family. Incest prohibitions are helpful conceptually because both generations seem to be implicated. The prohibition might perhaps serve to protect immature young from being physically overpowered and damaged by the elders, but it is thought to be more likely that it serves to force the young to seek sexual partners out of home, and so to diffuse the family's genetic resources.

II. PSYCHOLOGICAL PROCESSES AND ADOLESCENCE

A. The Role of Sexuality

Psychoanalytic views upon the nature of adolescence are rooted in the physiological changes that in turn require psychological adaptations. Freud (1905) points to the upsurge of sexuality in adolescence, and the possibilities presented to the youngster for full genital sexual experience. Freud noted that this possibility of genital heterosexuality carried with it a recrudescence, in the youngster's self-experience, of a wide range of sexual fantasies and urges, including incestuous longings. The revival of oedipal configurations of desire are suggested by psychoanalysts following Freud's tradition as a major feature of adolescence (e.g. Blos, 1962, Deutsch, 1968) presiding over the time of separation.

B. Identity Formation

Erikson (1950, 1968), in a major contribution to the understanding of the psychology of adolescence for the family therapist, concentrated upon the process of identity formation and the crisis that it implies and engenders. He pointed out that at the time of leaving the family of origin, a youngster must be heavily engaged in making choices that are going to be crucial parts of the definition of the person, both in the mind of the adult-to-be making the transition, and in the eyes of others. Choices about life-style and interests, social and geographical location, religious, professional, occupational, political orientations and allegiances and leisure affiliations, have to be made. The youngster in transition from adolescence to adulthood must make these choices in such a way that the future life will "fit" the psychology of the person. But the ideals and ambitions for the self that become approached or distanced by the possibilities of identities fulfilled or denied in the young person's life are chosen in relationship to that which has been received or rejected from the possibilities and ideals of the parents and other familial personages. The family will have offered overtly, or covertly in open or ambiguous ways, certain longings and expectations about choices for their offspring. Their children have to respond to these wishes or offerings by partial or total acceptance or rejection or by oscillation or compromise. Erikson notes the pain and discomfort of this process, and envisages breakdown in adolescence as either the result of being overwhelmed by the impossibility of finding an identifiable path for the development of a coherent self, or as part of the process of achieving an identity.

C. Family Responses

For the family therapist, the "classical" Freudian view of adolescence draws attention to the crisis for the family of the young and sexual adults who arrive with their longings for and ambivalences about their parents, putting stress for the parents on the sexual choices they made for themselves, and causing them to re-assess or re-affirm their commitment and need for each other. In the face of such stress, Anna Freud (1966) points out that the youngster may progress or regress. The family too, has, as it were, this choice and the parents and their adolescent youngsters may find a way of baulking at the change possibilities that adolescence provides. As will be mentioned later, much symptom formation in adolescence can be understood as an outcome of this process.

Erikson's views integrate with the theory of the family as espoused for example by Stierlin (1977) Boszormenyi-Nagy (1973) and the Milan Group (Palazzoli et al., 1978). Erikson shows us the adolescent struggling to find his or her own authentic identity among the welter of possibilities that society offers. Stierlin (1977) points to the specific qualities of the roles in the world that the adolescent may be required, and will expect of himself, to fulfil for his or her parents. Boszormenyi-Nagy (1973) emphasizes that the adolescent will feel compelled to take his loyalty for the parents' needs of him- or herself into the outside world and into the formation of the next generation families. The concept of loyalty is not specifically referred to by Palazzoli et al. (1978), but their work with disturbed adolescents within families constantly demonstrates allusion to the process whereby young adults express tension between espousing their own lives, or of pursuing a path in fulfilment of super-ordinate family rules.

The extensions of these psychoanalytic propositions into a beginnings of a family-systems viewpoint lead to a classification of the crises of the phase of the family life-cycle concurrent with later adolescence, which will be briefly proposed as a parallel to a division of styles of family therapy with older adolescents.

III. CHANGES IN THE STRUCTURE OF THE FAMILY SYSTEM IN THE PHASE OF THE SEPARATION OF ADOLESCENTS

The family system has to function to deliver its young to the outside world. During adolescence, therefore, the family has to develop the capacity to exist as an entity as a one generational, two-person system. Children tend to come in bunches, so that a family has a number of trials at facilitating this process. Many families may arrive at this phase with only a single parent being principally in charge of the child or children of the family, or there may be a distribution of the children of an originally married couple, between two or more re-groupings. For the purposes of these comments, the family will be discussed as though the above possibilities have not occurred.

A. Cues which Imitate Changes

At some time, in some way, the children and parents of a family recognize cues designating the possibilities of the children eventually growing. Welcomed or feared, these cues will initiate responses that, over time enhance or retard the process. During the transition, the offspring will achieve ejection velocity, and the parents will have devised ways of tolerating or enjoying each other's company without parenting of children as their major focus of common interest and activities. That is, they will enter the post-parenting phase of family life. In the course of this time, members of the grandparental generation may develop illnesses or infirmities that signal their death or they may die. The coincidence of grandparental infirmity or death, the clear identification by the parents of themselves being in the mid-life "plateau", and the move of children out of the home, are parts of a regular and predictable conjunction of life-cycle transitions, stressing a family enormously. These stresses are invaluable in enforcing system change, and are relatively unusual in that their trend is towards a simplification of some features in the systemic structure. This does not mean that the changes are regularly welcomed by any of the family members.

B.   Boundary Making

The simplification of the systemic structure can be elucidated in considering the boundary maintenance activities. The external boundary of the family has to be placed, in some ways, where the internal, inter-generational boundary had existed. As the children leave home, their access to the home becomes more restricted, and will be likely to become formalized, especially if geographical separation is great and contact infrequent. The children's right to take part in family decision-making will have been diminished, and that may require considerable work on the part of the parents, as their grown-up offspring, when living at home may have had high-level democratic voting privileges in most areas of family life.

The characteristics of the family communications system undergo a very interesting change during the leaving phase, because the children will become more like friends in the courtesy, respect and distance they are expected and will expect to maintain. Nonetheless they are family, and may have permission to show expertise in the workings of the family system. This is why it is so often extremely useful to be able to co-opt a grown-up adolescent who has moved out of the home during the therapy of a family presenting a youngster, stuck in the process.

The power and control systems of the family will show the imprint of the above-mentioned qualities. The boundary of the family may require definition by both parents to cope with, for example the intrusiveness of a child temporarily returned home. The manner in which control is exerted will be more as between equals and adults, rather than as between parents and children. This change can be quite striking, for an 18-year-old living at home may be required, by parental assertion, to conform to a family rule. Such a youngster who has left home will have to be treated quite differently.

IV. MODES OF PRESENTATION OF FAMILIES CONTAINING ADOLESCENTS IN THE PHASE OF LEAVING HOME

In keeping with the severity and multiplicity of the changes required of the family system to sustain this transition, the possibilities of casualty are correspondingly large. Many of the syndromes described in the mental health field can be seen as occurring at this phase of the life-cycle of the family. For example, it is in mid- to late-adolescence that many of the major "psychiatric illnesses" are first diagnosed. The psychoses, schizophrenic and manic-depressive, are descriptively rare before this time. Many such breakdowns can usefully be conceptualized as very major moves resisting the possibility of the family having to achieve a two-person status again. Major "neurotic" breakdowns such as anorexia nervosa and severe social phobias are equally clearly part of a retardation of the movement of the family into the post-parenting phase. In these conditions, the inability of the parents to function as a co-ordinated couple in enforcing appropriate life-cycle maturational activities in their disturbed child, protects them from being confronted by their fears that their marriage has no strengths without children. The presenting patient/offspring may seem, in this way, to feel that leaving home is impossible if the family, as represented by the couple, appears to be in danger of disappearing. Such a youngster may also appear to have a delegated function for the sibs whose separation is made possible if the "sick" member is made available to protect the parents from the twosome that they are believed to dread.

Other major disturbances of individual functioning occur in adolescence such as repeated attempted suicide, drug taking, educational drop-out and so on. But the adult generation also has specific casualty also at this time. The old category of "involutional melancholia" can be seen as occurring in this phase of the family life-cycle, while some forms of paranoia are also characteristically disturbances of the older members of families going through this transition. A family-systems viewpoint will often illuminate the resistance to entertaining the transition to the post-parenting phase.

V. IMPLICATIONS FOR THERAPY

Haley (1980) shows that a great deal can be achieved by the application of a rigorous problem solving, strategically orientated mode of therapy with youngsters and families at this stage of the life-cycle. It is the author's experience, however, that therapists should expect some failures if the parents are encouraged to establish clear generational boundary formation, for example, by the exercise of *force majeur*. The mobilization of power by middle-age parents against fully grown offspring can be amazingly effective, but there seem to be fewer occasions when this is as clearly possible as Haley suggests. The strategic aims of the therapy may more often require prescriptions of no change or other counter-paradoxical tactics, more regularly when working with older rather than younger adolescents.

Family treatments with this age group often seem to require, in the later stages, a formal mobilization of a counter-paradoxical systemic intervention to overcome the resistance of the parents to explore the possibilities of themselves having an available life together in the post-parenting phase.

REFERENCES

von Bertalanffy, L. (1950). The Theory of open systems in physics and biology. *In* "Systems Thinking", (F. E. Emery, ed.), 1969, Penguin, Harmondsworth, Middx.

Blos, P. (1962). "On Adolescence", The Free Press, Glencoe.

Boszormenyi-Nagy, I and Spark, G. M. (1973). "Invisible Loyalties", Harper and Row, New York.

Bowlby, J. (1969). "Attachment and Loss Volume One", Hogarth Press, London.

Bowlby, J. (1973). "Attachment and Loss Volume Two", Hogarth Press, London.

Bowlby, J. (1980). "Attachment and Loss Volume Three", Hogarth Press, London.

Deutsch, H. (1968). "Selected Problems of Adolescence", Hogarth Press, London.

Dolhinow, P. (1972). "Primate Patterns", Rinehart and Winston, Holt, New York.

Erikson, E. H. (1950). "Childhood and Society", Norton, New York.

Erikson, E. H. (1968). "Identity: Youth and Crisis", Faber and Faber, London.

Freud, A. (1966). "Normality and Pathology in Childhood", Hogarth Press, London.

Freud, S. (1905). "Three Essays on Sexuality", Standard Edition VII.

Haley, J. (1980). "Leaving Home", McGraw-Hill, New York.

Heard, D. (1982). Family systems and the attachment dynamic. *Journal of Family Therapy*, **4**, 99-116.

Palazzoli, M. S., Boscolo, L., Cecchin, G. and Prata, G. (1978). "Paradox and Counter-paradox", Jason Aronson, New York.

Stierlin, H. (1977). "Psychoanalysis and Family Therapy", Jason Aronson, New York.

Chapter 19

Grandparents, other Relatives, Friends and Pets

J. Byng-Hall

I. INTRODUCTION

The manner in which each generation is bound up with the extended family provides an important key to how each family functions. This chapter will explore how and when to work with past generations, and with others who are outside the nuclear family. Friends and pets will be included here, because although they are not blood members of the family, they often fulfil family roles. A dog might comfort a father, protect a mother, and be looked after by a child all during the same day.

The technical question of who the therapist should work with can be asked this way: When are inappropriate cross-generational coalitions (Haley, 1967) best tackled by having all the participants in the conflict present, changing the system within the session; and when is it best to strengthen appropriate generational ties by keeping another generation, say grandparents, out? One answer is that it is not an either-or process. It is a matter of balance and timing. The most common mistake family therapists make, however, is to leave the extended family out, even when they are behaving just as if they were part of the nuclear family.

II. WHEN SHOULD THE EXTENDED FAMILY BE INVOLVED?

A. Initial Interview

When possible, it is best to work with the system which is impinging on the referred patient day in day out. The whole system has to change if the symptom of that system is to disappear. Leaving parts of the system out slows this change down. For this reason I prefer to telephone the referred families, and invite those who are currently in the household to come. Often families will leave grand-parents, aunts, friends, etc. or whoever is outside the nuclear family behind, despite the invitation. Nevertheless, the invitation paves the way for future involvement. The extended family can be discussed in the first session to discover what roles they play.

B.   Home Visits

The surest way of involving the household is to go to the family home. This can provide some surprises. In one West Indian family, the 14-year-old, Jean, was admitted by her mother to an Observation and Assessment Centre. On admission she had been covered in blood, following a fight with her mother. The Centre's policy is to work in the home. Four generations were waiting there. Jean's grandmother let the social worker, the residential worker and myself in at the front door. She was clearly the boss. Nevertheless, Jean's mother was very angry with the workers for not talking to her first about Jean. There were many children and an older lady present. However, the intense conflict and rivalry between mother and grandmother had to be tackled even in the front hall, before eventually going through into the sitting room and meeting the others.

It appeared that grandmother had looked after Jean, the first born, since childhood, as is so common in the West Indian culture. Jean's mother had emigrated to England when she was one-year-old, and Jean and her grandmother followed three years later. Jean now only did what her grandmother told her. When asked how this presented problems, the grandmother explained that she was about to return to Jamaica so that she could die there. She intended to take Jean. Mother, almost exploding with fury, said she was going to keep Jean so that she could finish her schooling. Jean looked intensely anxious. At this point, grandmother burst into high pitched wailing which was heart-rending to hear. For about half an hour the work centred on helping grandmother to mourn. The elderly woman, who was grandmother-aunt, came over and mothered her, telling her to calm down, and not make so much fuss. This had a calming effect, and the great-great-aunt told her niece that she had to let her daughter decide about Jean. The family was doing its own therapy.

Grandmother and granddaughter had to mourn over their future parting. Mother was working and had six younger children. She could not look after Jean. The family decided that Jean's uncle (mother's brother) could manage her, and the next meeting was arranged to include the uncle. Further work on grandmother's impending departure was done, and the sadness was extended beyond the couple to include mother, uncle and all the children who were also sad and angry about her going. This brief family intervention finished with a discussion about Jean's placement with her uncle.

C.   Involving the Extended Family later in Treatment

Often the key role of other people becomes apparent only after the beginning of therapy. When should they be involved? Sometimes the nature of the problem requires their active assistance straightaway. In one family, the girl who was refusing school ran to maternal grandmother after being taken to school. In this case, the grandmother was invited to the second session, and everyone could see the sense in the request.

It is surprising how resistant middle-age parents become to asking their parents into a session once therapy is under way. Perhaps it should not surprise us so much. If the reader is to imagine taking his or her family of procreation to a therapist, share a family problem with him and then ask his parents to join in, the flavour of the anxiety might be appreciated. For this reason I take particular care to circumvent the resistance to involvement. Framo (1976) describes this resistance, but then makes a virtue of working through the resistance. His technique will be discussed later.

Where the family history and the intergenerational links clearly need work done on them, I ask the grandparents to come quite early in therapy (Byng-Hall, 1979). The task is very clearly defined. The grandparents are asked to contribute their knowledge and expertise to compiling a family tree (Lieberman, 1979). The family is told that the good things in the family as well as the painful areas will be sought out. If the family has experienced the therapist as supportive, they usually succeed in bringing their parents to the session. Contrary to family expectations, if asked they usually come. First an attempt is made to place the symptoms within an appropriate historical context. This is usually possible, especially if the theme expressed by the symptom is followed back several generations. The designated patient can experience enormous relief to find that his problem resonates with previous generations. Secondly, it provides a setting in which middle-age parents can, with the support of the therapist, establish the right to reinterpret the significance of the past. This process is called re-editing family mythology (Byng-Hall, 1979). To establish this right, is important because it symbolizes the transfer of authority to the next generation. These two aims make it important for the whole nuclear family to be present.

III. CLINICAL EXAMPLES

A. Grandparents are Invited to help establish a parent's authority

In one family the father found it difficult to establish his authority in his family of procreation. His own father had suffered and survived appalling hardships as a young man, and was unable to withstand any challenges from his sons. To fend off despair, this grandfather had demanded that he should be idealized by his whole family for surviving against all odds. In the family tree, the therapist took grandfather back in time to before the catastrophic period, and to easier and happier times. This provided safer ground for challenging the grandfather's view of something which had happened at that time. This was achieved when the two men, father and grandfather, agreed to differ on whether great-grandfather was thrifty or mean. This disagreement provided a big step from his position of father always being deferential. The fantasy that if grandfather was challenged he would crumble was not born out. From this point on, the father was much more able to control his own son. Confrontations could, he had discovered, be carried through to a safe conclusion.

B.   Grandparents are invited to Challenge a Myth

In another family, depression was particularly terrifying to the mother. When her son became depressed she panicked. In an earlier session, she had expressed her own view that her grandmother and one of her cousins had committed suicide. Her parents came in and helped compile a family tree. The therapist took the family tree back to include many strengths and creative aspects of the family. In my experience I have never found a family in which this has not been possible. The mother, with the help of her spouse, was now ready to challenge her parents' interpretation of these two deaths. Her anxiety could be understood when her parents were visibly shocked by the suggestion. However they did not refute the idea, and the depressed son discussed the possibility of suicide with his grandparents. The discussion opened up to include the terrible losses both these "suicide" ancestors had suffered. The topic was no longer taboo. The old couple were visibly relieved. The son gained considerable relief from being able to see his depression in an historical context. He could now understand both his mother's panic that he might be suicidal whenever he expressed gloomy ideas, but also that she could not openly discuss her worry because it was a particularly taboo topic in her own childhood. Her grandmother had died when she was 3½-years-old; old enough to know that something awful surrounded her grandmother's death which should be kept secret, but young enough for her parents to talk about it in front of her. The improved relationships between the generations paid dividends when cancer struck the grandfather, and mother and grandmother were then able to share their worries openly.

C.   Framo's Approach

Framo (1976) considers that much of the therapeutic work is done in overcoming the reluctance to face parents. For him, the actual meeting is merely the final step in the process. Thus his meeting with grandparents is late in therapy not early. When I sat in as an observer in a couples group that he was conducting (three marital couples who at other times in the week came with their children for family therapy), the strength of his argument was made clear to me. The member of the group who had, he reported, been disturbed, even childlike, previously was now the most composed. This man had met with his mother and an aunt in a session with Dr Framo during the previous week. He had clearly found the confrontation both much more rewarding and less frightening than he antici-pated. It was as if he had now reached his full stature within his family. He could now handle himself with the authority of a 45-year-old within the group and towards his spouse.

The wife in a different couple was planning to meet with her mother and father sometime in the near future. Although she was paying lip service to the value of the meeting, she had many good excuses why it could not be managed. Dr Framo enabled her to reveal her resistance, and help her come to terms with her anxiety which was high because the meeting with parents was unstructured and aimed at resolving problems. Thus the expectation was that difficulties would be addressed, and unlike the drawing of a genogram, there was no acceptable more neutral task defined for the session. Dr Framo only invites the offspring of the grandparents. The spouse and grandchildren are not included. In this way, the middle-aged parent is put back in his or her family of origin without the buffer of the family of procreation. The therapeutic effect seemed to me to be enhanced by the group structure. The achievement of the ultimate hurdle, meeting the family of origin, gained considerable group approval. It also defined the confrontation as the final test. Framo's technique of using a combination of nuclear family therapy, couple group and family of origin meeting seems to me to be very fruitful.

IV. UNCLES, AUNTS, COUSINS AND FRIENDS

In our culture, middle age carries many burdens. The value of strengthening the bonds in the same generation cannot be overestimated. This can provide parents with the strength to face difficulties in caring for either elderly parents or difficult children. It also reduces the tendency for parents to opt out of appropriate generational roles as in the reversion to a childlike role, while demanding that one of their children parents them instead. Cousins or close friends of the same generation, as well as uncles and aunts can be used to strengthen same generation bonds. To avoid anxiety about opening up old conflicts, specific middle age tasks provide a fruitful meeting point. Caring for ageing parents provides one such situation. Brothers and sisters (aunts and uncles of a child patient) can come together with this task in mind. A common finding is that siblings in middle age can frequently surprise themselves by the way in which they can come together, refinding some of the old joys and companionship which were present in childhood albeit entangled in sibling rivalries. This cannot automatically be expected to happen spontaneously and the therapist, as with the meetings with grandparents, often has to work to reduce resistance. The fear is that old conflicts will merely be reopened. Stating the positive, constructive aim of the meeting helps.

A. Clinical Examples

(1) The X Family: Sharing Grief

During family therapy treatment of asthma in a 7-year-old girl, the maternal grandfather died suddenly of a stroke. In the session following this, it became obvious that mourning was being avoided by a row which erupted between Mrs X and her brother. He was apparently furious that his sister had neglected their father, attributing his death to this neglect. Mrs X became preoccupied by her brother's unreasonable expectations of her when he had done nothing himself.

The therapist suggested a joint session. Mrs X immediately resisted this. Work had to be done with Mrs X to help her to see that she was feeling very guilty herself, and feared the accuracy of her brother's accusations. Mr X's help was enlisted in thinking of ways of inviting his brother-in-law which would not seem too threatening to him. He suggested that they should meet to discuss the future of their widowed mother. This worked, and brother and sister met. They were able, to their surprise, to grieve together. The therapist asked about the death of their grandfather. This revealed the fact that he had died in a state of neglect, which had led to many family recriminations. This generation resolved not to repeat that saga.

Sometimes families arrange their own contacts.

(2) The A Family: Recruiting Supports

The 13-year-old girl, Mandy, was beyond the control of her mother, Mrs A, who was slowly dying of multiple sclerosis. The question was whether Mandy should leave home. The work was done at the family home. Following a discussion about which family member could support her, her mother invited her first cousin, who had had a stroke three years before, following which she had had to put her child into care. The two women were able to weep about their losses, and to share the problem of how to be angry with limbs which no longer function.

The A family illustrated some of the advantages of working at the family home. The intensity of the relationships in this single parent/single child family was so high that friends and pets were needed to dilute the tension and support each individual. In one meeting Mandy was very truculent towards the therapist, and 10 minutes after the start of the meeting, she flounced out of the room, opening the front door where there were two teenage girls, whom she had obviously invited to be there. She had learned about recruiting supports. A game was then played over the next half-an-hour. The girls would ring the front door bell, Mrs A would hobble across the room shouting and waving her stick. The girls would giggle and run off. On one occasion, Mrs A hooked Mandy with her stick but was not strong enough to pull her back. My shouted interpretations were equally ineffective in bringing her in again. I realized I had to work with Mrs A. I suggested that perhaps she needed Mandy to make her get up and chase her in anger because then she felt alive, as if she was not ill at all. Perhaps this helped her avoid giving up and taking to her bed, as had happened before. This made her thoughtful, and she stopped answering the door. Surprised, the girls opened the door and stood looking in. I invited the two friends in to help us, saying that they would know what Mandy would like for the future. They came in.

The presence of the friends now enabled Mandy to express some of the things unsaid until now. She made coffee for her friends, leaving out the adults. This led to a discussion about her fury that she had to do the housework for her sick mother. Mandy became extremely abusive towards her mother. I asked the two girls what their mothers would have done. They would have hit her over the "lug hole". I said that perhaps Mandy longed for her mother to do that, both to punish her for her abuse but also to prove that she was still really strong.

Mandy moved across to sit on the back of the easy chair that her mother was sitting in, facing away from her mother, legs hanging down the back of the chair.

This had the effect of trapping her mother, because the chair would tip up if she stood up. From this position, Mandy launched another verbal attack on her mother, describing in graphic detail how when she was small, her mother had strapped her to a chair and tried to smother her with a pillow. Mrs A did not challenge this, but sat weeping.

The friends started trying to divert from the horror of what was being said by laughing and giggling. This raises a technical question about what responsibility the therapist has for outsiders with whom he does not have a clear therapeutic alliance. In this case, I asked if they wanted to leave, but they indicated that what they were hearing was not unusual for them. The flat was in the middle of a huge derelict tenement block.

After a while Mandy slid down, back first, leaving her legs hooked over the back of the chair. Mother and daughter were now very close, back to back. Mandy started up a giggling exchange with her friends about lesbianism. It turned out that Mandy frequently slept with her mother. It was now clear why Mandy ran away at night. The conflict mother and daughter felt was intense, they both desperately wanted and needed a very close relationship, but it became too suffused both with murderous rage, and sexual anxiety.

Towards the end of the last meeting with this family a neighbour and her teenage daughter came in, and offered to have Mandy to live with them. Right at the end, Mrs A's sister, brother-in-law and their children all arrived from Reading, and the details of the new living arrangements were made with the extended family taking over responsibility for monitoring this. The new arrangement provided a solution which was neither too close nor too distant for each of them. Mandy and her mother would be living in the same block but not in the same bed.

V.　ROLE OF PETS IN FAMILY THERAPY

A.　Pets as Sources of Information

Pets provide a valuable source of information. Family issues can often be starkly dramatized by pets, or in stories told about pets. In one session, Mandy placed her huge black rabbit on her lap, lying it on its back; she then leaned over placing her nose next to the animal's teeth. Mrs A told her to take her nose away, had she forgotten how the rabbit had bitten the leg right off the cat? On questioning, it turned out that the cat's leg had been damaged but not amputated in a fight with the rabbit. The therapist used this episode to discuss how Mrs A felt that her leg had been lost (multiple sclerosis); how both Mandy and she felt this was a result of Mandy's attacks on her; and how Mandy now felt she needed to be punished for this, which she demonstrated by inviting an attack from the rabbit. The primitive imagery would have been difficult to convey without this symbolic representation.

Dogs often reveal covert family interactions. They can be invited to the session or encountered in home visits. A huge ferocious Alsatian once met the therapist at the door. His barking was frightening. Waiting for the family to control it, the therapist noticed that the dog's tail was wagging in a very friendly way. Later this was used to illustrate how father's "bark was also worse than his bite". In another family, the dog was welcoming at every visit to the house, or indeed when anyone came into the room. The therapist slowly, however, became aware of something odd. The dog barked furiously whenever anyone tried to leave the room. Aggression in this family was expressed almost entirely by leaving. The presenting problem was the teenage son running away from home. The dog's behaviour was used as a powerful and convincing metaphor for this aspect of family life.

In one family, the dog was described as a member of the family, and so was invited to the session. She went up to each member of the family who was under stress, licking and comforting him or her. This provided the therapist with an accurate picture of where the anxiety was being experienced. It also helped members to be more sensitive to each other.

In another family, the 13-year-old girl was referred for a learning problem. During therapy she was given a poodle puppy for her birthday. She brought this puppy to the next session uninvited. Father in his brusque way had taken on the training of the puppy, claiming that within a week he had house-trained it. At one point in the session the puppy was seen to be performing under the therapist's chair. After the general merriment had died down, father accused mother of being soft on the dog. No wonder there was a puddle, the training he had given had been undermined. The therapist was able to point out the parallel between the girl's failure to learn and the puppy's education; illustrating that conflicting messages, coupled with unrealistic expectations, made learning almost impossible.

VI. THE USE OF VISITS TO AND FROM THE EXTENDED FAMILY

A. Family Reunions

Family visits, either arranged spontaneously by the family or encouraged by the therapists, can provide valuable opportunities for work. The therapist should keep an ear open for these opportunities. For example, the S family mentioned in passing a family reunion planned for the next month. They had been in therapy for 9 months at the time.

The S family originally came from Spain. Antonio, aged 16, had been referred because he was thought to have catatonic schizophrenia. His bizarre symptoms had followed an episode when, after a holiday to Gibraltar, he had challenged his very authoritarian father for the first time. He refused to do the washing up. His father had collapsed apparently dead on the floor, and his mother had screamed that he had killed his father by giving him a coronary. Antonio had rushed out of the room and gone into hiding, only to find out two days later that his father was medically perfectly well. The historical context of this family saga was established quite early in treatment. Mrs S's father, Mr E, had died of a coronary in Mrs S's presence shortly after she had visited Gibraltar only to be called home because of his failing health. Thus a similar saga had been re-enacted a generation later. Antonio's symptoms disappeared after a few sessions, but work continued on family relationships.

For the reunion, the family invited both maternal grandmother, Mrs E, now living in Argentina, and her son, Eduardo, now a successful engineer in Scotland to stay. This was brave because mother and son had not spoken to each other for 11 years as their relationship had deteriorated to an apparently irreconcilable point. Brother and sister had also seen very little of each other over the years. When the therapist heard about it, he invited the whole family to the clinic so that they could compile a genogram of the family. They were asked to invite their two visitors to bring all their family photos with them to London.

Much of the work had been done prior to the session. They had spent until the small hours of the morning pouring over old photos, swapping memories, and getting close to each other. Mrs E proved in the session to be an engaging, lively old lady. Her past was full of loss, illness and hardship. She had become the leader of her siblings, and rebelled against her parents. From the genogram it emerged that Mrs E, Eduardo and Antonio had each played exactly that particular role in each generation.

The three "rebels" made a link with each other, and explored the pain of being perceived as a rebel. Mrs E had been thought of as the ugly sister, but Antonio pointed out that in the photo of her in her twenties she looked very pretty. It was a very touching moment as grandmother and grandson gazed at each other. The values of being a rebel were then explored. Mrs E had led her family out of what she felt was bigoted ignorance, had become a nurse, and supported her brother's and sister's education. She had also led the family out of Spain. Those members who ignored or repudiated this leadership had been killed in the Civil War.

Towards the end of the meeting, Mrs E and her son Eduardo expressed some of their mutual anger and then made a reconciliation. Mrs S was now able to acknowledge how she had encouraged Eduardo to row with their mother, and secretly admired him for his bravery. By now Antonio's rebellion was securely placed within a historical context; it had a valued tradition behind it; it also made sense to everyone. It was no longer mad and terrifying.

B. Visiting Families

Grandparents or parents of adult clients can be involved even if they do not come to the Clinic. Clients can work on issues when they visit them. Bowen (1978) describes this process in detail. The father in one family worked over a period of a year towards learning more from his father about his mother's suicide which had happened ten years ago while he was abroad. He had to start talking about trivial issues before building up to more serious ones. He discovered that his mother had threatened suicide even before she was married. This perspective made him feel less guilty about having left home, which he thought had led to his mother's depression and suicide.

REFERENCES

Bowen, M. (1978). "Family Therapy in Clinical Practice", Aronson, New York.

Byng-Hall, J. (1979). Re-editing Family Mythology During Family Therapy. *Journal of Family Therapy*, **1**, 103-116.

Framo, J. L. (1976). Families of Origin as a Therapeutic Resource for Adults in Marital and Family Therapy: You Can and Should go Home Again. *Family Process*, **15**, 193-210.

Haley, J. (1967). Toward a Theory of Pathological Systems. *In* "Family Therapy and Disturbed Families", (G. Zuk and I. Boszormenyi-Nagy, eds), Science and Behaviour Books, Palo Alto, California.

Lieberman, S. (1979). Transgenerational Analysis: The Geneogram as a Technique in Family Therapy. *Journal of Family Therapy*, **1**, 51-64.

Part V

Intrusions in the Life-Cycle

Chapter 20

Loss, Mourning and Grief

S. Lieberman and D. Black

I. INTRODUCTION

The loss through death of a spouse or immediate family member such as a child or parent is one of the most stressful events we as human beings must face, as well as being a major disruption in the organization of family life. Grieving such a loss is nature's way of attempting to heal the wound which has been sustained, as evidenced by the occurrence of mourning in all primates, most mammals and some birds. Morbid grief is the process of improper repair, mourning gone sour like curdled milk. A description of morbid grief and its effects is illustrated by the following short case history.

A. Case History: Miss K

Miss K, a 20-year-old secretary, lost her 25-year-old fiancé. They had known each other since childhood, and had been engaged for two years. They would have married three months before he died if it were not for his illness (carcinoma of the larynx). Neither of their families would discuss the illness, but they were overkind and protective towards Miss K. She resented the silent, passive way the families seemed to be reacting. Very little discussion of the future took place between herself and her fiancé.

Her fiancé spent his last six weeks in a terminal ward in a large general hospital. Miss K gave up her job and was allowed to take care of her fiancé. In the later stages of his illness, he refused to have anyone else do anything for him. He died on Christmas morning with only his girl-friend present. She was given a strong sedative and seemed to be in a daze. She attended the funeral, but did not cry. Afterwards she returned to her office job but continued to feel that everything was unreal. She became detached from the world. She longed to discuss her bereavement with her family but could not. Her family showered pity on her, and she felt that they kept protecting her emotionally. She visited the grave of her deceased boy-friend daily as she had to pass the cemetery on her way from work. Eventually she suffered severe weight loss, depression and withdrew from people. She spent all her time in bed. Her relatives were very concerned about her.

Losses and an individual's reactions to them are not solely rooted in the person visibly suffering the loss. Losses have repercussions in the family and its relationships which are equally profound. The nuclear and extended families' reactions to and acceptance of loss, mourning and grief can hinder or help each individual family member. In this example, the nuclear family was unable to provide the correct emotional atmosphere, and it was fortuitous that a member of the extended family stepped in.

Miss K accepted an invitation to live with the family of her aunt. She spent the first week in tears and moods; eventually the crying became less, and long discussions took place about her fiancé's illness and death. These discussions occurred over and over again for at least 3 months. Almost daily there was a bout of crying. A great deal of resentment towards her parents was expressed, especially towards her father. Pictures of her dead boy-friend and his grave were displayed in her bedroom. She became brighter, more interested in life generally, and eventually took down the pictures in her bedroom and stopped wearing her engagement ring. After nine months, she met and became engaged to a new boy-friend.

At last contact, she felt that she had worked through the loss for her first fiancé, but knew that she would never forget her first love.

II. THE INDIVIDUAL'S REACTION TO LOSS

A. Stages of Feeling State and Behaviour

Before proceeding to discuss the effects of loss on a family relationship system, the effects of loss on the individuals who make up the systems will be reviewed. Mourning follows upon the loss of a loved one and is distinguished by changes in feeling state and behaviour which occur in stages. First, numbness and unfeeling shock intervene to provide a brief period of disbelief and unreality. Second, a stage of disorganization occurs during which physical symptoms such as "heartache", sighing, sleep disorders, palpitations and various digestive upsets may occur. These are accompanied by feelings of hostility, guilt, anger, despair and sorrow, which wash over an individual in waves or pangs of grief. Mental life becomes preoccupied with the deceased, and behaviour is disturbed by a loss of normal patterns of conduct, pining, searching behaviour and weeping. The third stage marks the resolution of the above disorganization, as the deceased ceases to occupy a central position in the mental life and new activities and behaviour fills the void.

Bowlby (1963) prefers to distinguish four stages:
(1) Shock
(2) Protest
(3) Despair
(4) Recovery
Parkes (1972) agrees with Bowlby that it is difficult to distinguish protest and despair as separate phases.

B. Morbid Grief Reactions

Morbid grief in the individual distorts or delays the normal grief process. In a clinical study of 19 patients suffering with morbid grief (Lieberman, 1978), the signs and symptoms were evaluated using a Morbid Grief Scale. The scale includes many of the most frequently observed reactions including: absence of expected reaction, delayed reaction, avoidance, panic attacks, anniversary reactions, overidealization, identification symptoms, recurrent nightmares, extreme anger, extreme guilt, prolonged grief and physical illness (Lindemann, 1944; Parkes, 1972).

Correlation of these items revealed three patterns. The first was an avoidance pattern in which avoidance of persons, places or things related to the deceased is combined with extreme guilt, extreme anger and the delayed onset of grief. The second pattern combined an absence of expected grief with idealizing the deceased and extreme anger directed towards others. The third pattern was the combination of prolonged grieving with recurrent nightmares and the development of a physical illness.

III. FAMILY REACTIONS TO LOSS

These individual reaction patterns cannot help but be reflected in the family system. The family system may operate like a tuning fork: vibrating in phase with the individual's pathology, or it may operate like a shock-absorber, damping down the pathological manifestations so that a loss may be properly mourned. When the family reacts to enhance or add to the pathology, a family system reaction to loss that parallels the behaviour of the individual occurs; avoidance, idealization and prolonged stressful grief patterns may be seen.

A. Clinical Example: Family Avoidance Patterns

Family avoidance patterns developed in the family of a 54-year-old woman who suffered the death of her mother in 1973 with great fortitude, but became increasingly housebound. In 1974 her sister died, and with that death, the patient was unable to walk out of the house alone at all. She feared she was going insane as her sister had done (her sister developed senile dementia prior to death), and stated she had seen people she mistook for her mother and sister in the street, which had frightened her and kept her from leaving the house.

Her husband and two children went along with her wish not to mention her mother or sister. They tried to protect her by being with her constantly, hiding pictures of her dead relatives, and avoiding contact with other members of her extended family. They completely avoided travelling to the village where her mother was buried.

B. Family Patterns of Idealization

Family patterns of idealization were evident in the family of a 64-year-old white retired widowed woman seen because of feelings of anxiety and depression and an inability to concentrate. Her husband had died 3 years before, and was described as "a wonderful man, a preacher who was very good and kind, a

husband who was perfect in every way". Life without him had become very
difficult, and she still missed him. Prior to his death, all had been well. She was
bitter about her children's reactions to her and to her husband's death. She even
blamed them for his last illness. When at last she was persuaded to invite her
daughter to the office, the meaning of her morbid symptoms became clear. Her
daughter was black, and for the first time she admitted that her husband was
black and that her parents had disapproved of her marriage and disowned her.
Later she admitted that she was pregnant when she married him, and that he had
left her with very little livelihood when he died. Her children felt that their
mother blamed them for their father's death, and they in turn felt angry towards
her and idealized their father.

C. Family Patterns of Physical Illness

A third pattern occurred in the family of a woman whose daughter died. During
the year following the death, she developed eczema and irritable colon. Her
prolonged bouts of crying and nightmares about her daughter's leg amputation
caused her son and husband to isolate her at home.

IV.   AMPLIFICATIONS IN THE SYSTEM

Patterns of response to loss deriving from individual reactions are complemented
by family system reactions to loss. Bowen (1976) describes one such reaction as
the "emotional shock wave". This is a network of serious life events in the
extended family occurring in proximity to the death of a significant family
member. Paul and Grosser (1965) describe a second pattern of family response in
the following terms:

> the inability to cope with loss might be characteristic of a family pattern acquired in
> a milieu where other family members showed a similar failing. This inability was
> usually expressed through denial of its significance on an affective level. Although
> the original losses may have occurred as much as 50 years ago, the response to them
> exercises a lingering effect on the present. Such losses were usually suffered by one
> or the other parent often before the birth of the identified patient. Affects and
> attitudes towards the lost persons had remained essentially unchanged and recent
> losses evoked similar reaction patterns. The current style of family life appears
> permeated with varying degrees of denial or warding off of losses and disappoint-
> ments. Major changes in family homeostasis, such as those which might result in
> separation or independence of its members are resisted.

Two other patterns exist which have been found to be manifested uniquely
in family dynamics and interactions rather than more isolated in the individual.

A. Family Substitutions

The first and most striking observation is that family losses are often followed
rapidly by family gains through marriages or births, as if in an attempt at restitution.

For example the Brown family, when paternal grandfather died, the following year saw the birth of five great-grandchildren and two marriages among the eleven grandchildren. The significance of the act of marriage or conception and birth lies in the replacement of those who have died. Replacements in a family can be conscious or unconscious, covert or obvious. The effect on the spouse or child who becomes the replacement may be negligible or catastrophic depending on the reality of their attributes, the strength of the projections, and the way in which the two match. Equally important is the conscious awareness of the container for the projections and the person seeking a replacement relationship.

The following is an example of the way in which the unconscious projection of a dearly loved but dead relative can affect the child who receives those projections. Miss S, a 17-year-old anorectic girl, was born 10 months after her paternal grandmother died. Her father had been very close to his mother as shown by their one enforced separation during the war. After the war he returned to the family home and remained there even after marriage. His wife became pregnant purposely in order to force him to move, a manoeuvre he never forgave her for. Shortly after the move and birth of his son, his mother became ill and died two years after. His daughter was born the year following her death. When she was born, he felt she looked exactly like his mother. She grew up with him treating her as if she were his mother and developed the same overclose relationship with her. When she became an adolescent, he stifled her independence while his wife was continuously angry and jealous of her daughter's closeness with her husband. She was unaware of the reasons for the growing tension at home, but when her body began to develop and it was clear that she would take after her mother's more voluptuous form, her father began to comment unfavourably. Her father's mother had been very thin all her life and she began to slim with her father's encouragement. The anorexic illness took over and she had to be admitted.

This example illustrates the unconscious use of a child as a container to be filled with the relationship patterns pre-established with a dead relative. Children who serve as replacements can face enormous difficulties related to their eventual growth into adulthood. Separation from parents is a particularly difficult task when the parent is projecting an unseparated dead relative onto the child.

B. The Destruction of Families

An unfortunate family pattern related to loss, is not an uncommon occurrence but tends to come to the notice of a family therapist too late. This is the destruction of families which can occur after a loss, either through further deaths, divorces, illnesses or separations. For example, Mr and Mrs D were happily married for three years until Mr D's father developed lung cancer. Mr D began to show jealousy, and became suspicious of his wife. He started drinking heavily. When his father died, he began to beat her. He started going out with other women. He rarely saw his mother or brother who lived nearby. His only sibling, an older brother also had several affairs, and his marriage was shaky.

Neither brother could discuss their father's death with their mother. Mr D denied that his father's death had any effect on his behaviour, although he also admitted that when his father became ill, he began to wonder for the first time in his life what life was all about.

When his wife threatened a divorce, he agreed to see his GP who referred them both for marital therapy. During the first meeting it became clear that Mr D was severely affected by the death of his father. He had shown a delayed response to the death (greater than two weeks) extreme excess anger, identification with personal traits present in the deceased's last illness and overidealization; four out of thirteen positive indicators of morbid grief. When discussing his father he began crying in the office, and his wife turned away. She was unable to support him when he showed his upset because of her own intense feelings of loss of her father-in-law. After this session, the couple decided to emigrate to Australia. They divorced after returning one year later.

V. FAMILY PATHOLOGY FOLLOWING LOSS

A. The Revealed Partner

Clinically, it is clear that family patterns of reaction to the loss of a loved one are present, but little systematic work has been attempted to discover the incidence of family pathology following loss. The work which has been done usually relates to widows or widowers only. There is an increased incidence of mortality of the remaining partner in the first year after bereavement estimated in studies to be 40 to 1200 times as great as in the general population (Parkes, 1972). Heart disease is particularly implicated as a constant factor. Other psychosomatic studies of the bereaved have established that they tend to consult their doctors more often, that 28% reported a marked deterioration in their health, that four times as many bereaved are admitted to hospital during the first year following bereavement, and that bereavement precipitates mental illness in a proportion of patients during the first year of bereavement.

There are important implications to draw from this work on the individual for the family system sustaining a loss. Not only must the family react to the loss itself, there is an implicit expectation after a loved one dies that further disasters are likely to occur in one or more close family members. In some families, this expectation leads to an overprotective stance in which fragile family members are given a cotton wool treatment which could prevent them from grieving normally. Other families react by increasing the tension and anxiety as they await further disasters while still others deny the loss either passively or actively.

B. Young Children and Their Reactions to Loss

(1) The Child's Conceptual Grasp of Loss
There is evidence that young children respond to the death of family members in a special way. Most of the evidence relates to the circumstances in which a child

loses one or both of his parents. About 1.6% of British children are orphaned of at least one parent (Finer, 1974), although the incidence is falling. The reaction of a child to the death of a parent depends on his stage of development, and on his previous and subsequent experience. A young child's understanding of death is limited by his difficulty in handling abstract concepts, by ignorance, and by lack of experience. There are only a few satisfactory studies of the growth of conceptualization about death (Anthony, 1940; Nagy, 1948). More recently, Koocher (1974) studied the development of the concept of death linking it with the Piagetian stages of cognitive development. These studies have their limitations, but there is general agreement that young children have difficulty in understanding the fact that death is final, and irreversible, and that the dead are different from the living or from objects which have never lived. They tend to think magically and to impute causation to events linked by time or to wishes. Their egocentric view of the world makes it likely that they will feel responsible for the death of someone for whom they harboured antagonistic or ambivalent feelings. They tend to concretize abstract concepts so that they have difficulty in understanding why, for example, Daddy does not return from heaven in time for dinner as he did when he went to Manchester. However, Bluebond-Langner (1978) has demonstrated that very young children with leukaemia can acquire the knowledge that they are going to die, suggesting that concept formation depends on experience. A child's bizarre ideas about death can be understood only by taking account of the limitations in his understanding and knowledge.

For example, a six-year-old was asked what happens to people when they die. "An angel comes down from heaven, cuts off their feet and puts the feet on a shelf in heaven to use for new people." This gruesome fantasy originated from an explanation about what happens to people's souls (soles) after death, which no doubt the adult concerned thought was understood!

(2)   Family attitudes to the child
The attitudes of the family, parents, grandparents and siblings have profound influences on how a child integrates his experiences. The twentieth century taboo on death, coupled with a reduction in the incidence of premature death, has made it difficult for children to acquire either knowledge or experience. Parents and other family members may have to provide manageable experience of death through the keeping of pets and attendance at funerals of distant relations. Whether they can do this depends on their own attitudes to death. The widowed mother who told her young son that "Daddy has chosen to go to Baby Jesus in Heaven", unwittingly left him wondering about how one copes with such a powerful competitor. Pattison (1976) has suggested that "death has become pathogenic because sociocultural taboos prevent children and their families from appropriately coping with death". He suggests that children can cope with the experience of death, but not with the family myth and mystification process.

Bowlby (1963) has suggested that children are more prone to pathological reactions to bereavement. Miller (1971) reviewed the psychoanalytic literature and concludes "that children, in comparison to adults, do not pass through mourning . . .", further, she finds that there is wide agreement that a particular set of responses tends to occur in children who experience the death of one of their parents. These reactions include unconscious and sometimes conscious denial of the reality of the parents' death; rigid screening out of all affective responses connected with the parents' death; marked increase in identification with and idealization of the dead parent; decrease in self-esteem; feelings of guilt; and persistent unconscious fantasies of an ongoing relationship or reunion with the dead parent.

All the studies she quotes are of symptomatic children undergoing psycho-analytic therapy which stated either prior to or subsequent to the death of a parent, so no firm conclusions can be drawn. Nevertheless, there is an impressive body of evidence (Black, 1978) that psychiatric disorder is significantly more common in bereaved children, both during childhood and adult life.

C. Absence of Parenting

One family-related explanation for this morbidity is that children must be parented, and the absence of one parent inevitably distorts their experience and makes it harder for them to learn how to be a father/mother, husband/wife, and an adult man/woman. Birtchnell, (1971) found that having a sibling of the same sex as the dead parent was some protection against the development of later psychiatric disorder, but that *being* an older same-sex sibling predisposed one to mental ill health. Brown *et al.* (1977) found that women who lose their mother in childhood are predisposed to depressive illnesses which is in keeping with these results. Widowed mothers may have to guard against making their eldest son a parental child and thus breaching the generational boundaries (Minuchin, 1974), and of course similarly widowed fathers with their daughters. But whether this increased morbidity is a product of the child's difficulties with expressing and resolving grief, or his adverse family experiences subsequent to the bereavement such as changes in income, housing, schooling, or family structure, and dealing with the grief of a remaining parent cannot be definitely answered at present and must await the outcome of further research.

VI.   FAMILY THERAPY WITH BEREAVED FAMILIES

A.   Operational or Forced Mourning

Forced mourning is used in family therapy to deal with families pathologically entangled in a reaction to loss.

Operational mourning or forced mourning is a therapeutic manoeuvre in family therapy based on the presumption that a family pattern of grieving is morbid and has stifled the growth and development of the individuals within that family. The primary goal of forced mourning is the conversion of a morbid grief reaction to a more normal one which is then followed to its completion. Making real the loss requires active intervention by the therapist by directed enquiry. The sharing of the strong feelings generated is an important new family communication pattern which is used to strengthen new relationships within and without the family boundaries. The therapy proceeds in three phases, the first of which is the detailed enquiry into the major losses sustained by family members. This includes enquiring as to the timing of the loss and the subsequent reaction to it.

(1)   Clinical Example: Mr and Mrs H
For example, Mr and Mrs H had not mentioned the existence of a child, Michael, who had died early in their marriage. It is in the collection of this sort of history that the geneogram (Lieberman, 1979) is a valuable aid. Directed enquiry into the death of Michael revealed that he was the cause of their marriage. Mr H had been in the army and returned there after Michael's birth. Michael's death was borne by his mother alone while her husband was attempting to get emergency leave to join her. They had never shared any discussion of feelings about him, his death or their own marriage forced by a birth and possibly released by a death. Kevin's birth 4 years later exacerbated the bouts of depression Mrs H had been suffering.

(2)   Stimulating Blocked Painful Feelings
The second phase of operational mourning is an inexorable and pitiless attempt to stimulate the painful emotions which are blocked. Mr and Mrs H were asked to visit the grave, to relive the exact circumstances of the final illness, to verbalize feelings of the most negative sort directed at Michael and each other in conjoint sessions including Kevin and their young daughter at times. The therapist must be willing to tolerate and stimulate the painful feelings stored within the individuals in the family without rancour or reproach. The moment arrived when Mr H, having been involved in an angry argument with his wife who insisted that he hadn't cared about Michael, suddenly began to cry. It was then that he revealed his trips to a spiritualist to attempt contact with his dead son.

(3)   Resolution of Grief
The third phase of therapy involves the resolution of the grief and a change in relationship patterns within the family. This was evidenced by the ability of Mr H to leave his wife in one of their stormy scenes at home which was played out in front of both his and her mother. Mr H had never before dared to separate from his wife. His ability to do so stimulated within Mrs H a new awareness of the love she had for her husband. He had altered a dependent clinging relationship into a more mature awareness of their mutual needs. They are continuing at present in therapy, and have been able to share much of their work with their children. A picture of Michael now hangs in their living room along with that of the other children, although important further work is still continuing.

B.   Family Therapy with Bereaved Children

Children, even very young ones, can be aided to express grief and to mourn (see Furman, E., 1974; Miller, 1971; Reeves, 1973; Harris, 1973 for individual treatment; and Black, 1974, 1980; Evans, 1976; Tuters, 1974; Clark, 1972 for family therapy) with a subsequent improvement in functioning. It is likely that their reported difficulties are due to adult avoidance of the task rather than to children's inability to mourn. It is painful for adults to contemplate childhood bereavement; it does violence to our fantasy that childhood should be a happy and conflict-free period. This avoidance can happen even with experienced therapists. Reviewing recently a videotaped interview with a family of children who had lost both parents, one of us (DB) was fascinated to note that she and her co-therapist, as well as the older children had failed to listen to the tentative but clear questioning of the five-year-old, "My mummy is dead, isn't she?", so intent were we to deal with a problem raised by the oldest child.

Furman (1980) describes the sensitive yet painful way in which a three-year-old is helped to know about his father's suicide, "His mindsickness made him so mixed up that he made himself die. The doctors tried to help his mindsickness but they couldn't", he was heard later to tell his friends, demonstrating that he had incorporated this reality. His friends then say: "Your dad was a great swimmer, wasn't he?" "Yes, this is one of the trophies he won. He was a great swimmer."

(1) Clinical Example: Brian and his Family
Brian, aged 12, had been unable to express any grief for his mother, who had died suddenly. Instead he angrily criticized his foster parents who were caring for him and his younger sister. They were not dressing her as his mother would have liked, not giving her the right schooling or the right religious upbringing. He thumped his chair angrily. His violence alarmed his social worker who tried to reason with him gently. But what was needed here was boldness (Parkes, 1977). "What you are really angry about is that you will never see your mother again", his therapist said. Abruptly the rage switched over to grief. He sobbed loudly, inviting what comfort the therapist could give. The loud protesting tears of grief came readily for the first time. When he recovered, he was able to relate more warmly to his foster parents and allow them to care for him instead of feeling he had to do all the parenting of himself and his sister.

Children learn their coping behaviour within their family (Paul and Grosser, 1965; Bowlby and Parkes, 1970). The effect of being brought up in families which suppress and avoid the expression of sad affects, is to produce a rigid family system in the next generation. The logical treatment for such dysfunctional systems is family therapy and this may need to involve three generations.

(2) Clinical Example: Katie and her Family
Katie, aged 8, was referred to one of us (DB) because the G.P. was concerned at the enmeshment of mother and daughter which he felt was impairing the child's development. The mother's concern was different. She wanted help for Katie's learning difficulties. The family consisted of mother (a part-time secretary) and Katie. Father had died when she was 2 years old. The referral had been asked for by father's mother, herself a widow, who was concerned about the damaging

over-protectiveness of mother and the constriction in her social life. The three were seen together.

Mother was unsure that they needed a psychiatrist, and kept her at arm's length with a bright, brittle defensiveness which was felt to cover prolonged and unresolved grief. She was close to and dependent on P.G.M., having poor relationships with her own parents who had been unsupportive throughout the years of her widowhood, as indeed they had been in her childhood. Mother felt her own life was over; she only lived for Katie. She had no joy from her work, friends or family. Two men were courting her; she strung them both along but made it clear there was no question of remarriage or involvement. Katie was unsure about her father's death, as she was about most things. In talking about father, she often used the present tense: "Dad and I both like the same foods, don't we Grandma?" An emotionally immature girl, she had few friends and struggled hard but unsuccessfully to learn at school. Could mother's unresolved grief be affecting Katie's learning ability and her maturation? Using techniques of forced or operational mourning, mother was pushed boldly to consider her life together with her husband, and P.G.M. encouraged to review her life with her son. Both women began to cry and Katie was helped to understand why. P.G.M. was asked to continue to meet with mother and look over old photos with the aim of grieving for what they had lost. Mother was sceptical but agreed to participate.

At the next session 3 weeks later, mother looked very happy. "Do you notice anything different about me?" She announced that she had got engaged and was to be married soon. She and P.G.M. had carried out the task that was set and had had a sad time. Curiously she then felt happier and had allowed her boy-friend to get closer. She could commit herself to him, and for the first time contemplate remarriage. Katie was delighted at the prospect of a new father, and referred to her own father only in the past. Mother was able to begin to recognize P.G.M.'s need for companionship and reciprocate some of the support, thus making the relationship more symmetrical. Follow up one year later showed that Katie was performing at an age-adequate level at school, and was not considered a problem there or at home.

Children's communications can be difficult for parents to understand, and misperceptions and misunderstandings are common. A parent's grief may alarm a child by its vehemence and unfamiliarity, and the family therapist can interpret the mother's behaviour to the child (Black, 1981). Family therapy can therefore be prophylactic, and should be considered in bereavements where there is a high risk of pathological reactions. These would include the loss of a parent in childhood, the loss of a child, loss during pregnancy (Lewis, 1979), loss by suicide, two or more significant losses in close succession, and loss in adults where there was a previous childhood loss.

C. The Death of a Sibling including Stillbirths

Children are often left out of the rituals around the death of a member of the family. In the case of sibling death, they may have entertained ambivalent or frankly hostile feelings which go unrecognized. The parents too may displace their feelings of guilt and self-hatred on to one of the surviving children which may in extreme cases lead to child abuse (Tooley, 1975; Lewis, 1979). If a stillbirth occurs, mourning may be particularly difficult for the family (Lewis, 1976).

(1) June and her Family

June, aged 7, had never been heard to speak at school, although at home she spoke occasionally. Her birth and early history were normal, and by 2 years she was speaking in sentences. Shortly after starting school, her mother had a stillbirth. June, who had been told of the expected birth, saw her mother return from hospital without a baby. No one in the family told her what had happened. It seemed like a conspiracy of silence. June was diagnosed as having elective mutism. It was possible by family therapy to help the family to communicate about the loss, to help them grieve, and to work through June's fears that she had damaged or killed the missing baby by her wish, expressed during the pregnancy, but then forgotten, that her mother should not have a baby. That her wish had come true had shown her that words were damaging and therefore not to be used lightly. Perhaps it was safer not to speak. Her family had demonstrated this to her by not speaking about the baby. Once they understood her misconceptions, they were able to help her to recognize that she had not killed the baby and her speech became normal.

D.   The Dying Child and his Family

We know of no family therapists who have treated families containing a dying child although individual psychotherapy with siblings has been reported (Rosenblatt, 1969) as was work with families containing a dying parent (Black, 1981). Dying children, especially in hospital, are isolated and cut off from their family, often feeling they have to protect and support their parents, and even their doctors (Bluebond-Langner, 1978; Howarth, 1974) rather than being able to count upon support for themselves.

(1)   Clinical Example: Simon and his Family

Simon, a 16-year-old boy with progressive muscular dystrophy which had crippled him considerably, and for which he had been repeatedly hospitalized, talked to his psychotherapist about the burdens which he carried which he felt prevented him from growing-up. His father would not face the fact that Simon's illness would soon kill him, and the parents became unable to communicate about anything. Mother suddenly developed a fulminating breast cancer and predeceased Simon. Although father then accepted some social-work counselling himself, he refused to discuss with Simon the mother's death or Simon's own "burdens". In this case, family therapy was offered but refused.

The only child may have particular problems in coping with his position as the only product of his mother's womb to survive.

(2)   Clinical Example: Jacqueline and her Family

Jacqueline, 10, an only child was referred for abdominal pain which had no organic cause. At a family diagnostic session, a geneogram elicited an odd reaction. Jacquie could talk freely about her maternal grandparents, but hesitated when asked about her father's parents. She peered intently into father's face. She said she was worried to talk about paternal grandfather who had died 4 years ago in case it upset Dad. The latter was amazed, and later work revealed that Jacquie saw herself as a powerful person who could hurt her parents, cause them to separate, and blight her mother's fertility (there had been a series of miscarriages and a separation). Family therapy sessions focussed on helping the parents to "cut her down to size", and relieve her of the burden of omnipotency.

Few research studies, even when allegedly focussing on families with a terminally ill child, actually interview the siblings or consider their needs (see Black and Sturge, 1979 for review). Black and Sturge conclude that life experiences are likely to have their impact modified by the interaction between temperamental variables, and sibling and parental attitudes and relationships. The concept of role assignment within families (Toman, 1961) seems a fruitful one for understanding and intervening preventively in families containing a dying or dead member, where loss or impending loss is producing family dysfunction. The restructuring of the family involves the reallocation of roles hitherto held by that member, so that a sibling may have to take on the role of the "clever" one left behind by the dead child; the eldest boy must take on the dead father's role, etc. Family therapy is the only technique which is likely to do justice to the complexities raised by the need of a family to adjust to loss (Bowen, 1976).

VII.   CONCLUSION

Within family therapy sessions the importance of loss, mourning and grief must not be under-emphasized. The painful emotions and their resultant blocks to family growth and development require delicate but firm handling to carry through the therapeutic contract.

REFERENCES

Anthony, S. (1940). "The Childs Discovery of Death", Routledge & Kegan Paul, London.

Birtchnell, J. (1971). Early parent death in relation to size & constitution of sibship. *Acta. Psychiat. Scand.* **47**, 250–270.

Black, D. (1974). What happens to bereaved children? *Therapeutic Education,* **2**, 15–20.

Black, D. (1978). Annotation:– The bereaved child. *J. Chil. Psychol. Psychiat.* **19**, 187–292.

Black, D. and Sturge, C. (1979). The young child & his siblings. *In* "The Modern Psychiatry of Infancy", (J. Howells, ed.), Oliver & Boyd, Edinburgh.

Black, D. (1981). Mourning & the family. *In* "Developments in Family Therapy", (S. Walrond-Skinner, ed.), Routledge, London.

Bluebond-Langner, M. (1978). "The Private Worlds of Dying Children", Princeton Univ. Press, Princeton, N.J.

Bowen, M. (1976). Family reaction to death. *In* "Family Therapy", (P. Guerin, ed.), Gardner Press, N.Y.

Bowlby, J. (1963). Pathological mourning & childhood mourning. *J.Amer. psychoanal. Assn.* **11**, 500-541.

Bowlby, J. (1972). *Attachment & Loss* (3 vols.) Hogarth Press, London.

Bowlby, J. and Parkes, C. M. (1970). Separation & loss within the family. *In* "The Child in His Family", (C. J. Anthony & C. Koupernik, eds), John Wiley, New York.

Brown, C. W., Harris, T. and Copeland, J. R. (1977). Depression & loss. *Brit. J. Psychiat.* **130**, 1-18.

Clark, M. (1972). A therapeutic approach to treating a grieving 2½ year old. *J.Amer. Acad. Child Psychiat.* **11**, 705-711.

Evans, N. S. (1976). Mourning as a family secret. *J.Amer. Acad. Child Psychiatry*, **15**, 502-509.

Finer, M. (1974). "Report of the Committees on One-Parent Families", HMSO.

Furman, E. (1974). "A Child's Parent Dies", Yale University Press, Newhaven.

Furman, E. (1980). A case of bereavement. *Psychoanalytic Quarterly*, **49**, 554-556.

Harris, M. (1973). The complexity of mental pain seen in a six-year old child following sudden bereavement. *J.Child Psychotherapy*, **3:3**, 35-45.

Howarth, R. (1974). The psychiatric care of children with life-threatening illnesses. *In* "The Care of the Child Facing Death", (L. Burton, ed.), Routledge & Kegan Paul, London.

Koocher, G. P. (1974). Talking with children about death. *Amer.J. Orthopsychiat.* **44**, 404-11.

Lewis, E. (1976). The Management of stillbirth: coping with an unreality. *Lancet*, **2**, 619-20.

Lewis, E. (1979). Inhibition of mourning by pregnancy: psychopathology & management. *Brit.Med. J.* **2**, 27-28.

Lieberman, S. (1978). 19 cases of morbid grief. *Brit. J. Psychiat.* **132**, 159-170.

Lieberman, S. (1979). Transgenerational analysis: The geneogram as technique in family therapy. *Journal of Family Therapy*, **1**, 51-64.

Lindemann, E. (1944). The symptomatology and management of acute grief. *American Journal of Psychiatry*, **101**, 141-149.

Miller, J. B. M. (1971). Childrens reactions to the death of a parent: A review of the psychoanalytic literature. *J. Amer. Psychanalyt. Assn.* **19**, 697-719.

Minuchin, S. (1974). "Families & Family Therapy", Tavistock, London.

Nagy, M. (1948). The child's view of death. *J. Genetic Psychology*, **73**, 3-27.

Parkes, C. M. (1977). What becomes of redundant world models? *Brit. J. Med. Psychol.* **48**, 131-137.

Parkes, M. (1972). "Bereavement: Studies of Grief in Adult Life", Tavistock, London.

Pattison, E. M. (1976). The fatal myth of death in the family. *Am. J. Psychiatry*, **133**, 674-678.

Paul, N. L. and Grosser, G. H. (1965). Operational mourning & its role in conjoint family therapy. *Community Mental Health Journal*, **1**, 339-345.

Reeves, G. (1973). Real life trauma & its implications for therapy. Treatment of children following the death of a parent. *J. Child Psychotherapy*, **3**, 11-26.

Robertson, J. (1952). [Film] "A two year old goes to hospital", Tavistock Child Development Research Unit, London.

Rosenblatt, B. (1969). A young boy's reaction to the death of his sister. *J.Amer. Acad. Child Psychiat.* **8**, 321-325.

Toman, W. (1961). "Family Constellation: Theory & Practice of a Psychological Game", Springer, New York.

Tooley, K. (1975). The choice of a surviving sibling as "scapegoat" in some cases of maternal bereavement—a case report. *J. Child Psychol. Psychiat.* **16**, 331-339.

Tuters, E. (1974). Short term contracts: Brief focal intervention in family mourning. *Social Work Today,* **5**, 226-231.

Chapter 21

Reconstituted Families:
Some Implications for the Family Therapist

M. Robinson

I. INTRODUCTION

Most families bring up their own children in nuclear family groups consisting of parents and their natural children. But these numbers are slowly diminishing and there are now large numbers of "families" of "parents" and "children" who spend a good deal of their conjoint family lives in alternative groupings, some of which might hardly be considered as "families" at all. Nevertheless, society, through various social institutions and what passes for family policy (haphazard as it frequently is), exercises a good deal of normative pressure towards the maintenance of this nuclear family group. At this time, approximately 1 in 10 are single parent families, consisting of deserted, divorced or widowed parents who have to, or who choose to bring up their children alone. Some of these single parents remarry, forming new nuclear groups, and others voluntarily or involuntarily give their children up to become members of other alternative family groups. It is on these reformed reconstituted family groups which this chapter focusses.

Reconstituted families consist of those family units who, for one reason or another, have come together in an attempt to reform a nuclear family of parents and children who are not equally legally and biologically related in the sense of consisting of a marital couple with their natural children, as is the case with natural nuclear families. Most reconstituted families which are reconstructed in this way consist of the "core" of a former originating nuclear family system, which may or may not have been a complete family unit of itself, plus an extra member (or members) who have been added, thus making up an apparently new nuclear family of two parents plus children, not all of whom are biologically related to both the parents.

It will already be apparent that reconstituted families are even more complicated than natural nuclear families, and that each is in the process of becoming reconstituted following its own particular pattern, but also sharing some characteristics with other reconstituted families. It is possible to distinguish three main groupings, each with various sub-types which share some of the main characteristic variables. These three main groupings are adoptive, foster and step-families, who are all reconstituted families who reform with at least some intent to remain together as a nuclear family group for some length of time. (The possible exception to this is the temporary foster home, here differentiated from short-term fostering.) The main distinguishing features of each of the three groupings will be described briefly, so that the similarities and differences can be considered.

II. VARIETIES OF RE-CONSTITUTED FAMILIES

A. Adoptive Families

Adoptive families are those which have added a child who is not the natural child of either parent. Traditionally the perception of an adoptive family is one in which an infertile couple adopt a baby, and thus it is by the act of adoption that the marital partners change from being a couple into becoming a family. But traditions have changed, and nowadays such a stereotype is only one among numbers of recognizable adoptive families. Due to a shortage of babies for adoption, many childless couples are adopting older children. In doing so, they are attempting not only to develop a family unit of their own, but also trying to assimilate into this developing group a child who already has some experience of family life, perhaps in a natural nuclear family or also in a foster home.

Other natural nuclear families are adopting children in addition to their own natural children, and these adoptive children are now more likely to be older children, some even handicapped in one way or another, than they are to be illegitimate babies. (These are now most likely to be brought up in single parent families, who are often later assimilated into step-families.) A third sub-group of adoptive families are those who adopt children of a different racial origin from their own. Many of these children are in fact multi-racial, and in such adoptive families, the initial and outwardly distinguishing feature is that the child's colour is different from that of the rest of the family, which in itself has implications for the reconstituted family group. Adoptive families who add to their number children from a different ethnic culture also have to take this into account within the culture of their own reconstituted family unit.

B. Foster Families

(1) Definition

Foster families are those families to which children who are not the natural children of the couple may be added, as a planned temporary measure (that is, short-term fostering), or for long-term fostering either with a view to adoption or for the duration of the rest of their childhood. Foster children may in fact be biologically related to the foster family, children in need of care being frequently fostered with aunts and uncles. But while there may be some familiarity of family culture, there may also be difficulties which stem from the history which lies within the family of origin (as was the case with Maria Colwell). Most foster families take in children who have already spent some part of their childhood in their natural nuclear family, and in the case of short-term fostering, it is expected that they will return to their own family at least in due course; but meanwhile the intent is that in some measure, they should become part of the foster family.

(2) Fostering Problems
This entails some degree of mutual accommodation within a reconstituted family group, even though the intention is often that the foster child should be regarded as a bird of passage, either retaining his or her personal identity as a member of another natural nuclear family group, or as a preparation for long-term fostering with a view to adoption. As well as the difficulties inherent in the issues of short-term or long-term fostering, and the capacities of the foster child and foster family to accommodate each other with a mutual sufficiency, there is also the vexed question of the relationships between the foster-child-in-the-foster-family, and the foster child in his own natural family. At the time that a child who has been subsequently fostered, was received into care, his or her own natural nuclear family must have been failing to care for the child adequately, although the reasons for such failure may have been temporary and remedial (see Bentovim Chapter 28). Two of the major problems for foster families are whether the foster family and the foster child are able to develop sufficient attachment for the fostering to be functional for all of them, and whether the child's attachment to his or her natural nuclear family (or more likely the residual members of such a family) can be maintained. This will be discussed further when capacity for attachment is being considered, but in the meantime Holman's (1975) concept of "inclusive" and "exclusive" fostering is a useful distinguishing feature.

(3) Inclusive Fostering
For a foster family where the foster child has considerable attachments to his or her own natural nuclear family, it is proposed that the fostering should be *inclusive* in that the child's relationships should be maintained with the original family. The implication is that there should be some kind of direct interaction between the foster-child-in-the-foster-family and the natural nuclear family.

(4) Exclusive Fostering
In the case of *exclusive* fostering, such contacts should not be required of the foster family, the decision being made according to the needs of the foster child. The implication here is that the more the foster child is absorbed into the reconstituted foster family, the less he or she remains attached to his or her original natural nuclear family. This question of whose needs should prevail is a moral dilemma in fostering, but also one in family therapy with reconstituted families, and will be discussed later.

C.   Step-families

(1) Definition
Step-families are those families where the additional member of the family is an adult who is not the natural parent of the children and has not previously been related to the custodial parent. There are however, some step-families where the incoming step-parent already has some legally recognizable affinity with the

family, as for instance when a widowed father marries his deceased wife's sister, who now becomes step-mother as well as aunt. Such situations, as with fostering children with relatives, have special familial features which have their roots in the parental families of origin. Some step-parents may already be natural parents in their own right, others may become an instant parent figure upon marriage and entry into the family. Some may bring into the family their own natural children from a previous family unit, others may leave behind them such children who remain in the custody of a previous partner. Thus the children in families where there are divorce chains, that is where both partners divorce and remarry, may find themselves concurrently members of two (or more) family units where, as is the case with inclusive fostering, the relationships between the family units may vary in quality.

(2) Legitimating Step-families
In the formation of a step-family unit, the fate of the original family group is an important factor. Some step-families are formed following the marriage of the single parent of an illegitimate child (or children) either to the child's natural parent or to another partner. I have elsewhere distinguished such step-families as *legitimating step-families*, although legally such a term only applied if the step-parent (usually a step-father) is either the natural father of the child, or an adoption order is made.

(3) Re-vitalized Step-families
Other step-families are those in which one of the natural parents has died and the widow or widower has remarried; I have described these as *revitalized step-families*.

(4) Reassembled Step-families
Step-families which are created following the divorce of the natural parents are increasing in numbers and in these *reassembled step-families* one of the natural parents (most often the natural mother) has the custody of the children who reside with him or her and the step-parent, while the non-custodial natural parent usually has access to the children, which may be exercised regularly or not at all.

(5) Combination Families
The final category of step-family, to which reference has already been made, is that of the *combination family* described by Schulman (1972), where each partner has natural children from a previous marriage who, whether they all live together or not, are in some degree of relationship with each other, as step-siblings to each other and step-children of their natural parent's new partner. In step-families where children are born following the remarriage, such children, while being the natural children of the new partnership, are half-siblings to those of the previous marriage or marriages.

III. THEORETICAL MODELS FOR FAMILY INTERACTION IN RE-CONSTITUTED FAMILIES

From a broad definition of the loose categories into which reconstituted families can be grouped, it will already be apparent to those engaged in family therapy that such families are by definition even more complex and confusing than natural nuclear families. Therefore, before commenting on some of the typical issues which underlie many of the difficulties in which reconstituted families find themselves, it is useful to distinguish a theoretical model which may be both clarifying and familiar. The one adopted here is the systems approach, which despite its many drawbacks, provides a model for differentiating family relationships and boundaries, and thereby creates a framework within which the therapist may focus and guide his intervention. What a systems approach fails to do is to provide an ideology of family treatment on which a therapist may base a therapeutic paradigm. For instance, one example of the ethical issues which occur again and again in family therapy with reconstituted families is that of a family situation where there is conflict between the needs of the parents and those of the children. The question of whose needs should prevail is always a difficult one, but where there are two (or more) sets of "parents" and children who have already been at risk, it is sometimes a situation where quick action must be taken, especially where family therapists have statutory responsibilities such as those in Social Service Departments and the Probation Service.

IV. THE SYSTEMS APPROACH

A. Here and Now*

Davies (1977) points out

> that all systems of living organisms are open systems and that characteristically an open system is defined as a system in an exchange of matter with its environment importing and exporting energy, building up and breaking down its component parts. Although stable, open systems are always changing, always evolving; although identifiable, classifiable, they present differences over time and in changing circumstances.

Walrond-Skinner (1976) writes of families as open systems.

> A system is not a random collection of components but an inter-dependent organisation in which the behaviour and expression of each component influences and is influenced by all the others . . .

She postulates that each family has

> a vital boundary which provides an interface both with its external environment and its own sub-systems and which circumscribes its identity in space and time.

---

*See Cooklin, Chapter 4

Perkins and Kahan (1979) develop this further. In discussing their comparative study of natural families *vs* step-families with step-fathers, and basing their thinking on the systems model of Kantor and Lehr (1976), they describe three systems that interact with each other and also the outside world.

> These three are the family unit system, the interpersonal subsystem and the personal subsystem. When two or more of these subsystems meet, each with its own boundaries and each with its own set of interrelated parts, they are said to be at an interface. The three subsystems of the family meet at interface both with each other and with the outside world.

Perkins and Kahan postulate that it is important for family system functioning that there is a congruence of perception between the interface of the interacting family subsystems where they meet both with each other and with the outside world. Their view is that interpersonal and intrapersonal problems develop where there is a lack of congruence at the interface. They suggest that in families where a family member is placed, or places himself or herself

> in the position of being inside the family perimeter, but outside the interpersonal subsystem, then he or she will have a different experiential domain from the other family members.

Such an experience will lead to the family member feeling dislocated and cut off from other members of the family.

In any family therefore, there is the family unit system, the interpersonal subsystem of parents and children, which incorporate further subsystems of parents as marriage partners and children as siblings. There are then the subsystems of each of the family members in their own right: a personal or intra-personal subsystem. Miller and Gwynne (1972) draw attention to the intra-personal subsystem, commenting that each individual

> has an inner world of thoughts and feelings that are derived from his biological inheritance and from what he had learnt and mislearnt from his lifetime and experience; he lives in an environment to which he has to relate himself in order to survive; and it is the function of the ego—the conscious thinking mind—to regulate transactions across the boundary between inside and outside.

B. Systems: Over Time

The usefulness of the systems model for family functioning is that as well as distinguishing the three interlocking systems within the family, it is also possible to differentiate between the "inner life" of the family and the outside life as part of the social world. What Perkins and Kahan's model does not emphasize is the process through time which, together with systemic influences outside the family, can and often does bring about changes.

(1) Bohannen's Approach

Bohannen's (1971) work is helpful here, in that he hypothesizes the occurrence of what he calls six stations in the process of divorce, all of which may be happening concurrently or consecutively in couples as they move from the initial estrangement to an ultimate regaining of personal autonomy. These six processes he describes as the emotional, the legal, the economic, the co-parental, the community, and the psychic divorces. It could be argued that many couples, particularly those whose children are still young, may not fully complete these processes for many years. It may not even be advantageous to themselves or their children that they do so, even though this may delay them gaining a new personal autonomy. There has been little research in the area of family breakdown and the capacity for investment in multiple family relationships.

(2)   Wallerstein and Kelly
Recent work by Wallerstein and Kelly (1980) carried out with well motivated and previously intact families at the time of their divorce, and followed up at 18 months and 5 years after, indicates that it takes at least that long for family systems to restabilize. They also found that the children in their study could make room for a visiting non-custodial father and a step-father and custodial mother; and that step-father only became the psychological parent, when the children voluntarily chose to replace their father in this way.

The model described by Perkins and Kahan seems to describe families who are only some way along this process, and does not take into account the economic and community aspects of the divorced couple. Bohannen on the other hand, does not consider the *family* perspective in his model, though it might usefully be considered in relation to whole families.

V.   APPLICATIONS OF A SYSTEMS APPROACH

A.   Introduction

The systems model as developed by Perkins and Kahan is based on their research into step-families where there are step-fathers following a divorce in which the non-custodial natural fathers continued to have warm relationships with their children and a civilized relationship existed between the former spouses. Nevertheless, it is a useful model to attempt to adapt to other step-families, and to explore in relation to all reconstituted families; although of course further research is necessary.

If Perkins and Kahan's hypothesis is correct and family members in the position of being inside the family perimeter but outside the interpersonal subsystem of the family find themselves in a dislocated situation, then it is at least possible that there may be similar phenomena following the addition of an adoptive or foster child into a natural nuclear family. They consider that in many of their step-families the step-parents

are caught in the intraspace, inside the family perimeter, but outside the inter-personal subsystem, that of the children. Step-children too, may be caught in the intraspace, without access to the marital subsystem.

B. Clinical Example: The J Family

The J family provide an illustration of this family situation. Mr and Mrs J married following his divorce from his second wife. Mr J's three children from each of his two previous marriages had strong bonds of loyalty to each other as the result of going through two divorces, the elder ones "teaching" the younger ones what to expect, and how to manage as the second divorce proceeded. The third Mrs J found herself in the role of wife to Mr J and cook/housekeeper to the children, who it might be said, regarded her as the next in a line of not very adequate "women in the house". They derided her cooking and complained that she talked down to them, and was really only interested in their father. She in turn felt overcrowded, pushed out, and much resented the hereditary burden of "expectations" that she had stepped into, wanting to create within the family a new and more co-equal sharing model for housekeeping.

C. Application to Adoptive Families

In would-be *adoptive* families where the couple are childless, there is a lack of congruence at the interface between themselves as a marital couple who would like to become parents and the outside world's perception of them as a childless couple. Similarly in couples with children of their own who would like to adopt others, there may be a lack of congruence, not only at the family unit interface with the outside world, but also either as between the married couple and their natural children or at an intrapersonal level of one of the family members.

D. Application to Foster Families

In *foster families* the situation is even more complicated, mainly because of the temporary nature of foster care (even long-term), and the concomitant effect of uncertainty on relationships between the foster child and foster family. Child care practice tends first to emphasize the possibility of congruence at the interface of the intrapersonal system of the foster mother and the possible foster child. Secondly, the emphasis is on congruence at the interface of the interpersonal subsystem of potential foster mother and foster father. The third important consideration is the congruence at the interface of the marital interpersonal subsystem and the intrapersonal subsystem of the potential foster child. It is relatively unusual for the family unit system to present a congruent interface to the outside world with regard to the advent of a foster child, or even to present a congruent interface between the whole interpersonal subsystem and the family unit system as regards the including of the foster child within the interpersonal subsystem. Often such congruence is not altogether achieved, and there remain two distinct interpersonal subsystems: one which includes the foster parents as natural parents and their own natural children.

VI. THE SOCIAL CONTEXT OF RE-CONSTITUTED FAMILIES AND PROFESSIONAL INTERVENTION

A. Introduction

The discussion so far has focussed only within the boundary of the family unit system, the interface between this and the other subsystems within it, and the interface between all three family systems and the outside world. It will be apparent that in reconstituted families the congruence between them and the outside world is a particularly important factor, and that society impinges on them in ways which are unusual in natural nuclear families. It is therefore necessary to discuss the social context in which reconstituted families are placed.

B. The Needs and Rights of Children

Statutory family policies have remained very chary of intervening directly in the inner family life, and many of the social institutions within which family policy has developed were originally created to maintain and support this privatized sanctity.

For instance, the whole structure of housing and income maintenance policies demonstrate at least the intention to give priority to families with young children, despite the haphazard nature of their growth and co-operation with other social institutions. A study of the development of the education and social service policies reveals a gradual shift from protection of the family unit against the ravages of the industrial revolution when children were considered the possessions of their parents, to present day policies which recognize the needs and rights of the child as an individual.

Statutory intervention in inner family life initially developed for the protection of children at risk from negative societal influences but also from inner family breakdown. Of course the two are intimately connected, and there is a continuous debate as to which has the greater responsibility. Nevertheless, it has long been recognized within family policy that it is necessary for some children to be removed from their families in order to rescue them from what has been proven to be an inner family life which is deleterious to their development. The whole question of the statutory removal of children is a highly controversial one which has many implications for the family therapy approach (see Bentovim, chapter 28).

It is however, important to recognize that in the case of all reconstituted families, with the possible exception of revitalized step-families, the state takes some interest in the provision of proper care for the children. Statutory intervention in the inner life of reconstituted families is haphazard and at times inconsistent, as will become evident later, but the possibility of such intervention is present, and serves socially to differentiate those reconstituted families from natural nuclear families. Such social differentiation inevitably reinforces the inner family experience of being different or even counterfeit, in that they are aspiring to acquire an inner family unit of systems so that they can pass as if they were a natural nuclear family.

C. Adoption and Fostering Situations.

In the case of the addition of children by *adoption* or *fostering* the statutory intervention takes the form of some kind of assessment of the family unit system in order to see whether or not it "comes up to scratch". From the perception of the inner family, it is not always clear on what criteria such judgments are based; and many resent such intrusion, although they may not dare say so, feeling that this may go against them. The representative of statutory intervention in *adoptive* and *foster* families is usually a social worker, and it is he or she who will be working at the interface of the family unit system with the outside world. While the individual social worker has a particularized role and is part of the social service system which has prescribed policies for adoption and fostering, he or she also has an intrapersonal system in their own right. All these factors inevitably influence the shared task, which is to achieve some degree of congruence at the societal/family unit interface with regard to the possible adoption or fostering. Inevitably the social worker is perceived as a person of considerable power; in the case of a possible adoption, that of someone who can give or withhold the child which they want. It could be argued that for this reason, as well as to protect the needs of the child who is to be adopted, the state has devised the system of a further social worker (acting as guardian *ad litem* for the child) who also assesses the family unit system and makes a report to the court, where the ultimate decision is made regarding an adoption order. It will therefore be seen that in *adoptive* families, at least during the period of assessment and the granting of the adoption order, the social workers involved become very much part of the family unit system.

For *foster* families there is a similar period of assessment in which the social worker will be attempting to establish not only what kind of individual foster child could best be assimilated into the potential foster family, but also their capacity to make short- or long-term commitments. Here again, although not always, there are often two social workers, one aligned with the family unit system and endeavouring to understand their perceptions, and another who is aligned not only with the intrapersonal system of the potential foster child, but also with the remaining interpersonal system of the child's natural nuclear family. Certainly this is often the intended policy; it is not difficult to see why such a complex, important and painful procedure too often falls down. Where there are two social workers, each initially aligned with two separate and distinct family unit systems (or partial systems), then it will be clear that the congruence which can be achieved at the interface between the two social workers is a crucial factor in the process. It is also easy to see that in a situation where a foster child is in the family, any difficulties between the various foster family unit subsystems are likely to produce echoes which will resonate along the systems with which each of the social workers is aligned. This is unfortunately not always recognized.

Even more unfortunately, either one may carry out the whole process of assessing, matching and supporting the new unit of foster-child-within-the-foster-family, or one of the usually hard pressed social workers will diminish or terminate their contact with the foster family once an apparently successful placement has been achieved.

D. The Social Context of Step-families

It has already been indicated that it is in the creation of the step-family unit system that the inconsistencies of statutory intervention are fully revealed. Unless a family is already known to some care-giving agency, there is no statutory involvement in legitimated or revitalized step-families. It is only where the children concerned may have already been under the statutory supervision of the local authority, or perhaps on probation, that the state evinces any interest in the reconstitution of such families. Of course, because such incomplete families may be at risk, it is possible that they may be receiving the support of a social worker from a voluntary agency caring for the unmarried mother and her child, or from the medical social worker at the hospital caring for the dying natural parent, but it is unlikely that such workers will have the statutory powers which could lead to state intervention around the time of the remarriage.

In the case of reassembled or combination step-families, state intervention is, if anything, even more haphazard although again the children in such families may already be under some kind of statutory case.

E. Divorce and Professional Intervention

It is at the time of the divorce between the two natural parents, rather than on the occasion of the remarriage of either or both partners, that the possibility of statutory intervention is considered, albeit fleetingly. At the time of granting the decree nisi, the divorce court judge is required to consider the arrangements proposed for the minor children of the divorcing couple, and before the subsequent divorce absolute, he must issue a "certificate of satisfaction" stating either that these arrangements are satisfactory, that they are the best that can be made under the circumstances, or that it is not practical to make any arrangements for the children.

The judge may decide to interview the children himself within the privacy of his chambers, or he may ask the Court Welfare Officer to provide a report. Either of the divorcing partners may also request for such a report by the Court Welfare Officer, who would then attempt to make an assessment which would include, where practicable, the wishes of the children as well as those of the parents. Unless requested by the judge, involvement in conciliation procedures over custody and access of the children is a voluntary matter, and it is only when these arrangements are specifically set out by the court during the divorce proceedings that statutory intervention becomes a possibility.

In fact, Eekelaar et al.'s (1977) study of custody after divorce showed that of 652 cases in England and Wales, in only 11.3% was a Divorce Court Welfare

Officer's report available. A breakdown of figures in cases where custody was uncontested compared with those where it was contested, showed that a report was available in 8.2% of the former and 53% of the latter. Of course divorced couples may subsequently return to the divorce court to request that such custody or access orders may be made, and the number of such orders is quite small in relation to the large numbers of divorces and remarriages which involve children. The statutory involvement of the Court Welfare Officer (usually a probation officer) is limited to initial or subsequent requests for recommendations regarding custody, and although they may, and quite often do provide support during the period following the divorce or custody order, they are not statutorily required to do so. Murch's (1980) study of families in divorce proceedings found that a number of Court Welfare Officers went beyond providing a report for the court and provided casework help, and that this was appreciated by a sizeable minority of the parents who experienced it.

It will therefore be apparent that whereas in all *adoptive* and *foster* families the state impinges on the inner life of the family unit system, at least for a short crisis-oriented period when the reconstituted family group is initially attempting to become a family unit system, it is relatively unlikely that it will do so at the same stage of development for step-families. It is of course possible that newly reconstituted step-families are referred to statutory agencies but, not infrequently, the focus then has a partialized child-care orientation rather than a recognition of the particular needs of the step-family.

VII. COMMON AREAS OF DIFFICULTY

In the discussion of theoretical models, it has already been pointed out that individual family members may find themselves cut off from the rest of the family and, while remaining within the family unit system, are out of touch with some of the interpersonal subsystems within the family. The possibility of there being two distinctive interpersonal subsystems within the family has also been discussed. But such hypothetical models of dislocated family systems and the resultant possible manifestation of problems can only serve as informative guidelines within which the family therapist must focus with greater precision when it comes to therapeutic intervention. Family therapists also need to consider the phenomenological form in which these problems are likely to become manifest, and bearing this in mind, to select nodal points for actual interventions. There are two main areas in which many reconstituted families find themselves in difficulties. The first is the area of family loss, aspects of which are important to all families, but for reconstituted families there has been an actual loss within the lifetime, if not the cognitive living memory, of all the remaining family members. The second area is the capacity of family members for developing new attachments and here again this is of obvious importance for all families. Where reconstituted families differ is that within the lifetime of at least one of the individual family members a major loss has occurred, one which may well have been preceded by a series of traumatic experiences and one of such severity that the individual's capacity for developing mutual and trusting relationships has been impaired.

VIII. LOSS

A. General Aspects

Murray Parkes (1975) has written widely about the importance of mourning in adult life, basing the stages of mourning on his research findings in studies of widows and widowers. His work has been used as the basis from which much understanding has been developed in other areas of loss than that of the death of a loved person. He describes the process of mourning as a series of stages which individuals must go through, though in their own individual ways and time, so that personal autonomy can be ultimately regained and the capacity for making new attachments released. The mourning process is initially one of denial, or avoidance of the recognition that the loss has occurred. The work of the Robertsons most clearly demonstrated in their films of children who are separated from their families and hospitalized, this tendency to deny what is happening. As the realization of the loss begins to become more apparent, the bereaved person feels alarmed, and these feelings may be accompanied by the physiological accompaniments of fear. At this time there is often restless searching, in an attempt to seek out the lost person in some form.

Bereaved people at times apparently reproduce symptoms which are either similar to those of the deceased, or which replicate the manner of their death. The children with whom the Robertsons worked became protesting, clinging and whiney. At these times there are also often outbursts of both anger and guilt, frightening both because of their unpredictability and the intensity of the feelings aroused. These angry feelings may also be directed at the very people who are trying to help; adults for instance, may find themselves outraged at the hospital staff whereas before the death they had found them both caring and competent. Children may regress to earlier tantrums or hostile and withdrawn, sullen anger. The guilty feelings of reproach may lead to internal feelings of loss of self and phantasies of mutilation.

As the grieving begins to become apparent to the bereaved person, there is an intense sadness, which at times gives way to despair, a sadness which seems to occur suddenly and inexplicably at sudden reminders of the loss. Gradually, in a mourning process which is following its normal course, the periods between the bouts of sadness lengthen, and the bereaved person begins to find themselves forgetting for short periods in which they begin to regain a capacity for enjoyment, which they had felt was lost for ever. As they begin to recover and turn towards building a new life without the lost person, they experience feelings as if they were recovering from a serious illness which has been both physical and mental. On recovery, many people find they have acquired new characteristics and strengths they did not hitherto possess (see Lieberman and Black, Chapter 20).

B. Loss and Divorce

Many people in fact never fully recover from serious loss, but some significantly fail to grieve sufficiently, and this has serious repercussions for their future family life. In Pincus' (1976) account of her work with married couples, she points out that repressed mourning unresolved in childhood may become resurrected within the marital relationship, where the old failures to grieve lead to new problems. She writes

> Divorce, like death, means loss and bereavement. Marriages that ended in divorce may be regarded as failures, yet unless some new insight has been gained through the pain of this failure, here too the previously unhappy pattern of interaction may be almost compulsively re-enacted in a new marriage.

C. Loss in Divorce and its Effect on the Children

The recent work of Wallerstein and Kelly (1980) distinguishes various processes through which individual family members pass during divorce and its aftermath. Many of these are connected with the various losses experienced as part of this process, as for instance the reduced economic state which often leads to women going out to work; and the need to take on a new role as head of single parent household, plus major responsibilities for child care, which are onerous and exhausting. In almost every family there was one, if not two angry parents whose anger often spilled over into mutual vilification, either directly or via the children. For some of these parents which they describe as "embittered chaotic", the anger was apparently unabated 18 months or even 5 years later, and Wallerstein and Kelly hypothesized that this covered a severe depression. Emotional estrangements and sexual frustrations had characterized many of these marriages, and about half the men and a third of the women launched into new social rounds and sexual activity, some of it quite frenetic. Many of the parents were also quite evidently depressed, at least for a time. Depressed non-custodial fathers for instance, either avoided visiting altogether, or were driven by their guilt to visit with a flurry of intensity which they could not sustain. In general, there was a diminished capacity for parenting, particularly for the younger children, most of whom had been given no satisfactory explanation and had no adequate understanding as to why their parents were divorcing.

There were common experiences among all the children, and others which were age-specific. In general, the experience of the children seemed to be that divorce is a time of anger, fear, worry, sadness, loneliness, yearning for the departed parent, of conflicting loyalties and of feeling rejected. Most of the children did not feel guilty about their parents divorce, although almost all of them had phantasies of bringing them together again. As might be expected, children in the 3–5 age group also showed bewilderment, regressive behaviour, macabre phantasies, considerable emotional needs and attempts at mastery through play. Children of 6–8 showed fear sometimes amounting to dis-organization and inhibition of aggression towards the departed parent, which was expressed openly towards the custodial parent. But the 9–12-year-old children, while apparently coping with poise, courage and clarity revealed underneath an anger which was divorce-specific and remained unaltered at the 18 month follow-up. Particularly vulnerable in this age group were the pre-adolescent boys, who had often been particularly close to their fathers and were also being neglected by their custodial mothers who characteristically gave their attention to the younger children and the girls. The 13–18-year-old age group showed characteristic anger, some of which was age-related, loyalty conflicts and mourning and particular worries about sex and marriage. Some of them were surprisingly realistic about money matters, and some dealt with their fluctuating perceptions by a strategic withdrawal from the family.

D. Loss in Adoption and Fostering

Even in *adoptive* families where the adopted child has been introduced into the family as a baby, there has been the loss of the natural mother, the effect of which remains as yet unknown. For children who are adopted later, or placed in long-term *foster* families, there may be not one, but a series of losses ranging from the original loss of one natural parent to the loss of a family unit, perhaps the privation of a family unit which never was complete, all of which may also include a cumulation of losses from children's homes or foster homes. For children who have experienced such serious and multiple losses, it may be impossible either to face or to work through the mourning processes, and they may remain damaged as personalities who cannot assimilate what for them have been disastrous experiences.

E. Loss in Adoption: Case Example

Jane, for example, was adopted at 4½ following abandonment by her natural mother and a series of foster and small group home placements. She was referred at 14 for violent fights with her adoptive mother. The social worker saw these as a response to current family tensions relating to the transitional pressures within a family which was attempting to contain a developing adolescent. The parents however, and especially the adoptive mother, continually, and in a concealed way, linked the difficulties back to Jane's origins and history prior to living with them. They had never told her very much about her history and were reluctant to do so, referring her back to the social worker for individual discussions. Following the referral, Jane's behaviour became so disturbed that she was briefly admitted to an adolescent unit. The family then firmly reorganized itself around the idea of Jane as a "damaged child" and refused to do any more work on how the adolescence as a whole might be handled, nor would they become involved in helping Jane to work on the loss of her previous "families". The parents' way of coping seemed to be to separate the two sets of familial experiences, thus cutting off to an extent Jane found intolerable.

Others, while remaining partially damaged by their experiences, can come to terms sufficiently with their loss experiences to risk once again attempting to form new attachments, even though they may remain transient and superficial.

F.   Loss in Step-families

In *step*-families, the loss situation is often extremely complicated. Where the natural parent has died, most people would expect the remaining partner to mourn the loss, as they probably would also the children who are older. But it is surprising how many people do not consider that young children also experience the death of a parent at a very basic level, and too often they deny the child the right to grieve by insisting that they are too young to remember or understand. In step-families which have been created following desertion and divorce, or even a planned and relatively civilized divorce, there is still mourning to be done. Each of the individual family members has to grieve at an intrapersonal level for what they have lost, and at the interpersonal subsystem, there may be different experiences of loss for the sibling subsystem which they do not feel able to share with the now remarried custodial parent. The custodial parent may find that, surprisingly, he or she is mourning for the lost family unit, and yet find this difficult to face or to share because of their guilt about their own part in breaking it up. They may even find themselves grieving for the loss of the marital subsystem or deeply concerned about their previous spouse; yet how can they share this with the new step-parent? Many of the early problems of step-families lie in their failure to acknowledge and share with each other their grieving for the loss of the former interpersonal subsystem and the resultant changes in the family unit; and if a sensitive and perceptive family therapist can find ways of opening the system out so that these feelings can be shared, the natural healing processes may be completed by the family themselves.

G.   Loss in Step-families: Case Example

For instance Mr G had married the widow of his great friend (who had committed suicide) thereby becoming step-father to two children with whom he already had good relationships. His own three children remained in the custody of his first wife. The second Mrs G had not been able to mourn the death of her first husband fully, nor to help her children to do so; moreover, she felt immense guilt in relation to the breakup of Mr G's first family. He, in turn had not expected to find himself so cut off from his own children, and had expected his new wife to become as close to them as he was to her children. This family, as the result of various individual, dyadic and family interviews, were able to face and to share at least to some extent, the grief and guilt they all felt, which thus openly acknowledged could begin to run its natural course.

IX.   CAPACITY FOR ATTACHMENT

A.   General Factors

By definition, reconstituted families are those where family members are in the process not only of developing attachments to the new member, but also of redefining the family unit system and the interpersonal subsystem within the family. Despite the immense amount of research in the area of child development, into the effects of separation from natural mothers, and of being brought up in institutional care, we know surprisingly little about the development of bonding processes *within the family*. Much of what is known about early *child* development remains the subject of controversy. However, a recent review and discussion of the state of research in this area by Pilling and Kellmer Pringle (1978) does yield some definitive facts. They consider that an infant's relationship to his or her care-giver begins very early and that the child's congenital characteristics do affect the interaction through their influence on the care-giver. They conclude that

> the infant becomes attached from about the third quarter of the first year to people who interact sufficiently with him and deeply attached to those who are sensitive to his signals and who provide the most social stimulations for him.

While other attachments follow soon after the first, there is no agreement as to whether the child has one major attachment (usually to the mother) and other subsidiary attachments, or is equally attached to two or three people. There have however, been insufficient longitudinal studies to be able to state with certainty that early attachments are linked with later behaviour.

B. Children who move from Institutions to Families

With regard to children who have been in institutional care, it is known to be beneficial to their adjustment if they can form a stable tie with an adult; but that frequent changes of care-giver may lead to difficulties in forming relationships with future care-givers. The quality of substitute care provided is also important. Adcock and White (1977) in writing of planning and decision-making for children in care, base their recommendations on Rutter's work, and stress the importance of the child's experiences before separation; the quality of experience in foster care; the transition from care to back home and the understanding given to him on return. In addition, it is important that the children are not further exposed to stresses and unhappy situations. Tizard's recent work (1977) on the *adoption* of older children throws some light on fostering. Although the number of *foster* children in her research were small, she is able to differentiate three distinct kinds of relationships between the foster child and foster parents, though nothing about their relationship with the natural children of the family. These relationships are described as those who "foster as a charitable act"; "fostering in the hope of adoption"; and "experienced foster parents". This last group sometimes make a deep mutual attachment to a particular child and effectively become a "pseudo adoptive family". She writes

> There was in fact an element of selflessness in the foster parents which one could not help admiring—they lavished the same devotion on quite disturbed children as did the adoptive parents, although these children were not and would probably never be 'their own'. In all these instances the children had no contact, or only minimal contact with their natural parents. Provided that the foster family could

be confident that the natural mother would not reclaim her child they were content not to push the issues of adoption.

Tizard's study of children was concerned with those children who had spent the early years of their lives in residential nurseries, compared to those who were adopted early (between 2 and 4) or late (between 4½ and 7) and those who were restored to their natural parent early or late. Her research shows that though there are often difficulties, and that for some parents there is lasting regret at missing the early years, determined, consistent, committed and sensitive parenting can lead to the development of mutual attachment in a significant proportion of *adoptive* families. Where the adoptive parents' motivation was sufficiently strong they were able to tolerate the limitations and degree of regression which older children seem to need in order to begin to make a mutual attachment. Tizard concluded that

> the subsequent development of the early institutionalised child depends very much on the environment to which he is moved. This seemed to be as true of attachment behaviour as of emotional problems . . . our evidence suggestions that what is more important is that he should be reared by parents, both of whom really want him, and are prepared to devote time, energy and thought to him.

C.   Attachment, Divorce and Step-families

Wallerstein and Kelly's five-year follow-up after divorce showed the important influence of the following components, various combinations of which seemed to have affected the outcome: the way the parents had been able to resolve their own conflicts and anger; the custodial parent's handling of the child and the quality of relationships within the home; the quality of the child's relationship with the "visiting" parent and the way this had kept pace with the child's developing needs. The age and sex of the child seemed less important in the outcome, but the child's strengths and deficits, his or her present resources such as intelligence, capacity for phantasy, social maturity, ability to turn to peers and adults, and the absence of continuing anger and depression all had some relevance; as did the pre-divorce history within the family, and the availability of a supportive human network. By this time, about half the children's parents had remarried, but the study seemed to reveal very little about the relationships within the reconstituted family.

Future research will need to find the answers to many questions about the development of attachment behaviour in *step-families*. If it is possible to assume that the individual capacity for attachment has sufficient potential for each of the reconstituted family members, then two key questions need to be answered. First what is the effect on the parenting capacities of the parental couple, where one of them chose to become the marital partner of the custodial parent, rather than to "foster the children with a view to adoption"? And secondly, how possible is it for children to develop and maintain sufficiently deep attachments for what and to whom? Wallerstein and Kelly's research seems to indicate that children can maintain sufficiently deep attachments to more than one set of parents. Indeed their findings disagree with those of Freud *et al.* (1973), and they recommend that wherever possible divorcing parents should be helped to shape post-divorce arrangements which allow for and encourage continuity in parent–child relationships.

X. SOME NODAL POINTS FOR INTERVENTION IN RE-CONSTITUTED FAMILIES

A. Introduction

In the previous discussion of models for family interaction and in considering the areas of possible difficulty, two key themes have been developed. First, the capacity of individual newly reconstituted families to recover from previous loss experiences sufficiently to develop new attachments is crucial. Secondly, it is essential that the newly developing family unit system must, almost from its inception, develop the ability to maintain open interactions with other family systems closely connected with it, as well as sufficient trust in interactions with social systems available for support. For those in the caring professions who come into contact with reconstituted families at this early and vulnerable stage, a family therapy approach may enable and reinforce the development of congruence at the boundaries of the family unit system and those of the outside world with whom open interactions are critical.

There are several nodal areas where therapists may gain entry to the inner life of the family unit system and which, in discussions with the family, may enable supportive help to be given. These nodal points may be revealed according to the pattern of interaction within any individual family and are not therefore discussed in any order of priority.

B. Names

First names and surnames are important in all families, but in reconstituted families, the names of individual members and also those which denote their relationships to each other are one of the ways in which they are differentiated from natural nuclear families. In *foster* families and *step*-families, the first names of the children have not been given them by both the parental couple, and frequently these names denote elements of the natural family history from which the children come. Even in *adoptive* families where the adopted children are very young, they have usually already been given a name, which has either been retained as a first or second name, or has been changed altogether. Surnames are another aspect of dissonance within the family relationships. It is only in *adoptive* families and *step-families with step-mothers* that the family will all have the same surname; and this fact is often of immediate and lasting embarrassment or even shame. Mrs G for instance, could not bring herself to wear a wedding ring, and continued to be known by her previous married surname, which was of course that borne by her own children. Many families in fact try to cover this difference by using the same surname, even though strictly speaking, this is not legal. Finally, there is the vexed question of the names which are given to the role relationship within the family. Most children can fairly quickly come to terms with the concept of foster, step or half brother or sister; it is the symbolic meanings which lie behind these terms which are more difficult. But the question of nomenclature for the foster, adoptive or step-parents often remains a long-lasting and thorny issue which is also exacerbated by the actual or psychological presence of the natural parents.

C. Access

(1) In Adoption
The *adoption* of a child is legally considered to have extinguished all previous natural relationships, and apart from Scotland, where adults who have been adopted as children have long had the right to find out about their natural parents, the question of access to natural parents has not arisen. However, recent legislation (1975 Children Act) has extended this opportunity to such adults over the age of 18 and subject to safeguarding counselling procedures. The numbers who pursue their inquiries about their natural parentage to the point of meeting their parents is small, but the anxieties around such a possibility now lend a shadow to the family life of adoptive families.

(2) Fostering and Access
As will be clear from the previous discussion, and particularly from the comment about inclusive or exclusive fostering, the question of access by natural parents is one of particular difficulty for *foster* parents. This is a matter over which they have little control, as what powers there are to constrain the access of natural parents to their children in foster care are in the hands of the social workers who, not surprisingly, are frequently reluctant to stop such visiting.

(3) Reassembled, Combination Families and Access
It is in reassembled and combination *step*-families that problems of access seem to cause the most difficulty, as even when the amount of access is laid down by the court, the custodial parent has to return to the court in order that access conditions, which are being abused or refused, are in fact carried out. But in the great majority of cases, conditions of access have not been laid down legally, but left to negotiations between the custodial and non-custodial parents and may continue to be an area of wrangles and disputes for the whole of the children's childhood as the following example shows:

(4) Case example: Susan and her Family
Susan lived with her mother and step-father following a very turbulent divorce between her parents when she was aged 3. The violence of feeling between her parents was so great that all communication was by letter, not even by the phone. Her father was only able to have access to her via "doorstep deliveries" with no

conversation. Negotiations about holidays took place between step-father and father. On one occasion when Susan was not delivered back, the mother and step-father sent the police round to collect her, preferring to do this than face the alternative violent scene they feared.

(5) Access and the Extended Family

The question of visits by or to natural parents is not the only area of access which may cause difficulty for reconstituted families. By the very fact that there has been some previous breakdown in the natural family, it is often the case that other relatives, particularly grandparents or aunts and uncles, have been particularly involved and attached to the children in such families, in the period between the breakdown and the reconstitution of the family. These key relatives are often very important members of the extended family system, and their attitudes to the developing reconstituted family are often crucial in the early stages of attachment.

Access is an issue in which passions run high, and as has already been indicated, are apt to spill over in ways which are disadvantageous and distressing to all concerned. Murch (1980) in a discussion on cathartic listening comments

> Insofar as both solicitors and welfare officers are part of the legal machinery of divorce, it can be argued that through their agency the response of the law to parents in conflicts is emotionally appropriate. Legal machinery has within it powerful symbolic authority — particularly in the form of an independent judge and court, imposing their presence on the psychological background. It often seems to help people contain and yet not deny, powerful and aggressive feelings.

D. Territory

(1) Where is Home?

The question of which place is "home" is an initial problem for all reconstituted families, and there is some evidence of a hierarchy of attachment to particular places of residence. While it is obviously important that the reconstituted family have sufficient time to develop individual and familial attachments to the place in which they reside, it is also necessary for the member who is being incorporated to have sufficient personal physical space which they can consider their own. It is not only the question of the home and surrounding locality which is problematic, but also material belongings such as clothes and toys for the children, and furniture and furnishings for the adults.

E. Possession

Arguments about material goods, hi-fi sets, casseroles, and things chosen and brought together may furnish much of the material of inter-family interviews. For children, even the temporary loss of a toy which symbolizes particularly strong attachment to their lost or left behind natural parent, can be deeply upsetting. Mother's determination that her child should not be beholden to a "previous" father for anything led to her refusal to say who had given her daughter the bicycle that "Santa Claus" had left for her. The child, no longer believing in such things, knew this to be a ploy to refuse her father even a limited place in their lives, and attacked her mother for her inability to buy her what she wanted and for not telling the truth, and this led to the daughter realizing that her mother had also been untruthful about a number of other issues. Helping mother to talk with her daughter about her own feelings regarding father's role in the new family enabled boundaries to be more clearly defined and he was less feared as a seducer of the child's loyalties.

For foster parents, multiple gifts of expensive toys or unnecessary additional clothing, the anger or competitiveness of the natural parent, may be apparent and difficult to manage. In the case of step-families, the constant reminder of a home previously occupied and furnished by the custodial parent with their previous spouse may lead to repeated pangs of jealousy.

F. Example: the F family

An example from the F family shows how issues of unresolved attachment can reach strange proportions in terms of household arrangements. Mr F insisted on his younger second wife, Samantha, keeping the house exactly as his first wife had furnished it, even to including a cabinet case of "show" objects they had collected together on their holidays. He also insisted on Samantha being courteous and hospitable to his first wife who frequently dropped in for drinks and stayed for supper. One day Samantha threatened to leave unless all the things were removed; packed them up in several packing cases, and put them outside the front door, where they remained for three days. Now all are back in their "rightful" place.

G. Financial position

While the question of financial circumstances is important in the case of *adoptive* families, there is not the opportunity for the development of financial tangles developing between the reconstituted family and the natural or extended family as there is in *foster* and *step*-families.

The matter of expensive gifts which may be considered unsuitable within the family life-style of the reconstituted family has already been mentioned, but there is also the question of payment for the care of the children and/or the upkeep of the home.

(1) Foster Families
In *foster* families, there is the payment of a boarding out allowance, and for older children a pocket money allowance and sums of money for clothing. The natural parents of children in care are also expected to contribute to their keep, and this is assessed and payments made to the local authorities. These facts in themselves constitute grounds for the development of tensions between the reconstituted family unit system and those outside, but it may also be the case that the foster

children may in fact have more money spent on them or available to them than the natural children of the foster family.

(2)   Step-families
In *step*-families, the whole area of maintenance payments is one fraught with difficulty, as very few men can afford to maintain two families at the level to which the family members are accustomed to live. This usually means arguments or tensions over the amount of the maintenance payments for the mother and children (whether or not she has remarried), and often a failure to make regular contributions, even when these have been laid down by court order.

XI.   THE USE OF A FAMILY THERAPY APPROACH

A.   Introduction: Gaining Therapeutic Access

How can those adopting the family approach use these nodal points in such a way as to gain therapeutic access to the family system? Here the agency setting within which the therapist is working is important, as much of the information concerned with these nodal points is an integral part of initial assessment procedures. In some reconstituted families, particularly those with a long history of involvement with care-giving agencies, there will be such information contained in the records, but this remains to be made available within the therapeutic relationship between the therapist and the family. One way of gaining access to these nodal points is for the therapist to construct a *geneogram* together with the family. In reconstituted families this is usually particularly complicated, involving as it does the interconnections of at least two family units with their own historical antecedents. But even more important, the construction of such a geneogram is a particularly delicate and sensitive activity, as it involves opening up areas of considerable pain, many of which have been repressed with considerable strength and for good reason. There are also likely to be gaps of knowledge and experience which cannot now be filled, and these too are the cause of grief and anger. Nevertheless, if the family members are interested and willing, the use of geneograms, built up sensitively and over a period of time, do allow a focus for the therapy.

It is only possible to give a brief example of the use of a family therapy approach with two kinds of reconstituted family.

B.   Family Therapy and the Adoptive Family

(1)   Clinical Example: the D Family
This family, the D family, were referred to another therapist and myself for a private consultation by the adoption section of a local authority social services department. It has been written up more fully elsewhere (see Robinson, 1976 for complete details) but is useful to quote here, as we worked closely with the

adoption social workers who, of course, had the power to make the recommendation to adopt.

The Ds had been approved as potential adopters but had a long wait, during which Mrs D became more and more preoccupied inwardly with the coming baby, and Mr D felt more and more pushed out of what had been a close marital relationship. He had an affair, more by way of an SOS than because he was particularly involved with the lady, and on discovering this his wife returned to her family for a few days to think things out. Unfortunately, during this time the baby for whom they had waited so long became available to be placed, and the rift in the marital relationship was apparent to the adoption worker, so that they lost the opportunity to adopt this baby.

(2) Initial Work with the D Family
The therapists saw the couple together and agreed with them that the focus of the therapy should be a marital one, though the question of the possibility of adoption could be reconsidered later. Initially the therapists worked individually with the couple, the wife's therapist working with her disappointment at her infertility and the loss of the available baby. The husband's therapist worked with his ambivalence about wanting to have a child at all, and in particular with his resentment at having to be assessed as fit for parenthood.

(3) Later Work with the D Family
After three or four separate interviews, the therapists worked with the couple as a foursome, exploring and reinforcing the strengths within the marriage and reconsidering the possibility of parenthood, for a further five sessions. The therapists considered that their own criteria for successful parenthood should be made explicit to the D's, and when they felt confident enough to be honest with them about this, this provided a further focus for therapeutic work. Finally, at the request of the Ds, they were reassessed for adoption, accepted by the local authority, and eventually a baby was made available to them. As they both liked it, they decided to retain the name given to her by her natural mother. The therapists remained in touch with the Ds after the adoption, although less intensively and more informally than in the previous therapeutic work. About a year after the apparently successful establishment of an adoptive family, Mrs D had what appeared to be a very self-destructive and short lived affair which seemed to be related to her resentment at the amount of commitment which mothering entails, but also her resentment at her husband's attachment to the baby, a girl, which was certainly excessive. After a further period of work, particularly with Mr D, the couple resumed their attempts to become a family, and at this stage moved away.

(4) Comment: the D Family
It will be seen that in the D family, the therapists first of all worked at the interface of the intrapersonal system of the individual marital partners, later and with their agreement, shifting the focus, working with them together towards the achievement of congruence at this interface. It was only in the final stages of the

first period of treatment that the therapists worked with the focus on their potential development as a parental subsystem. It may be that this stage of the work was not particularly successful, although the second period of therapy seemed to indicate that sufficient strength had developed within the family unit system for the interpersonal system to survive the destructive vicissitudes which both partners appeared to have brought from their families of origins and which appeared to have been reinforced by their infertility.

C.   A Family Therapy Approach to Step-families

(1)   Clinical Example: the B Family
Work with the step-family B was first commenced in the child guidance clinic to which the son, S, was referred at the age of six, only a few weeks after his father and step-mother had married following the death by suicide of his natural mother. It was S who discovered her body, and as he appeared to demonstrate no feeling about this event, but was having destructive temper tantrums, the parents were worried. The family were seen by two therapists, in fact it was one of the early families which they saw together, and one of them worked with S, the other working individually or together with the father and step-mother. Both the therapists had occasional interviews with the whole family.

(2)   Initial Work with the B Family
At the time, the clinic accepted the family's definition of S as the identified patient, and the work with the parents was consistently child-focussed. The case was closed after about two years of weekly treatment, during which S was apparently able to work through the death of his mother. The father and step-mother were able to work through their guilt and at some later stage, perhaps in adolescence, S should be told of his mother's suicide following their affair. After a chance meeting with step-mother in the street, the author was invited to have social drinks with the B family and met S, now a young man of 18, and their own child, T. All seemed to be going well, although the parents revealed that the mother's suicide had still not been discussed with S though they felt he might know. S remembered little of his therapy except how angry he had been; he was now planning to go to University and working hard.

(3)   Later Events and Work with the B Family
Some 18 months later, step-mother managed to trace me, and begged me to see her again as the marriage was in difficulties. After an initial meeting in which we agreed to work on her marital difficulties and whether or not she wished to continue the marriage, we have continued to meet weekly. Father refused all further offers of help, though clearly he had never come to terms with his own feelings about the death of his first wife, though through step-mother's support and insistence, he did discuss this with S. Step-mother left father and set up home with T, eventually joined by maternal grandmother, a foreigner who lived abroad and had recently divorced her second husband.

Again at step-mother's insistence, father maintained paternal contact with T, and S had his own room and a base in each of the two homes. There have been no legal proceedings to date; father maintains T (Mrs B is a successful career woman in her own right) and access to T, achieved by mutual negotiation, is now fairly regular. Mrs B prided herself on the civility and maturity with which she felt the separation had been conducted, and was dismayed and disconcerted to find herself demonstrating intense aspects of a grief reaction some 6 months after she had left father. She was momentarily jealous of discovering he was having an affair with a much younger woman, despite embarking herself on a sequential series of affairs (always making sure another man was "in the wings" before she terminated the previous one), in which for the first time, she discovered her own potential as a sexual woman.

S went to college, but on each visit home in the vacation, he and step-mother have a series of bitter rows followed by reconciliations in which they appear able to face the strength of their feelings for each other, both positive and negative, as well as being able to share their feelings about mother's suicide. Step-mother has been able to support T in her own grief over the break-up of her parents' marriage, but in doing so, has found herself trapped in single parent motherhood in which she feels deeply inadequate and guilty. This, together with her recent concern about her ability to have a lasting and mutually-fulfilling relationship with a man, is our current area of work.

(4)   Comment on the B Family

When first seen, the therapists adopted a child-centred approach to the therapy, although this was within the context of the family unit. With hindsight it was clearly a mistake not to find ways in which the father and step-mother could have informed S about the suicide of his mother, as the guilt and grief around this area has festered throughout the family life of this reconstituted family. While current therapeutic work is being conducted mainly at the intrapersonal system level with Mrs B, the experience of the earlier, more family-oriented therapy has enabled the therapist to adopt an approach which recognizes the importance of paying attention to the intrapersonal and interpersonal systems within the whole family unit system. Mrs B herself recognizes this now, and considers that this was the reason why she sought me out when she realized she needed further help, as she felt that I had helped her to take on the step-parent role, and would understand how things were for her now.

It is too soon to make any judgment about what the future holds for this reconstituted family, which came together in destructive circumstances, now revealed to have their roots in the family history of both Mr and Mrs B, but at least it seems possible that S will be able to seek further help at University, and that Mrs B is struggling to achieve some kind of family security for herself and T.

REFERENCES

Adcock, M. and Robinson, M. (1976). Brief Marital Counselling and Adoption, *Child Adoption*, **83**, no. 1.

Adcock, M. and White, R. (1977). Assumption of Parental Rights and Duties. A.B.A.F.A. London.

Bohannen, P. (1971). "Divorce and After", Doubleday Anchor, London.

Davies, M. (1977). "Support Systems in Social Work", Routledge & Kegan Paul, London.

Eekelaar, J. and Clive, E. with Clarke, K. and Raikes, S. (1977). "Custody After Divorce", Centre for Socio-Legal Studies, Wolfson College, Oxford.

Goldstein, J., Freud, A. and Solnit, A. (1973). "Beyond the Best Interests of the Child", Free Press, Glencoe.

Holman, R. (1975). The Place of Fostering in Social Work. *British Journal of Social Work*, **5**, 8-10.

Kantor, D. and Lehr, W. (1975). "Inside the Family", Jossey Bass, San Francisco.

Miller, E. and Gwynne, G. (1972). "A Life Apart", Tavistock, London.

Murch, M. (1980). "Justice and Welfare in Divorce", Sweet and Maxwell, London.

Murray Parkes, C. (1975). "Bereavement: Studies of Grief in Adult Life", Penguin, Harmondsworth, Middlesex.

Perkins, T. and Kahan, J. (1979). An Empirical Comparison of Natural-Father and Step-Father Systems. *Family Process*, **18**, 176-181.

Pilling, D. and Kellmer Pringle, M. (1978). "Controversial Issues in Child Development" Paul Elek, London.

Pincus, L. (1976). "Death and the Family", Faber, London.

Robinson, M. (1980). Step-Families: A Reconstituted Family System. *Journal of Family Therapy*, **2**, 45-70.

Robinson, M. (unpublished). "What's in a Name".

Robinson, M. and Adcock, M. (1976). Brief Marital Counselling and Adoption. *Child Adoption*, **83**, 49-53.

Schulman, G. (1972). Myths that intrude on the adaptation of the step-family. *Social Casework*, **53**, 135-137.

Tizard, B. (1977). "Adoption: A Second Chance", Open Books, London.

Wallerstein, J. and Kelly, J. (1980). "Surviving the Breakup: How Children and Parents Cope with Divorce", Grant McIntyre, New York.

Walrond-Skinner, S. (1976). "Family Therapy: The Treatment of Natural Systems", Routledge & Kegan Paul, London.

Chapter 22

Handicap and Family Therapy

D. Black

I. INTRODUCTION

What does "handicap" mean? What provision should a caring society make for people with handicaps? What contribution can the family therapist make to the well-being of handicapped people and their families?

In this chapter I will briefly review the literature on handicap with special reference to children, examine the relevant concepts developed by family theorists, and assess the contributions that family therapists can make to the total provision for families with a handicapped member.

II. SOME BASIC ASSUMPTIONS ABOUT HANDICAP

A. Definition

The various definitions of handicap (see Younghusband *et al.*, 1970; Pless and Pinkerton, 1975; Rutter *et al.*, 1970) all emphasize the concept of handicap as something to be applied to functioning rather than people. The same disability may handicap different people to different degrees. Thus one of the effects produced by arthritis is limitation of movement. This disability, even if slight would severely handicap a violinist, but might be negligible in a telephonist. Someone who is handicapped in some of his functioning, is not necessarily handicapped generally. Pless and Pinkerton (1975) stress that the notion of generalized handicap imposed by a specific disease is unjustified and has unfortunate psychosocial consequences. Both the disabled person and the non-disabled may view the former as more limited than he is. They point out that this phenomenon of "spread" (Wright, 1960), i.e. a generalized devaluation of body function and even of self, can be more handicapping than the original impairment itself, and that a "marginal" disability, because it keeps the individual in the community, may be harder to adjust to than a severe one which forces him to come to terms with his limitations.

Rutter and his colleagues (Rutter *et al.*, 1970) examined the prevalence of handicapping disorders in 10–11-year-olds under four headings: intellectual, educational, physical and psychiatric; and used strict criteria which included the concepts of severity and duration. "Handicap for most of the children studied meant a considerable interference with their ability to lead a normal life." (p. 351).

417

A handicapped individual therefore is one whose functioning in one or more areas of his life is retarded, impaired or distorted by a disorder which is permanent or present for a substantial period. Handicapping disorders may be physical, intellectual, psychiatric or educational. Commonly there may be a combination of handicapping disorders. A person with a disability interacts with his environment. His family is the most important matrix in which he is embedded and is the most important determinant of outcome in terms of adjustment. The concepts developed by family theorists are very relevant to our understanding of the effects of disability on individual and family functioning, but have rarely been applied to the study of people with handicaps and their families.

Is it true, as Sheridan (1965) suggests, that "in the background of every individual handicapped child there is always a handicapped family", or when we find such a handicapped family, could more skilful or plentiful services have prevented or mitigated their disabilities?

B.   Prevalence of Handicap

The most comprehensive epidemiological study of childhood disorders (Rutter *et al.*, 1970) found that one in every six children between 9 and 11 years had a chronic or recurrent handicap, physical, intellectual, educational or psychiatric. A quarter of the handicapped children had at least two handicaps; 90% of the intellectually retarded children and 29% of the physically handicapped children had other handicaps as well. In over half the children, the disorder was associated with some disorganization of family routine. In some there were impaired family relationships, and over half the parents expressed some dissatisfaction with the services available to them. These figures can be regarded as minimal population estimates and reveal the widespread existence of handicap in a developed society, and the relative inadequacy of health, education and social services to meet the needs of the families. Educational help was insufficient, and while the strictly medical aspects of treatment were fairly adequate,

> parents felt they needed more guidance in the individual management of the handicapped child; more moral support and advice in coping with the disturbed family situation and relationships sometimes associated with the handicap . . . , and more tangible help to relieve them of the mental, physical and financial burden of caring for and living with severely handicapped children. (Rutter *et al.*, 1970, p.356)

C.   Services for Handicapped Children

Improvements in medical care and other social measures have brought benefits to children's health and physical well-being in the last half-century, and have thrown into relief the problems of handicap. While the aim of society must be to prevent handicapping disorders wherever possible, the role of health, educational and social services in diagnosis, support, advice and treatment and other services to the handicapped and their families has only recently received systematic attention (see Kellmer-Pringle, 1964; Dinnage, 1970, 1972; Pilling, 1973; Court, 1976 for summaries of research). The establishment of comprehensive Paediatric Assessment Centres in Great Britain, staffed by professionals from many disciplines, has improved the ascertainment of handicapped children, and in the best centres (e.g. Brimblecombe, 1974; Goddard and Rubissow, 1977) a continuing treatment, support and education service to families is offered which is already reducing the need for permanent hospital beds for handicapped children.

A major problem in the field of handicap is the misuse of costly resources by parents peddling their child round from hospital to hospital in the hope of finding a cure. The causes of this phenomenon are complex: failure of communication on the part of the professionals involved in the diagnosis; lack of an ongoing treatment and management plan which is comprehensible to the parents, and a failure to help the family in their task of mourning the loss of the normal child they expected.

D.   Case Example: Florence

(1)   Basic Facts

Florence was 3½ years-old when she was referred by the consultant paediatrician because of several behaviour problems. He wondered if she was autistic. Severely retarded in speech and language, she had no symbolic play, was waking several times a night and screaming, was negativistic in behaviour and would scream when her 1-year-old sister was present. She did not play with other children, and there were temper tantrums on mild frustration.

The family were from Ireland, and father was a bus conductor. Neither parent was bright, and they had few family supports here. They were caring parents, but father coped by getting very angry if people didn't do what he wanted. Mother seemed very depressed. An incredible number of people had become involved with this family (see Fig. 1).

They had seen all these people frequently, but seemed confused and unable to tell us what was wrong with Florence. Susan (1 year) seemed developmentally normal. Seen as a family, the following sequence became apparent. Father or mother would ask Florence to do something. She did not respond. Father's voice would grow gradually louder, to a shout. Florence, seeming anxious, would throw a toy at her sister, who would run to mother and cry. Florence would get a smack for being "bold", an Irishism for "naughty". She would cry and try to go to mother; Susan would push her away; she would hit Susan and in return be hit and shouted at by mother.

Father's exasperation made him look ill; he shouted that no one would tell him what was wrong with Florence. Most of the confusion was semantic. He had been told she was slow and backwards, but understood that to mean a delay in development which would eventually disappear. "Why couldn't she have some schooling now, so by the time she was five she would have caught up?", he asked. What was the *reason* for her backwardness, is what he meant by "what was wrong", and it was clear that they did not know.

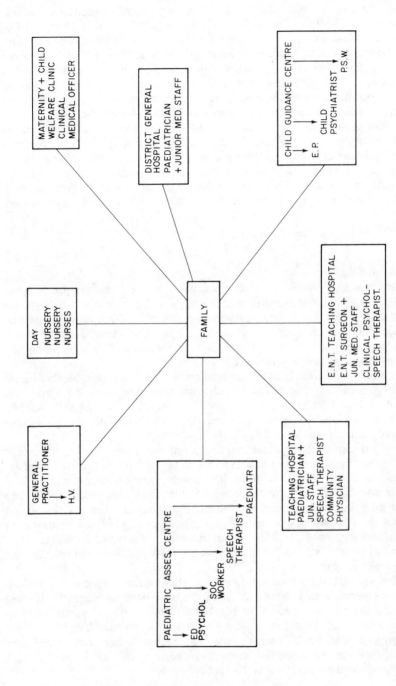

Fig. 1. Florence's professional network.

(2) The Therapist's Tasks
There were two tasks here: to establish a diagnosis, and then to help the parents
to understand its implications. Could Florence understand gesture? We got the
parents to communicate their wishes silently. Florence was eager to please. She
carried toys from mother, to Susan, to us, when she understood father's
instructions given by gesture alone. The parents could experience at first hand
the way in which Florence was locked into herself because of limited understanding. With help from other specialists, a diagnosis of specific severe speech
and language disorder in a mildly retarded girl was made, and a contract for four
family therapy sessions made. These sessions enabled us to work on
communication within the family and with the professional network; on specific
disordered behaviours (such as sleep disturbances) which were remediable, and
to facilitate the expression of the parent's grief when they finally understood that
they had a child with a severe handicap.

When last seen by us one year after referral, Florence was understanding four
or five words with meaning, making good social contact, and was able to play
with her sister and peers. Her parents had stopped peddling her round to several
hospitals, and although they were under considerable strain, family life appeared
happier. The problems of coping with this severely handicapped child will of
course be lifelong, but it seemed as if the family therapy had been able to convert
the aggressiveness and blaming into grief, and then into understanding and
acceptance, so that they no longer attacked or rejected Florence or their advisors,
but could tackle their problems in a more adaptive way. The family continues to
receive much professional support.

In this case, there were communication problems between Florence and her
family, between the parents, and between them and the many doctors they had
seen. Family assessment helped to establish the diagnosis, and family therapy
was needed to maximise communication within the family and with their
advisors. The establishment of a firm diagnosis, with its implications, provoked
an appropriate grief reaction in the parents, which could be worked through,
releasing more adaptive behaviour.

(3) Implications for Services
Services for handicapped children like Florence and their families should be
comprehensive and long-term. There are advantages to the families and to the
professionals in the establishment of a centre from which all the services needed
can function so that there can be an association of the different relevant
disciplines over time, and an opportunity for the cross-fertilization of ideas.
Services must start with the diagnosis and ascertainment of handicapped
individuals, and will therefore involve hospital and community paediatricians
and other hopsital specialists, and will also involve in counselling (including
genetic counselling), treatment and support some or all of the following:
medical, psychiatric and local authority social workers, health visitors, general
practitioners, hospital and community nurses, physiotherapists, occupational
therapists, speech therapists, clinical and educational psychologists,
psychotherapists, and consultants in paediatrics, neurology, child psychiatry,

mental handicap, and genetics, as well as junior medical staff. Such a team should be headed by a consultant paediatrician with a special interest in handicapped children, and children and their families, once registered with the service should be able to use it as needed. The provision of short stay "respite" accommodation, of more permanent residential care which is child-centred (Tizard et al., 1975), of information about benefits available (such as mobility and attendance allowances, and grants for house adaptation), and about the availability and suitability of day and residential schools and pre-school play-groups, nursery schools and day nurseries, is essential if severely handicapped children are to develop their full potential without impoverishing or exhausting their families.

Unfortunately, few districts can boast a comprehensive service, but if the recommendations of the Court Committee to establish district handicap teams is implemented, the prospect for the handicapped and their families should improve.

III. IMPACT OF HANDICAP ON CHILD, FAMILY AND COMMUNITY

A. General Effects of Disability

The extensive literature on the effects of handicap can only be briefly summarized here. Interested readers are referred to reviews by Barker et al. (1953), Pless and Pinkerton (1975), Dinnage (1970, 1972), Pilling (1973) and Kellmer-Pringle (1964). The literature on sibling reactions to handicap is reviewed by Black and Sturge (1980). The psychological problems in physically ill and handicapped children are reviewed by Fox (1977) and Steinhauer et al. (1974). The problems of adolescents are reviewed by Freeman (1970) and Dorner (1976), and there are numerous studies of the families of children with single handicapping conditions, of which Jan et al. (1977) on visual impairment, Hewitt et al. (1970) on cerebral palsy, Burton (1975) on cystic fibrosis, and Gath (1978) on Down's Syndrome may serve as excellent examples.

B. Effects on Parents

The parents attitude to their child's handicap has been found to be the most important factor in the family's successful adaptation. Parental attitudes are of course influenced by many factors. Table I attempts to summarize the research findings.

Significantly high rates of both physical and mental ill-health have been found in parents of handicapped children, especially those with other adversities, (financial, housing, employment etc.). The good marriage may be strengthened by the stress of a handicapped child, but the strain on a weak marriage may be too great. Handicapped children may also keep a bad marriage going. These factors may be equally balanced, and there is little hard data showing an increased rate of marital breakdown.

Table I. Summary of research findings.

Factors affecting adjustment to handicap.

(1) Large families more tolerant of handicap.
(2) Catholics less guilty than Protestants.
(3) Parents more accepting of handicap when child is young than later.
(4) Parents more affected by handicap in boys than girls.
(5) Adjustment better when good counselling available early and practical help given.
(6) Younger siblings are more affected by parental absences in hospital.
(7) The following ameliorate the adverse effects of handicap:
     (a) mildness of handicap.
     (b) large age gap between handicapped sibling and the rest.
     (c) moderate family size.
     (d) a good marriage.
     (e) good financial and community support.
(8) Life-threatening diseases increase family vulnerability.

C. Effects on Siblings

The effect of handicap on siblings are similarly balanced. The development of beneficial traits such as tenderness, compassion, generosity and protectiveness tending to occur as often as adverse traits and symptoms. A child may imitate or identify with his disabled sibling, to the extent that it impairs his development. This may be an attempt to gain more parental attention, or a genuine empathy with the sibling (Black and Sturge, 1980). Diseases which are familial or life-threatening appear to affect siblings adversely. Certain handicapping conditions may even affect the size of the family itself, parents limiting their families after the birth of a handicapped child.

D. Effects on Others

The effect of handicap on grandparents appear to have been studied rarely, if at all. The effect on the community has not been systematically described. The myth of the accepting and tolerant primitive community is belied by the tradition of exposing handicapped infants, and the high rates of infanticide and abandonment right up to the present century. The allocation of public funds nicely illustrates public attitudes. The mentally and physically handicapped have always had the crumbs from the table of the acutely ill, and the recent public outcry at the exposures of the inadequacies of Britain's Health Service in caring for the mentally handicapped (e.g. the Normansfield Enquiry 1978) was a muted and short-lived one.

The effects on physicians and other professionals of handicap are interesting. The priorities have always been with the acute illnesses. The concept of a continuing role for paediatricians and others in the care of the handicapped has really only developed in the last 10-15 years, as the acute diseases have receded.

E. Effects of School

One section of the community needs special consideration: children spend much of their early life at school. What is the interaction between them, their non-handicapped peers and their teachers? Facial deformities have been shown to render children unpopular (Richardson, 1971; Lansdown, 1975), and so has obesity, which is often the consequence of the immobility imposed by some physical handicap. Strong arguments exist for and against segregation of the severely handicapped in special schools (see Anderson, 1973, for the "anti" arguments, and Fox (1976) for the "pro" ones.) If children are in special schools, they rarely meet non-handicapped children. Teachers and children in ordinary schools do not have the opportunity to become familiar with the problems in living that face the handicapped child, or to develop desirable attitudes to the disabled. It is more difficult to provide a wide enough range of educational facilities for young adolescents with physical handicaps at a special school. Furthermore, the regular withdrawal from lessons for the physical treatment of the handicap may deprive the handicapped child of the education he needs if he is to have a chance of independent adult life.

F. Effects on the Child

Summarizing the research findings, we can say that the effects on the child himself depend to some extent on the age of onset and the nature and severity of the handicap, but much more on the quality of parental and professional (including educational) care. A disability can prevent or disrupt the early formation of bonds which we believe to be essential to emotional health (Bowlby, 1969), either because of separation because of treatment needs (admission to special care units, removal to specialist hospitals etc.) or because of parental rejection, or depression. The disability itself may handicap the development of relationships, either by producing in the parents a "too perfect" adaptation to the child's needs (Bentovim, 1972), or in the case of children with sensory impairment or brain damage, especially, behaviour problems stemming from poor impulse control, frustration and insecurity which the parent can find no way of mitigating. The child thus becomes unrewarding to the parents and is relatively neglected or rejected.

The problems of frequent hospitalization are the same for the handicapped as for the normal child, and may produce an anxious, clinging and phobic child, who is passive and dependent with a constricted, fearful personality. The effect of frequent pain and of limitations in movement imposed by some diseases, can also cripple personality development and produce a demanding and querulous child.

That 29% of physically handicapped children are educationally retarded too may indicate the difficulties that both parents and teachers have in providing a rich and varied experience for them. Their educational failure serves further to lower the child's feelings of self-worth already damaged by increasing awareness of his disability.

Some parents over-protect their handicapped child, which impairs the development of autonomy, and prevents normal sibling interaction. The sibling may not be free to resent, fight with or compete with his handicapped brother or sister (Jan *et al.*, 1977), and the disabled child then cannot give up his fantasies of omnipotence, a necessary step in the development of social relationships.

The social isolation that the family finds imposed on it, or that it imposes on itself because of rejection, guilt, depression or over-protection (so that for example the parents never go out because they cannot trust a baby-sitter), further limits the child's opportunities for the development of social skills.

The rates of psychiatric disorder are raised in mentally, physically and educationally handicapped children. Children with chronic physical handicap in the Isle of Wight study (Rutter *et al.*, 1970) showed a rate of psychiatric disorder nearly twice (11.6%) that of the general population. If the handicap affected the brain (e.g. epilepsy, cerebral palsy etc.), the rate of psychiatric disorder was 3-4 times that of the general population. However there was no specific association between the type of psychiatric disorder and the physical handicap, nor was there an association between the severity of the handicap and the incidence of psychiatric disorder. Only 10% of children with handicapping psychiatric disorder were in fact receiving any psychiatric treatment.

G. Adolescence and Handicap

The cognitive changes associated with puberty, bring the possibility of increases in disturbance in the handicapped youngster, especially the physically handicapped. He begins to face the implications of his disability. Can he support himself, will he be attractive to the opposite sex, can he marry, have children, become independent of his parents, like his non-handicapped peers? Since the rate of psychiatric disorder is raised in adolescence in the general population, and epidemiological studies of the handicapped adolescent are not available, there is no clear evidence for an increase in problems in the handicapped adolescent specifically. Pless and Pinkerton (1975) suggest that there is limited evidence that suicide and suicidal intent is more common in physically ill adolescents, but that there is little evidence for a specific increase in problems of the handicapped at adolescence, greater than in the general population. We urgently need good studies in this area.

Freeman (1970) indicates the problems that physically handicapped young people have to face. There may be an actual deterioration in their physical conditions, they have to give up fantasies of a cure, social isolation may increase at a time when sexual maturation brings problems of impulse control, which heightens family and neighbourhood concern. Indiscriminate affection is no longer acceptable. The problems of leaving school and finding work, difficult as they are in themselves, bring with them the changeover of professional staff as well. Probably the majority of adolescents with handicaps and their families, would benefit from skilled counselling at this time.

H.   Handicap and Adulthood

So far, we have focussed on the handicapped child and his family, as indeed do most of the research studies. Marriage rates are lower in the handicapped, rates of psychiatric disorder and unemployment higher, and the handicapped are more likely to be in low-level jobs (see Pless and Pinkerton, 1975 for a review). The effect on children of parental handicap and chronic illness was studied by Rutter (1966), who found a significantly increased rate of chronic or recurrent parental illness in psychiatrically disturbed children. The mechanism of the association is probably through the stresses on family and marriage imposed by the disorder (finance, job difficulties, separations, personality disorders arising from chronic handicap, and death). Disabled parents are more likely to die during their children's childhood with all the implications for the children that carries (see Chapter 20, Loss, Mourning and Grief). The quality of affectional relationships seems to be the best predictor of whether the children will be affected by the parent's disability.

Adult handicap may be accentuated to maintain a bad marriage, or to bind families together in ways that can be dysfunctional. Changing practices in the treatment of psychiatric patients by adult psychiatrists can affect family functioning, and those professionals working with children and their families must liase more with the adult services.

I.   Specific Effects of Disability

So far, we have described the effects of handicap in general terms. There are consequences specific to certain diseases and to certain phases of the family life-cycle to which brief attention must be paid, although it is beyond the scope of this chapter to describe the consequences of each individual disorder. Travis (1976) has summarized the problems for children and their families of each of the major chronic illness, and Gath's (1978) account of the effects of Down's Syndrome has applications to most of the mentally handicapped.

IV.   CRISIS INTERVENTION AND FAMILY INTERVENTION

A.   Crisis Periods and Handicap in the Family Life-Cycle

All families are vulnerable at times of crisis, and Caplan has suggested (1964) that they are also more open to change. He distinguished times of potential crisis in the life of each individual as "normal crises" at times of transition e.g. marriage, birth of the first child, going to school, leaving home, starting work, retirement, death of parents; and the crises which are not common at all, such as the birth of a handicapped child, the death of a spouse or child, marital break-up, loss of job or house, etc.

Dare (1979) has taken these concepts further by suggesting that the more there are family members at important critical transitions or phases in their lives, the more likely it is that the family will be encountering stresses and need for adjustment and change that springs largely from the fact of the multiplicity of individual crises.

The work of Rappoport (1963) in identifying phases in the life-cycle of families is relevant to an understanding of crisis in families.

The special potential crisis periods for families of a handicapped child are:

  (i) At diagnosis.
 (ii) When the parents realize the implications of the impairment for the child and family.
(iii) When a decision about placement has to be made (hospital, school etc.)
 (iv) When a decision about future pregnancies has to be made.
  (v) During subsequent pregnancies.
 (vi) When the prospect of promotion or job change involves moving away from family, neighbourhood and professional supports.
(vii) When the handicapped child goes to primary school, and when he would have changed to senior school, had he not been handicapped.
(viii) If there is a significant deterioration in the disorder, so that it becomes life-threatening or terminal.
 (ix) If the child dies.
  (x) When the child fails to negotiate a normal developmental stage (talking, walking, reading etc.)
 (xi) If another child in the family develops the same or another disorder.
(xii) At the onset of puberty.
(xiii) When leaving school and starting work (or not starting work).
(xiv) If the child requires operation(s).
 (xv) If the child goes into residential care.

At all these times, it may be possible to intervene briefly to make a positive contribution to the welfare of the family. All these potential crisis periods are additional to those normally experienced by every family and the likelihood of two or more hazardous times concurring is high.

B. Family Therapy and Crisis Intervention

The family therapist who is part of the handicap team is well placed to intervene swiftly with a family in crisis who is known to the centre. The child psychiatrist, social worker, psychotherapist and psychologist may have acquired family therapy skills, and others (health visitors, general practitioners and physio-therapists in particular) are recognizing the advantages of learning these therapeutic techniques to help their patients.

(1) Case Example: Douglas and his Family
Douglas, aged 8 was referred to a child guidance clinic because of enuresis, and behaviour difficulties at school. There was a strong family history of Huntington's Chorea, a familial disorder affecting 50% of the children of victims. It causes involuntary movements of the body, personality deterioration, psychosis,

eventual dementia and death (Fig. 2). The paternal sister had first developed the
disease, and mother was convinced her husband was showing early signs.
Unspoken was the concern that Douglas was the next victim. The marriage was
an unhappy one, but mother was caught in a bind: she could not confront her
husband honestly about her unhappiness if he was a sick man. His tense

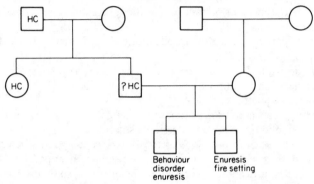

Fig. 2. Douglas' geneogram.

constricted personality, the result of much suffering in childhood at the hands of
a deteriorating irascible father, led him to avoid emotional commitment to his
wife and family, and he denied that he had any worry about inheriting the family
disease. The complaints about Douglas were ill-formulated, and the parents
spent the whole time talking about the marriage so that he seemed to be being
offered as a passport to marital therapy which was what was offered. During the
course of six sessions, the parents began to face together the implications of the
family disease and to plan appropriately. Father had a vasectomy and made
realistic plans with his wife for that eventuality. Freed from the unspoken dread,
they turned to getting some enjoyment from each other: mother was clearly
impressed by the caring way father had made his plans and could relinquish her
ambivalent protectiveness which had of course been patronizing, and make
demands on him for a reciprocal relationship. Douglas was no longer a cause for
concern, and his mild symptoms improved.

The crisis of hospital admission, especially for operation can cause a temporary period of individual or family malfunctioning even in the most stable
families. In the following case, two crises, i.e. father's unemployment, and
Dennis's admission, coincided.

(2) Case Example: Dennis and his Family
Dennis, aged 9, was referred by his cardiologist having developed somatic
symptoms of anxiety while awaiting an operation to improve his chronic valvular
heart disease, which had stunted his growth and prevented normal activities. He
had had 16 previous admissions. The middle of three children, father was

unemployed and expressed great fury at the referral: his son was not mad, and anyway why drag the whole family an expensive 70-mile journey? However they could be engaged by the offer to do some rehearsal for the operations which were clearly a realistic worry for them all.

In the course of these sessions, each member of the family was asked to role-play Dennis and then his own role in the family system during the forth-coming hospitalization for surgery. Dennis was strikingly passive, and could not even indicate where his heart was. His drawing (Fig. 3) indicated a view of himself as isolated and deformed. The role-play enabled others to voice for him the common fears—of injections, pain, abandonment, and death which he could not articulate. All the family had some personal experience of hospitals, and it relieved them to be able to express anxiety and know it was accepted and considered normal by the therapists. Dennis had a success-ful operation and his behaviour was normal. His mother in a letter acknowl-edged that the family sessions had enabled Dennis to "sail through his time in hospital".

Fig. 3.

Dennis's symptoms were due to anxiety with which his parents and medical and nursing staff could not help. We intervened by short-term family therapy, and also by some counselling on the ward so that Dennis had oral premedication and mother accompanied him to the anaesthetic room and stayed with him till he was unconscious. In family sessions we explored areas of anxiety in Dennis and his family, and helped them all to find roles for themselves in his "scene", and thus gain mastery over their fears and helpless feelings. The forthcoming operation was rehearsed, and time was spent helping them to anticipate what would happen and prepare themselves.

The use of a family approach at times of crisis may prevent the development of secondary disability in children and their families. It is possible that Dennis might have added a psychiatric disability to his chronic cardiac disorder and that in the former example, Douglas's mild developmental delay could have led to educational disability and a conduct disorder had not family therapy tackled the underlying anxieties and tensions.

V. FAMILY THEORY AND THERAPY WITH HANDICAP

A. The Place of Family Theory and Therapy

The treatment needs of handicapped children and their families are as complex and diverse as the disorders from which they suffer. No attempt will be made here to consider the full range of resources, physical, psychological, educational or social, needed, but to look specifically at the contribution of family therapy. It must be emphasized that such therapy is but a small contribution to the overall treatment provision, but may be effective in enabling a family to free itself from blocks to its development and improve family functioning.

In the previous section we looked at the effects of handicap on individual family members, but family theory has much to contribute to our understanding of the effects of handicap on the family system, for example, the concept of role assignation (Toman, 1961). In a handicapped family, the eldest girl is assigned the role of caring for the other siblings, and has been shown to be at greater psychiatric risk (Farber, 1959; Gath, 1974). A non-handicapped child may be appointed by the family to achieve all the parental aspirations, and may feel himself to be "special", or have a messianic mission. This overvaluing of one child throws particular stresses on the child and on the homeostasis of the system. The family assignment of the role of "handicapped" or "stupid" to the child with a disability may lead to an exaggeration or "spread" of his disability so that the child becomes handicapped more severely or in more spheres than he need be. The handicapped child himself may receive the "special" label either overtly or by implication, and is not submitted to the normal rough and tumble of family life. In Minuchin's words, the sibling subsystem is,

> the first social laboratory in which children can experiment with peer relation-ships. Within this context children support, isolate, scapegoat and learn from each other. In the sibling world children learn how to negotiate, co-operate and compete. They learn how to make friends and allies, how to save face while submitting and how to achieve recognition of their skills. They may take different positions in their jockeying with one another and those positions, taken early in the sibling subgroup, can be significant in the subsequent course of their lives. (Minuchin, 1974, p. 59)

If the role assignment becomes rigidified by attitudes to handicap, the flexibility necessary for the development of social skills is not present in either the handi-capped or the non-handicapped sibling.

Non-handicapped children, especially older ones, may cross the generational boundary to become a parental child (see Sandra below), with the ensuing dangers of skewing the marital relationship and forcing premature and distorted maturation of the child so affected.

B. Effects of Particular Handicaps

Sensory handicaps in particular may produce enormous problems of communication within the family. Shapiro and Harris (1976) describe the use of family therapy with deaf patients. A deaf and hearing co-therapy team treated a family containing a suicidal adolescent girl who was deaf. Individual therapy had been unsuccessful and because of the intrusiveness of other family members, a family evaluation was made. Although the girl had been deaf since infancy, the parents had never learned to communicate with their daughter. The authors suggest that the girl was scapegoated in order to mask the guilt and anger provoked by her handicap, and to detour the marital conflict. The girl misinterpreted family laughter as directed at her, and her resultant distress was misconstrued by the family as bad behaviour. The role of the therapist in patiently unravelling these distortions of communication is described, as are the considerable difficulties of communicating with deaf patients.

Communication problems may occur because of retarded development, or because of cultural or language differences between parents and/or between the family and their advisors.

C. Family Therapy and genetically inherited Handicap

An important use of family therapy with genetically inherited handicaps is to aid the family to explore the implications of the familial disease. Martindale and Bottomley (1980) give a detailed description of their work with one of these families, in which they were able to involve the extended family and help them to help the next generation to understand and cope with the effects on the family of a disorder which causes personality deterioration, psychosis, severe physical disablement, and eventually death (Huntington's Chorea). The outcome of such sensitive work might be, they suggest, that afflicted families would choose to eliminate the disease (which affects 50% of a sufferer's children) by adopting children rather than conceiving their own. They demonstrate the reluctance of professionals to counsel families adequately, and in particular the difficulty that everyone has in believing that young children could have any real understanding of the implications of the disease. Yet it was the youngest children in the family they describe who were the first to talk about their fears of developing the disease, and the first to reveal their plans for coping as parents: by adopting a child. In view of Rutter and his colleagues' (1970) finding that children with hereditary disorders are more vulnerable to psychiatric disorders, and Atkin's (1974) poignant description of the agony that siblings and their parents suffer when they observe the first signs of the familial disease affecting the second child in the family, family therapists should be developing their work further to help such families.

One aim of all those who are involved in helping the handicapped, is to prevent secondary handicaps.

Family attitudes to handicap may be determined by their experience of it in their families of origin. The use of geneograms (Guerin, 1976; Lieberman, 1979) to explore the meaning for each family of having a handicapped member is illustrated in the following case.

D. Case Example: Michael and his Family

(1) Presentation of the Family
Michael, aged 9, was referred by the educational psychologist because of odd behaviour in his ESN (M) school where he had been placed at the age of 5. He made no social contact, and was "nervy, jumpy", and over-active. He couldn't concentrate or settle to anything.

He was a non-identical twin, and his brother Martin was of superior intelligence. The parents were highly intelligent: both working full time in professional occupations, so that Martin assumed the care of Michael after school until mother came home one hour later. Father had a physical handicap. A diagnosis of infantile autism was established. Mother broke down into tears when we offered a diagnosis, expressing guilt and relief in equal measure. There seemed little communication between the parents.

We noted that the mother treated father as if he were also a child, and that she related more to Martin as a spouse. For example she always insisted on going with father to his specialist because "he wouldn't ask the right questions". He had never learned to drive, assuming that his handicap would prevent it. When we queried this, she said that he would only take lessons if she arranged it.

We were concerned about Martin who seemed to be a parental child. He did not play with the toys, appearing as a too serious unjoyful, responsible older brother although they were in fact the same age. The family were immigrants and had few family supports. Mother's parents had disapproved of the marriage which was to a man of lower social class and she had had to wait a long time for her father's permission to marry. Father's family were stigmatized by other handicaps; Michael was said to be like him, Martin like mother.

(2) Family Therapy Process
We offered a contract of family therapy sessions with the goals of improving the parental relationship and alliance, relieving Martin of the burden of parenting Michael, helping the parents to accept Michael's handicap, and giving specific help with the management of Michael's behaviour. I can only illustrate some of the highlights of this family's treatment which included drugs and behavioural techniques, all in a family setting.

For example, they wanted to work on Michael's long-standing tendency to scribble over everything including important papers brought home from work. We explained the difficulty Michael had in distinguishing important paper from drawing paper, and suggested a behaviour therapy programme in which he was given pink paper and encouraged to scribble on that, but a firm "no" was always given to any other paper he tried to use. He was rewarded at first when using pink paper. This behaviour improved in a few days. The problem of Martin's parentification was tackled obliquely by strengthening the parental alliance.

The male therapist agreed to take the lead, and model more assertive behaviour with me, the older and more senior therapist. My acceptance of his leadership we felt might then enable mother to accept father's tentative attempts to lead which had hitherto been squashed by her.

The male therapist encouraged father to explore the possibility of learning to drive: to "help his wife" with the chauffeuring. She offered to find out about driving schools for the handicapped, but was firmly blocked by the therapist. By the next session father had begun driving lessons which he had arranged himself.

(3) Use of Geneograms

We then used geneograms to examine the concept of handicap in the family. Geneograms are an elaborate form of family tree in which the family are invited to draw parallels between people through the generations on the basis of shared characteristics, either actual or fantasied. In this way family myths can be exposed and challenged. In Michael's father's family, there had been handicapped people in three or four generations, and the tradition in their country of origin was that the siblings had to care for them at the expense of their own happiness. Caring for father, disabled as a child, had caused father's eldest brother to neglect his wife who had left him. Martin was being moulded into the same role as a caretaker for Michael.

The family worked hard on their geneogram, enjoyed the exploration of their family history and retelling it to the boys; even Michael realized that something important was happening, and sat still without his usual stereotypies (Fig. 4).

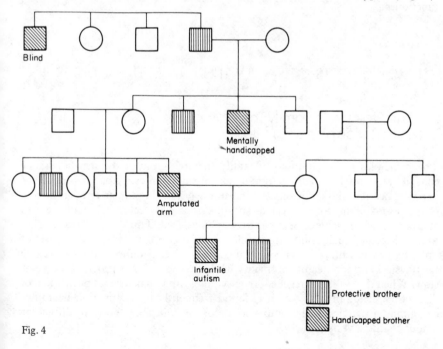

Fig. 4

Father had lost his arm at 15 because of a bone infection and was considered too handicapped to live independently. Paternal grandfather had detailed the oldest son to have him live with him and his new wife. The brother had lavished inappropriate and overprotective care on father, and his wife had become jealous and left him. Father had felt it to be his fault, and seemed condemned to repeat the family history with his own sons. He had chosen a wife who had perpetuated his brother's care but who also exacted a price for it: an unhappy, dominating woman whose alliance with Martin pushed father into the handicapped child subsystem with Michael. The genograms made the parents aware of how much they had followed the family tradition. But their courtship had in fact been a rebellion against the traditions of their culture, and they recognized that it was their guilt about this rebellion that had bound them to perpetuate the other tradition. After working on this myth, the parents were able to make better caretaking arrangements which relieved Martin of his parenting role.

We were delighted when he began to use our toys in an age-appropriate way and with evident enjoyment. Michael made considerable strides during this time in his social behaviour and his ability to concentrate and learn at school.

Why had it taken so long for Michael's autism to be recognized and referral to a child psychiatrist arranged? Could the passivity of the parents, based on their fatalism derived from their own cultural and family traditions have infected their professional advisors too? Certainly, even with this severely handicapped boy, it was possible using a family approach to improve family and individual functioning.

VI.   ASPECTS OF FAMILY THERAPY WITH HANDICAP

A.   The Process of Family Therapy in Handicapped Families

The principles and techniques of family therapy apply to the families under consideration no less than to non-handicapped families. What distinguishes handicapped families is the repeated need to work through their grief at the loss of the normal child they expected, and this need may recur again and again as another hoped for achievement has to be relinquished. Thus parents may appear to have accepted their child's limitations, only to grieve anew when the onset of puberty, or adult life, reveals how limited he will be. Families continue to hope for physical and intellectual normality while they experience progress, however slow. When the ceiling is reached, renewed mourning may have to be facilitated. The other major process which is found frequently in dysfunctional families containing a handicapped member is the use of a disabled child to diffuse or detour conflict (Minuchin, 1974).

B.   Case Example: Sandra and her Family

(1) The Family
Sandra, an adopted child, was 4½ when she was referred to the school psychological service by her middle-class parents because of long-standing severe
temper tantrums and backwardness in speech and social development. At that
time, the educational psychologist and social worker were involved, and after
psychological assessment had revealed mild intellectual handicap, the social
worker saw the mother regularly over the next 2 years for counselling and advice
about management. Sandra's learning difficulties increased when she entered
junior school, and eventually at 9 years, she was transferred to a school for mildly
educationally subnormal children. (At this time, her intelligence quotient on the
Wechsler Intelligence Scale for Children verbal scale = 72, Performance
scale = 61. Full scale IQ = 64.) She settled well there, but when she was 11
years, the school doctor referred her to the child psychiatrist because of
behaviour difficulties at home which were increasing. She shouted and screamed
unbearably when she couldn't get her own way, and was persecuting the cat by
squeezing his neck.

A family diagnostic interview was offered and accepted. The parents were in
their 50s, and had an older, adopted boy of 14, Tony, who was very bright. The
adoptive mother was obese and in poor health. The father was a quiet man who
seemed calm and placatory. Tony was clearly a parental child. This extract is
from the fourth family session. In the previous sessions, a behaviour programme
had been set up to reward Sandra for not shouting, which had been successful, so
that the family life was happier.

(2) Extract from Fourth Session (15 minutes from end)

Tony: The main problem is that I try to stop Sandra from making mummy
    angry. But if I do, Dad gets cross with me and tells me off: sends me to my
    room, so Dad and I quarrel. I'm good at stopping Sandra from getting Mum
    cross: better than Mum is.
Dad: [to Tony] I don't want Sandra not to like you—I don't want you to have a
    bad relationship. I know that when you boss her, Sandra dislikes you.
Mum: I know I shouldn't do it, but I really invite Tony to help and appreciate it
    when he does. When Sandra is angry and attacks me I can't cope: she is quite
    big now.
Dr Black: Can you describe the sequence of events. What are you doing when
    Sandra gets angry?
Mum: I am lying down in my room watching TV. Sandra comes in for a cuddle.
    At first things are O.K. We're both enjoying it, then Sandra starts to get
    silly, tries to turn off the TV, or starts nagging or mucking around and I get
    angry. At first my anger mounts slowly, but eventually I am screaming at
    Sandra, but she won't obey me or take any notice.
Tony: When I hear Mum screaming I get worried because of her heart.

Dr Black: What's that?
Mum: I had a heart attack and get blood pressure. I've been told I mustn't get
    excited. Anyway I'm in a terrible state after one of these shouting matches.
    I know I shouldn't shout and lose my temper, but it is almost impossible.
    I need Tony to help.
(Dad says nothing. Sandra has been very quiet, looks from face to face, seems
anxious.)
Dr Black: It seems to me that Sandra's not the only handicapped member of the
    family. Mum is handicapped in the control of her temper, Dad is handicapped
    in coming to her aid, Tony is handicapped in not knowing what he should
    do. Can you, Mum and Dad talk together about how to change things?
Dad: Maybe I'm not the ideal man.
Mum: [to Dad] I know that you think I really should control my temper.
Dad: Yes. I think you should. You're an adult and you should be able to control
    your temper and control Sandra.
Tony: [attempts to join parental subsystem] I would like to have Dad's per-
    mission to go and help Mum, because I can control Sandra, I can get her out
    of the bedroom. (Dad is silent).
Dr Black: [redraws the generational boundary to exclude Tony] I guess this is
    something that Mum and Dad will have to discuss together and decide how
    they would like it to be dealt with. If Dad and Mum make the decision that
    Tony should be involved, then Tony would obviously be glad to help, but I
    feel it would need to be the parents who decide that. In the meantime Tony,
    I guess you'll have to see whether being a child in this family has any
    compensations.

(3) The Next Session
The next session with the parents alone had been planned some time before,
because they were bothered about Sandra's burgeoning sexuality and wondered
if she could be sterilized, as they felt she might easily be seduced and violated.
During this exposition father had sat with his back to mother and I asked why.
Father admitted that he had felt agonized after our last session because of the
realization of the burden they had put on Tony to be grown up before his time
because they couldn't control Sandra. They had in fact been able to talk about
this, and had given Tony clearer instructions which were working well. For the
first time Sandra had controlled a temper herself. Mother turned to me to tell me
how embarrassed she had been all her married life because of father's social
incompetence. He refused to make any small talk and so she rushed in, talking
nineteen to the dozen, when they had company. Really she was at heart a quiet
person, and she resented being forced to be loud and loquacious. She felt she was
a very incompetent parent. She could only talk to children as if they were adults.
Father was much better at coming down to their level. She realized that she was
really making Tony into a parent for herself, and she felt awful about this. Father
seemed surprised at this outpouring, and turned around to face her. With some
encouragement they began a dialogue in which their tender feelings for each
other could be recaptured.

(4) Comment

Although individual casework had helped mother to come to terms with her infertility and with the fact of Sandra's handicap, father and the children had been excluded from the treatment. The generational boundaries had not been firmly established because of the intellectual discrepancy between Tony and his parents on the one hand, and Sandra on the other. Mother's unhappiness in her marriage and her ill health had led her to put pressure on Tony to husband and parent her. The system had always been a vulnerable one, but it was probable that what precipitated the breakdown in family functioning was the onset of puberty in both children which reactivated incest fears, rivalry between father and son, and envy in mother of father's close relationship with Sandra.

What would restore system stability was an improvement in the marital functioning. In fact Sandra was being used to detour marital conflict. Some improvement in her behaviour, using behavioural techniques forced the parents to look at their own relationship. The will to work on what they found was fortunately present. In the past, early attempts by therapists to redefine a problem identified by parents as in the child, as a marital problem has resulted in their losing the family. In this case, the improvement in the marital relationship was achieved by using family therapy. This resulted in generally improved family functioning and a diminution in the symptoms of the identified patient. The anxiety about Sandra's sexual development reflected the dysfunctioning in the marital subsystem, and subsided once attention was paid to the marriage.

In this case the process of family therapy enabled a long-standing marital problem to be exposed and helped. Individual therapy previously had not revealed the problem.

VII. CONCLUSION

Family therapists working in this field need perhaps more than those working with other families, to have a good family and professional support system, and to spend only part of their professional day in such taxing work, if they are to bring to it an enthusiasm tempered with compassion and reality. Living with a severely handicapped child is a constant and unremitting strain for parents, and although we can use our skills to improve family functioning, it is imperative that we remember the burdens these families bear. They have much to teach us about courage and endurance, and about how to find pleasure in the almost imperceptible development of the most handicapped children. In the words of Bentovim (1972)

> physical or mental impairment should not handicap the future emotional adjustment and development of the child.

Children with handicaps need not produce handicapped families.

REFERENCES

Anderson, E. M. (1973). "The Disabled Schoolchild: A Study of Integration in Primary Schools", Methuen, London.

Atkin, M. (1974). The "doomed family" — observations on the lives of parents and children facing repeated child mortality. *In* "Care of The Child Facing Death", (L. Burton, ed.), Routledge & Kegan Paul, London.

Barker, R. G., Wright, B. A., Myerson, L. and Gonick, M. R. (1953). "Adjustment to Physical Handicap and Illness: A Survey of the Social Psychology of Physique and Disability", Social Science Research Council, New York.

Bentovim, A. (1972). Handicapped pre-school children and their families — effects on child's early emotional development. *British Medical Journal,* **3**, 634-637.

Black, D. and Sturge, C. (1980). The young child and his siblings. *In* "Modern Perspectives in the Psychiatry of Infancy", (J. Howells, ed.), Oliver & Boyd, Edinburgh and London.

Brimblecombe, F. S. W. (1974). Exeter project for handicapped children. *Brit. Med. J.,* **74**, 4, 706-709.

Burton, L. (1975). "The Family Life of Sick Children", Routledge & Kegan Paul, London.

Caplan, G. (1964). "Principles of Preventative Psychiatry", Tavistock, London.

Court, S. D. M. (1976). "Fit for the Future. Report of the Committee on Child Health Services", H.M.S.O., London.

Dare, C. (1979). Psychoanalysis and Systems in family therapy. *Journal of Family Therapy,* **1**, 137-151.

Dinnage, R. (1970). "The Handicapped Child: Research Review. Vol. 1. Neurological Handicap". Longman in association with National Childrens Bureau. London.

Dinnage, R. (1972). "The Handicapped Child; Research Review. Vol. 2. Physical and Sensory Handicap", Longman in association with National Childrens Bureau, London.

Dorner, S. (1976). Adolescents with spina bifida. *Archives disease childhood,* **51**, 439-444.

Farber, B. (1959). Effects of severely mentally retarded children on family integration. *Monographs of the Society for Research in Child Development,* **24**, 2.

Fox, A. M. (1976). Special educational needs of physically handicapped children. *Childcare, Health and Development.* **2**, 45-71.

Fox, A. M. (1977). Psychological problems of physically handicapped children. *British Journal Hospital Medicine,* **22**, 479-490.

Freeman, R. D. (1970). Psychiatric problems in Adolescents with Cerebral Palsy. *Developmental Medicine and Child Neurology,* **12**, 64-70.

Gath, A. (1974). Sibling reactions to mental handicap; a comparison of the brothers and sisters of mongol children. *Journal of Child Psychology and Psychiatry,* **15**, 187-198.

Gath, A. (1978). "Downs Syndrome and the Family", Academic Press, London and New York.

Goddard, J. and Rubissow, J. (1977). Meeting the needs of handicapped children and their families. The evolution of Honeylands. *Childcare, Health and Development,* **3**, 261-273.

Guerin, P. J. (1976). "Family Therapy — Theory and Practice", Gardner Press, New York.

Harris, J. (1980). Personal communication.

Hewitt, S., Newson, J. and Newson, E. (1970). "The Family and the Handicapped Child", Allen and Unwin, London.

Jan, J. E., Freeman, R. D. and Scott, E. P. (1977). "Visual Impairment in Children and Adolescents", Grune and Stratton, New York.

Kellmer-Pringle, M. L. (1964). "The Emotional and Social Adjustment of Physically Handicapped Children", National Foundation for Educational Research, London.

Lansdown, R. and Polak, L. (1975). A study of the psychological effects of facial deformity in children. *Childcare, Health and Development*, **1**, 85-91.

Lieberman, S. (1979). Transgenerational analysis: The geneogram as a technique in family therapy. *Journal of Family Therapy*, **1**, 51-64.

Martindale, B. and Bottomley, V. (1980). The management of families with Huntington's Chorea. *J. of Child Psychology & Psychiatry*, **21**, 343-351.

Minuchin, S. (1974). "Families and Family Therapy", Tavistock, London.

Normansfield Inquiry (1978). Committee Report. H.M.S.O., London.

Pless, I. P. and Pinkerton, P. (1975). "Chronic Childhood Disorder: Promoting Patterns of Adjustment", Henry Kimpton, London.

Pilling, D. (1973). "The Handicapped Child; Research Review. Vol. 3. Mental Handicap", Longman in association with National Childrens Bureau, London.

Rappoport, R. (1963). Normal crises, family structure and mental health. *Family Process*, **2**, 68-80.

Richardson, S. A. (1971). Children's values and friendships: A study of physical disability. *Journal of Health and Social Behaviour*. **12**, 253-258.

Rutter, M. (1966). "Children of Sick Parents", Oxford University Press, London.

Rutter, M., Tizard, J. and Whitmore, K. (eds) (1970). Education, Health and Behaviour. Longman, London.

Shapiro, R. J. and Harris, R. I. (1976). Family therapy in the treatment of the deaf: a case report. *Family Process*, **15**, 83-96.

Sheridan, M. (1965). *The Handicapped Child and his Home*. National Childrens Homes, London.

Steinhauer, P. D., Mushin, D. N. and Rae-Grant, Q. (1974). Psychological aspects of chronic illness. *Pediatric Clinics of North America*, **21**, 825-840.

Tizard, J., Sinclair, I. and Clarke, R. V. G. (1975). "Varieties of Residential Experience", Routledge & Kegan Paul, London.

Toman, W. (1961). "Family Constellation: Theory and Practice of a Psychological Game", Springer Publishing Co., New York.

Travis, M. (1976). "Chronic Illness in Children", Stanford University Press. California.

Wright, B. (1960). "Physical Disability: A Psychological Approach", Harper & Row, New York.

Younghusband, E., Birchall, D., Davie, R. and Kellmer-Pringle, M. L. (eds) (1970). "Living with Handicap: A Report of a Working Party on Children with special needs", National Bureau for Co-operation in Child Care, London.

Chapter 23

Physical Illness and the Family

B. Lask

I. INTRODUCTION

Physical illness may affect all families, our own included, at any time. It is a rare family that has not been so affected. The family therapist must be aware of both the impact that such an intrusion may have on the family, and the role of the family in the cause, aggravation and maintenance of physical illness. This is true of all illness whether it be "purely organic", psychological or psychosomatic. (Such terms are best avoided, as any distinction is arbitrary and potentially misleading. Organic, psychological and social factors require due consideration in all illness.) Following a review of the literature, I propose a conceptual model of interaction between illness and the family in which I show how physical symptoms or illness play an integral part in family homeostasis. Some case examples are provided to illustrate the clinical application.

II. REVIEW OF THE LITERATURE: INDIVIDUAL VIEWPOINT

Few would dispute that psychological factors are relevant in the precipitation and maintenance of a wide range of physical illness. The evidence for this has been comprehensively documented (Lipowski et al., 1977). Until recently, most emphasis has been placed on the roles of stress and specific personality character-istics. These linear views state that stressful events create emotional arousal which disrupts the endocrine and autonomic nervous systems with resultant physiological changes. Further, specific personality characteristics predispose individuals exposed to stress to specific illnesses (Alexander et al., 1968).

Grolnick (1972) states that the vast majority of stressful events are inter-personal and involve significant relationships, most commonly in the family. He criticizes the hypothesis linking personality-type to specific illness by pointing out that there are many more illnesses than specific personality profiles, and that "it is fallacious to assume a linear correlation between events at the levels of physiological and psychological integration".

III. REVIEW OF LITERATURE: INTERACTIONAL VIEWPOINT

In the last few years, much more consideration has been given to the inter-actional model (e.g. Watzlawick and Weakland, 1978). Most illness is of multifactorial origin. Asthma, for example, results from an interaction between stress, infection and allergy on a labile bronchus. Even the common sore throat conceals subtle processes. Mayer and Zaggerty (1962) have shown that a major determining factor as to whether or not a child who has acquired a streptococcal infection in his throat becomes ill, is the presence of acute or chronic family stress. Thus instead of asking whether a sore throat is due to streptococcal infection we should ask "If this is a streptococcal sore throat, why has this child become ill at this time?"

The literature on illness and interpersonal interaction concentrates upon both dyadic and family interaction (Meissner, 1966; Grolnick, 1972).

IV. DYADIC INTERACTION

A. Parent-Child Dyads

The purported findings are at best unconvincing and often absurd. For example, patients with *tonsillitis* are "overly dependent upon their mothers" (Schellack, 1957) while *hyperthyroid* patients are also "over dependent upon their mothers, but deny this because of their ambivalence" (Alexander, 1961). Alexander also found that children with *arthritis* have "aggressive and demanding mothers", and a year later Finch and Hess (1962) reported that children with *ulcerative colitis* have "aggressive and dominating mothers". The fathers of children with *ulcerative colitis* are "passive and ineffectual", and the fathers of children with *rheumatoid arthritis* are "gentle and inconsistent" (Finch and Hess, 1962). The relationship between children with *ulcerative colitis* and their mothers is "nearly symbiotic and tremendously ambivalent" (Titchener *et al.*, 1960). *Cancer* patients have "an unresolved emotional attachment to their mother" (Perrin and Pearce, 1959), and *asthmatic* patients have "dominating and narcissistic mothers" (Bastiaans and Groen, 1955). The reverse side of the coin has also been examined: *arthritic* mothers "tend to dominate their children" (Alexander, 1961).

The majority of these studies lack elementary scientific precautions such as clearly defined terms, blind assessment and control groups. There are only three published studies of parent-child relationships in physical illness that warrant detailed consideration.

Block (1969) has questioned many of the deeply entrenched myths regarding the psychopathology of parents of asthmatic and schizophrenic children. She compared the parents of
(1) schizophrenic children, with those of
(2) neurotic children, and found no differences between them.
Further, she compared the parents of
(3) asthmatic children, with those of
(4) congenitally ill children,
and was unable to find any distinguishing characteristics.

In a study of the parents of 100 asthmatic and 100 physically disabled children,

Fitzelle (1959) found no quantitative or qualitative differences in psycho-pathology between the two groups. Williams (1975) compared two groups of asthmatic children, of differing severity, and matched them with two control groups, one of normal children and the other containing children with a chronic chest disease (cystic fibrosis). Using carefully defined terms, and reliable and valid tests, he found that asthmatic children had "an excessive dependence-independence conflict with an intensive mother–child bond, and core anxiety around the threat of separation". He concluded that these themes were specific to asthma regardless of severity.

It is difficult to know what to conclude from all these studies. Certainly there is no evidence whatsoever to suggest specific personality types of modes of interaction between parent and child in physical illness. It is just possible however, that asthmatic children experience more separation anxiety than others.

B. Object Loss

The literature is well-endowed with reports of the loss or the threat of the loss of significant relationships shortly preceding the onset or exacerbation of physical illness. Grolnick (1972) quotes reports of object-loss associated with ulcerative colitis, rheumatoid arthritis, leukaemia and various "psychosomatic conditions". Meissner's earlier but more fruitful review (1966) quotes references to object loss being important in tuberculosis, anaemia, arthritis, hypertension, duodenal ulcer, ulcerative colitis, leukaemia and cancer. Paulley (1976) considers object-loss central in multiple sclerosis.

For such reports to have meaning we need to know the incidence of object-loss in other physical disorders not mentioned, as well as in psychiatric disturbance, and in the general population. The absence of control data and the wide range of pathological processes included render most of the above reports suspect. The findings of Stein and Charles (1971) are more credible. They discovered that diabetic adolescents had a significantly higher incidence of loss than did a matched non-diabetic control group. They advanced the hypothesis that juvenile diabetes occurs as a consequence of psychological stress in a physiologically susceptible individual.

C. Husband–Wife Dyads

The spouse dyad literature is more helpful in that the methodology is generally more satisfactory; no claims for specificity are made, and the findings have practical value. Researchers have concentrated on the relationship between the illness and marital equilibrium.

Kellner (1963) reported that a wife's illness followed a husband's almost twice as often as vice-versa. Witkin (1965) suggested that it is more common for one spouse to manifest psychosomatic symptoms at any one time than for both to do so, while Kreitman (1964) has shown that the spouses of psychiatric patients had more physical symptoms than those of a control population. Similarly, Cobb

(1972) found in a study of 49 couples in which the wife had rheumatoid arthritis and the husband had a peptic ulcer, that the wife's controlling behaviour dovetailed with the husband's need to be controlled.

Hoebel (1977) has shown that the efforts of the wives of heart-attack patients to modify the latter's type A, high-risk behaviour (Friedman and Rosenman, 1974) often play a role in maintaining that behaviour (see also p.447). Significant and possibly life-saving changes can be brought out by effecting a change in the wife's problem-solving behaviour. Wikran *et al.* (1978) compared the patterns of communication of the parents of children with asthma with those of children with congenital heart disease using an experimentally-induced communication conflict. The heart-disease parents had a very efficient communication as did two-thirds of the asthma parents. However, one-third of the latter group had an extremely inefficient communication.

The complexities of such studies have been commented upon by Stewart and Lask (in preparation) who, using a similar experimental design, found no difference in communication patterns between the parents of children with "psychosomatic" disorders and the parents of other clinic-attenders.

V.   FAMILY INTERACTION

The reports on family interaction may be grouped as follows:
(a) Affective style,
(b) Typology,
(c) Homeostasis,
(d) Contagion,
(e) Reaction to illness,
although there is considerable overlap between them.

A.   Affective Style

For many years, individuals with psychosomatic disorders have been described as unable to express negative affect, and the same has now happened to families. Goldberg (1957) has described families with a psychosomatic member as using mechanisms which contribute to family cohesion, but oppose the expression of negative or dysphoric feeling. Jackson and Yalom (1966) studied eight families of children with ulcerative colitis, and concluded that they were restricted. Gehre and Kirschenbaum (1967) have described "repressive families" giving rise to "repressive symptoms" such as headaches, enuresis, stomach disorders and phobias, while Looff (1970) stated that families containing children with psycho-physiological reactions had particular difficulty in the verbal expression of affect.

B.   Typology

With so much written on individual and dyad typology, it is inevitable that the family typology bandwagon should roll. The study referred to above by Jackson and Yalom was biased in its selection of families, did not include controls for chronic illness and had small numbers, but the findings are similar to many clinical reports. The families were severely socially-restricted, and restricting of each other in the range of permissible behaviour. They had a feeling of sameness that seemed almost like solidarity (Wynn's pseudomutuality). Jackson and Yalom's report was unusual in this area in that it contained a detailed critique of the research design and a caution about the validity of the findings.

Lask and Kirk (1979) did not find any specific typology or common patterns of interaction in their study of asthmatic families. Indeed although the families were matched for social background, pathology, severity and length of asthma, directly opposing patterns of interaction were found. Rees (1964) and Pinkerton (1967) have reported similar findings.

Minuchin *et al.* (1978) and their colleagues at the Philadelphia Child Guidance Clinic have done as much as any group to advance our understanding of family interaction and physical illness. They have described a general type of family constellation that encourages somatization of emotional conflict. Three factors in conjunction are considered necessary for the development of severe childhood psychosomatic illness:

(1) a physiologically-vulnerable child;
(2) an enmeshed, overprotective and rigid family who are unable to resolve conflict;
(3) the ill child plays an important role in the family's conflict-avoidance.

Detailed clinical observations are provided to support the hypothesis, and the work is considerably strengthened by the inclusion of some remarkable biochemical studies. The level of free fatty acids (FFA) in the blood is an indicator of stress, and Minuchin and his colleagues studied these levels in groups of children with labile and well-controlled diabetes, during stressful and non-stressful phases of family interviews. The parents' FFA levels were also recorded. Raised FFA levels in diabetes are early precursors of diabetic coma. FFA levels were significantly higher in the labile children during stress, and took significantly longer to return to normal. This finding could not be replicated for stressful events outside the family interview where there was no difference between the groups. Further, when a parent's FFA level was raised, and he or she brought the child into the conflict, the parent's level dropped to normal, while the child's rose and failed to return to normal during the recovery period. Hence the emotional arousal related to family conflict in labile diabetic children produced a significant physiological change. Parental arousal can be alleviated at the expense of the child. This pattern may well account for the lability of the diabetes.

As the authors state, the significance of these findings cannot be over-emphasized. There is a clear parallel between family interaction and physiological events. It is therefore all the more frustrating that details of the methodology for rating family interaction are not available. References are made to the analysis of the family diagnostic interview and family tasks, but until such important work can be fully evaluated and replicated, the findings relating to the family characteristics remain unproven.

Despite these criticisms Minuchin and his colleagues have clearly demonstrated the relationship between family conflict-avoidance and labile diabetes. It is of interest that these findings could not be replicated in asthma or anorexia nervosa, although the authors state that "therapeutic observations of such patients have validated the generalisability of their hypotheses, as have the strikingly successful therapeutic results".

Loader *et al.* (1979) have tested the Minuchin "enmeshment hypothesis" and the "affective hypothesis" (see p. 444 *Affective Style*) for families with eczematous children. Using carefully-defined terms and reliable and valid measures, they found that most but not all families fitted in with one or other or both of the proposed interactional patterns, but that the hypothesis of a specific family, "the psychosomatogenic family", was not supported. Their findings complement the studies of individuals where specificity hypotheses have proved to be over-simplified.

C. Homeostasis

This term refers to the *balance* of forces within a family: disturbance of one part affects the whole and sets in motion compensatory events to re-establish equilibrium (Hopkins, 1959). The idea that physical illness plays a major part in the homeostatic equilibrium of a family is not new (e.g. Richardson, 1948), but it has yet to be fully researched. The phenomenon has been described by Jackson and Yalom (1966) in ulcerative colitis; Lask and Kirk (1979) in childhood asthma; and Minuchin *et al.* (1978) in childhood anorexia nervosa, labile diabetes, and recurrent abdominal pain.

D. Contagion

Linked to the homeostatic idea is the commonly-reported phenomenon of illness contagion. Illness in one member produces illness in another (Dunbar, 1954; Hopkins, 1959; Kellner, 1963; Peachey, 1963).

E. Family Reaction

Contagion is but one of many possible reactions to illness. Apley *et al.* (1978) have reviewed the effects on the family of acute and chronic childhood illness, while Schonfeld (1966) has described the effects of having a handicapped child, and Gath (1978) has studied in depth the effect on families of the birth of a child with Down's syndrome (mongolism). One of her most important findings is that the quality of the marriage is a major determining factor in the family's adaption, and that marital breakdown is less frequent where there has been an early therapeutic intervention.

Reddihough and her colleagues (1977) interviewed 43 asthmatic children and their parents, and found that there were basic misconceptions about the disease and its therapy. Fears and anxieties were expressed about death and permanent damage to the heart and lungs. The disease caused a burden to all members of the family, especially the mother. The child was not able to discuss adequately his asthma with the doctor. (This last finding should really be phrased: "the doctor was unable to discuss adequately the asthma with the child," for any failure in communication between doctor and patient is a failure of the doctor's part.) The authors conclude that treatment should include more time spent with the child and family to relieve many of their anxieties.

Gath (1977) has drawn attention to the effect on the siblings of the birth of a child with Down's syndrome. Lask and Kirk (1979) have noted that the siblings may be more adversely affected psychologically than the asthmatic child, and Crain et al. (1966) reached a similar conclusion about diabetic families. Lavigue and Ryan (1978) have shown a high rate of sibling disturbance when examining children with chronic illness, dependent to some extent upon sex and age.

VI. THERAPY AND ITS EFFECTIVENESS

Despite the massive literature, credible and otherwise, on the relationship between illness and the family, and the obvious importance of therapy, there are relatively few reports of techniques or outcome studies. Richardson (1948) was one of the first to urge consideration of the family in all its complexities. Satir (1964) has claimed she uses family therapy regardless of the diagnosis, and Senn and Solnit (1968) have always attempted to modify parental and family patterns of reacting to stress. Carey and Sibinga (1972) and Mechanic (1977) have warned that neglect of the family may delay recovery, and Reddihough and her colleagues (1977) have recommended that more time be given to the treatment of asthmatic families as a whole.

Hoebel (1977) has described the treatment of the wives of Type A coronary artery disease patients. He found that effecting a change in the wife's problem-solving behaviour led to a modification in the family system and consequently in the husband's behaviour. Nine wives were treated and the families were followed-up one month after the end of treatment. Seven wives had improved, and their husbands had also improved on one or more parameters such as Type A behaviour, smoking, amount of exercise, and obesity. Two wives had not changed and nor had their husbands.

The Philadelphia team have described in detail the family treatment of asthma (Liebman et al., 1974a), anorexia nervosa (Liebman et al., 1974b) and psychogenic abdominal pain (Liebman et al., 1976). They claim spectacular results for their therapy, but the details are not available. Hughes and Zimin (1978) have also described the family treatment of psychogenic abdominal pain, while Tomm et al. (1977) have outlined their approach to the family treatment of childhood diabetes.

Bingley and her colleagues (1980) have described the use of a family approach to all children with primary or secondary emotional problems on a general paediatric ward. During a one-year period, 96 children were so treated, and two-thirds of these had improved at a one to two-year follow-up.

The only controlled trial of family therapy for physical illness is that reported

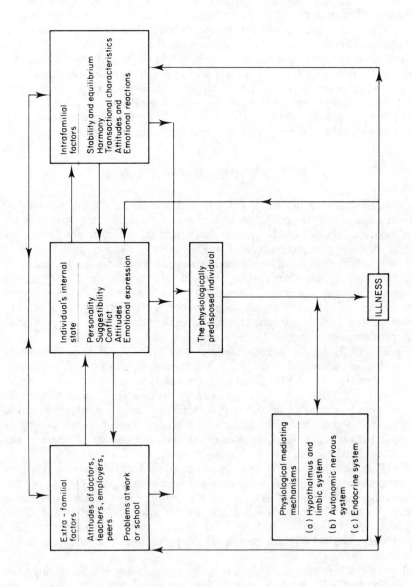

Fig. 1

by Lask and Matthew (1979) in which the effectiveness of family therapy as an adjunct to standard medical management for childhood asthma was evaluated. At a one-year follow-up, the treatment group showed a significant improvement on various parameters when compared with a control group. The therapy was relatively short (a total of 4½ hours in 4 months) compared with the Philadelphia approach of about 75 hours during one year, but the authors concluded that this approach is of value in selected cases of childhood asthma.

VII. GENERAL COMMENTS

What stands out in this literature review is the poor research methodology. In only a small minority of the studies are terms clearly defined and groups matched and controlled. There is rarely any evidence of reliable and valid measures being used. Most of the reports of family interaction contain descriptions only of dyadic interaction. Random allocation to treatment and control groups is mentioned in very few studies.

VIII. CONCEPTUAL MODEL OF INTERACTION BETWEEN ILLNESS AND THE FAMILY

There is a complex interplay between the individual, his illness, the family and extrafamilial factors, which may be conceptualized as an open system. Within this system there is no specific causal factor, and due consideration is given to the relative contribution of each of the elements identified in the circular process (Fig. 1). As I have discussed this model in detail elsewhere (Lask, 1980), I shall only summarize it in this chapter.

A. The Physiologically Vulnerable Individual

Stress of any nature is a potent trigger for a wide range of psychophysiological responses (Fig. 2). Most people have a "target-system" or "target-organ" (part of

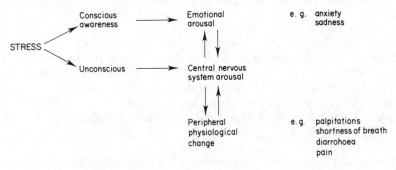

Fig. 2

the body already primed to respond to stress in a pathological way, e.g. the labile bronchus of an asthmatic, the labile cranial arteries of the migraine sufferer) or an already diseased system or organ e.g. narrowing of the coronary arteries. Prolonged or severe stress, whether it be physical or psychological, may thus precipitate an attack of asthma, migraine, angina or other symptoms. An elegant illustration has been provided by Tal and Miklich (1976), who demonstrated how the bronchospasm of an asthmatic may be induced by instructing the subject to concentrate on the recall of an incident associated with intense anger or fear.

B. The Individual's Psychological State

Various aspects require consideration:

(1) Personality Typology

There is very little evidence linking specific illness to personality-type despite considerable effort to do so (e.g. Alexander et al., 1968).

However, the personality-type may precipitate or aggravate a problem in an individual who is already predisposed to a specific illness. For example, coronary artery narrowing (arteriosclerosis) is a very common condition, which starts soon after birth, but angina or coronary thrombosis does not affect all people with arteriosclerosis. Behaviour patterns associated with a high risk of coronary thrombosis have been identified (see above pages 7 and 15). Friedman and Rosenman (1974) have shown that a high-risk coronary-prone behaviour pattern (Type A) can be distinguished from low-risk (Type B) behaviour. Type A individuals are aggressive, competitive, ambitious, restless and experience a profound sense of urgency. Type B individuals are free of these characteristics.

It should be noted that not all Type A individuals suffer coronary thrombosis. For this to occur there is required an *interaction* between the presence of arteriosclerosis, Type A behaviour, and possibly one or more other factors such as smoking, unhealthy diet and lack of exercise.

(2) Emotional Expression

Psychosomatic theory has long held that those individuals who suffer psychogenic physical symptoms are unable to express negative affect (e.g. Nemiah and Sifneos, 1970). One of the few convincing studies in this area is that of Stewart (1962), who was able to show that "delinquent" youths, who seldom suppress discordant affect, are spared psychosomatic illness. Unfortunately much of the research in this area is methodologically suspect, and there is no evidence for such views as that of Pincus and Dare (1978), who consider asthma to be "the literal suffocation of the anger which cannot be expressed". It is true that many asthmatics have difficulty expressing anger, as do many non-asthmatics, but a large number are well able to give vent to their anger.

(3) Suggestibility

The degree of suggestibility of any person plays a part in determining the course of his illness and the response to treatment. This concept comprehensively reviewed by Rachman and Philips (1978) applies particularly to symptoms such as pain, disorders like asthma, and the use of symptomatic treatments.

(4) Attitudes
The "patient" may respond to his illness with a wide range of attitudes to not only his illness, but also the doctor and his treatment. This attitude-spectrum is outlined in Fig. 3. Either extreme represents an unhealthy adjustment, and is likely to be part of a pathological process within the system. The concept of the attitude-spectrum and its associated emotional responses such as anger, guilt, despair, fear or resentment has been comprehensively described by Pless and Pinkerton (1975).

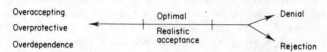

Fig. 3

(5) Conflict
Whether the concept of conflict is applied to something happening between the ego and the id, or to the difficulty a child has in deciding whether or not to go to school where he might be punished for not doing his homework, or to a dispute between two individuals, or to the position of a child whose parents are those two individuals, there is no doubt that conflict is a central feature of our everyday lives. Among the many "defence mechanisms" for coping with conflict is that of "somatization". This term was first used by William Stekel, and later Freud (1905) when referring to what we now describe as hysterical conversion. I use it to describe the process by which distress is expressed in physical terms. Between 50% and 70% of a general population consult their doctors with functional (non-organic) somatic complaints (Langner and Michael, 1963), and the persistent somatizer has received full recognition (Lowy, 1977). The significance of somatized conflict in the interaction between illness and the family has been fully documented by Minuchin *et al.* (1978).

C.   Extrafamilial Factors

The attitude-spectrum (Fig. 3) applies also to important persons outside the family such as employers and teachers, peers and friends, and doctors and nurses. Any of these may be overaccepting and overprotective, or rejecting or denying. Further the "patient" may become overdependent on, or rejecting of the doctor and the treatment (Lask and Kirk, 1979).

Consideration must also be given to other relevant extrafamilial factors such as examinations, interviews and changes of job, school or housing.

D.   Intrafamilial Factors

There is only limited practical difference between the consideration of a family with physical illness, and one without illness. A careful assessment of the family is required with attention being paid to all the relevant aspects of its structure and function, including its stability, harmony, equilibrium and transactional characteristics. The illness requires due consideration in the same way as any other aspect of the family system. Note will be made of the role of the illness in the family, the attitudes and reactions to it, its effects on family life, and its relevance to family homeostasis.

E. Comment

It will be seen from the case illustrations below that using the conceptual model described, there is no requirement for specificity in terms of attitudes, personality-types, family constellations or transactional characteristics. The wide range of each of these is recognized, and the interaction between the various components is emphasized. There is no insistence that the illness plays a vital part in family equilibrium, but there is allowance for that very possibility. The model is equally applicable to children or adults, and allows for illness in more than one person. Finally, it is applicable to all illness at any point on the spectrum from primarily organic to primarily psychogenic.

IX. CLINICAL APPLICATION

The family therapist's approach to illness in the family should be the same whatever the reason for the family being seen, whether the illness is seemingly incidental, or it is taking its toll on the family life or because there is doubt as to its cause. Although the significance of the environment in the precipitation and maintenance of the disorder may vary, the physical manifestation is genuine, and of intense importance to the "patient" and his family. The therapist can use discussion of the illness as a method of observing the mode of function of the family system.

A. The Differing Role of Illness

The first three examples illustrate the differing role of illness in the family and the range of reactions to it.

(1) Clinical Examples: The A's "Denial Patterns"
A middle-class professional couple, the A's, had adopted two children after failing to have children of their own. When these children were 7 and 5 respectively, Mrs A developed multiple sclerosis. The illness ran a typically fluctuant course with periods of normality and other times when Mrs A was confined to a wheelchair. Neither parent could admit to the severity of the illness or to the effect it was having on the children. For example, Mr A would allow his wife to take the children on holiday to remote areas of the countryside despite her considerable difficulties. Any suggestion of weakness or vulnerability in any member of the family was suppressed, and perfection was demanded.

As the elder child, Jim, approached adolescence and started seeking some autonomy, his age-appropriate behaviour was forbidden, and his mother increasingly infantilized him in an attempt to keeping him as a "perfect" and conforming child. His reactive protests increased in severity until eventually he ran away and committed a variety of offences. There was an immediate relapse of the multiple sclerosis with subsequent return of the wayward son to the family fold, and renewed promises of good behaviour. This repetitive pattern led ultimately to Jim being taken into care.

This extreme denial of the severity of the illness was an unhealthy adaption to a handicapping condition, and it was linked to the unrealistic and impossible demand for perfection which forced one of the children into a delinquent mode of behaviour. His delinquency coincided with relapses of the disease, which remitted on his return. A close interaction can be seen between multiple sclerosis, the denial, the demands for perfection and the delinquency. The opposite extreme to denial, overacceptance and overprotection plays a major part in the next example.

(2) The B's Conflict as a Regulator
Michael B, 14, the youngest of four siblings, had refused to go to school since the repair of a leaking heart valve 2 years previously. His elder brother, Nick, 16, had had a shorter period of school-refusal the year before Michael's operation. Two elder daughters had left home, but returned during their holidays. The family were devoutly religious. Mr B, a fitter in his late 50's, had a fixed knee joint, having been shot through the knee during the war, and walked with a heavy limp. In addition he had a peptic ulcer. At the time of referral, family life was dominated by Michael's school refusal and all the usual and unsuccessful attempts to overcome this. The family had taken no steps to get him back to school for a year after his operation, saying that because he had been so ill, he should not be pushed. Once they started trying to get him back they were frightened by his violent refusal to return. In family sessions any discussion of this was accompanied by Michael screaming, raging, and throwing himself on the floor. The therapist challenged the parents' tendency to give way, and he then became the target of a united family attack. A further challenge of this rigid defensive pattern led ultimately to Mr B saying it was wrong to have all this arguing and fighting, it was un-Christian, the family did not do it at home, and they were really all very happy. Mrs B, crying, told the therapist how she had to "keep the peace to stop Michael having a heart-attack", and her husband from "bursting his ulcer".

In this family, unrealistic attitudes to illness had played a major role in its pathology. Michael's congenital heart disease and Mr B's war-wounds had added to the strains of a family in which anger and confrontation were not permitted. The ensuing stresses and bottled-up feeling had probably contributed to Mr B's ulcer which in itself accentuated the problem. Mrs B's overprotection of the sick with desperate attempts to control the situation had brought her to the edge of a breakdown.

(3)   The C's: Avoidance Patterns
Roy C, 7, was referred for assessment of overactive and disrupted behaviour.
There were three other children, Emilia 14, Alan 12, and Karen 3. Mrs C had
suffered from long-standing recurrent thrombosis in the leg, for which she had
been offered surgery. Roy, the only member of the family who made demands or
expressed anger, seemed to dominate family life, and Mr and Mrs C were unable
to assert any limits. Fears of Mrs C's illness and resentment of her refusal to
accept treatment were denied. Only Roy's behaviour brought the family to a
hospital for help. The therapist made a strong recommendation that Mrs C
should accept surgery. She refused and cancelled the family's next appointment.
Roy started lighting fires, and Alan developed anorexia nervosa.

Although the referred child's symptoms seemed to be the most powerful factor
in the family system, it is more likely that these were a reaction to the mother's
denial, as they did at least bring her to medical attention. As a result of the
failure to help instantly, there was an escalation of symptoms and the onset of
another illness in a different member of the family.

B.   Interventions in Family Problems relates to Physical Illness

The therapist's intervention in the above example was made without careful
consideration of the family system. It had the same impact as the referred child's
behaviour, so threatening the mother that she withdrew from this treatment also.
The therapist acted using his medical knowledge without appreciating the part
that the mother's illness played, and so he failed to help. The role of the illness in
the family must be included in the formulation, in the same way as would be
other interruptions in family life such as bereavement, adverse social influences,
loss of employment or move of house. The aims of treatment, and the strategies
and interventions used should be determined not by the quality of the illness,
but by its role in family life. Focussing on the illness may be a necessary strategy,
but the illness may be an important part of family homeostasis, and the therapist
may need to "de-emphasize" the illness and concentrate specifically on the
family relationships. The next two examples illustrate the different interventions
necessary in the treatment of the same illness in the same sex and age-group.

(1)   The D Family exploring Feelings about Illness
Fiona D, the middle one of three daughters aged 18, 10 and 8, was referred
because of severe life-long poorly-controlled asthma. Another daughter had died
of asthma, aged 4, 12 years previously. The family was warm, close and
harmonious. Mr D, a managing director in his 40s, and also an asthma-sufferer,
was the spokesman for the family who tended to agree with everything he said.
The family avoided disharmony, saying they preferred to agree on everything.
Mrs D would often speak for others, while Mr D would help any dissenters to
see his correct, point-of-view. Any discordant feelings were in this way
controlled and rationalized. The therapist made little impact initially, and
previously-made plans for Fiona to go to boarding-school came into effect.

While away at school, she had no asthma attacks, and during the holidays she had fewer frank attacks, but her chest was still very tight, and she was unable to take any exercise. Fiona told her parents that she had enjoyed the "grouse sessions" at school when, in the dormitory in the evenings, the girls would have a good moan about everything, without fear or reprisal, or denial of their feelings. Her parents were impressed by this, and told the therapist during the next session that they attributed her improvement to this. Fiona denied this was the case, and her father rationalized her into accepting that it was. The therapist challenged Mr D's recurrent denial of Fiona's feelings, and Mrs D immediately defended her husband by stating that as the asthma was now behind her, he must be right. The therapist asked Fiona whether her mother was right in saying the asthma was behind her, and Fiona said that she preferred to call it a phase of improvement. Mrs D immediately started telling Fiona that she would feel more comfortable if she could see it not as a phase of improvement but as a cure. The therapist asked Mr D to point out to Mrs D what she was doing. From here on the family made a game of using signals to indicate those times when one person was rationalizing to deny another person's feelings. Fiona's breathing steadily improved over the ensuing weeks, and she was eventually able to stop her medication.

In this family, the main interventions had been exploration of feelings about the asthma and a challenge of the tendency to deny and rationalize. It could be argued that there was a need to explore fears of death, given the tragedy of the death of another daughter, but the family had readily put the therapist off the scent using the same process of resistance. The enmeshment and conflict avoidance seemed to be major maintaining factors in the illness. In the next example, conflict was also very important.

(2) Exploring Conflict around Illness
Mary, 8, a Sri Lankan child, had on two occasions required resuscitation after her breathing had stopped during asthma attacks. Attempts to help her through individual psychotherapy had failed, and the whole family was then referred for therapy. Seven family members attended: the parents Mr and Mrs S, Patrick 10, Mary, Anita 5, and the maternal grandparents Mr and Mrs V who came to England shortly after Mary's parents had married and who had lived with the family since. The grandmother started the session by stating that the real problem was that she and her son-in-law did not get on; in fact they had not spoken since Mary was born. They held strongly antagonistic views to child-rearing, and all three children were caught up in this conflict. If one child was hurt, Mrs V would start comforting, and Mr S would stop her, insisting that the children must learn to fend for themselves. When Mr S was disciplining a child, Mrs V would comfort. Mrs S, her loyalties divided, but tending to agree with her own mother, was unable to discuss the problem with her husband, and so the silent conflict continued.

The therapist encouraged the protagonists to discuss their differences using himself as a go-between. He soon felt constricted, caught up between warring factions. He instructed the parents that they must decide how the children should be handled, and that no-one else must interfere once the decision had been made. Further, he insisted that the father and grandmother stop using the children as a weapon in their own conflict.

Four marital sessions were arranged to help the parents explore their own difficulties, reach some decisions on handling the children and consolidate the changes. They were able to use these constructively, and they developed a satisfactory *modus vivendi*. The intergenerational conflict remained unchanged, but the grandmother stopped interfering with the management of the children. Mary had had no further asthma one year after the end of therapy.

(3)   Exploring the Interaction between Illness and Family Functioning

The final example demonstrates how important it is to understand the inter-action between illness and family functioning.

A 35-year-old teacher, Mrs R, divorced her husband two years after he had developed a crisis of identity which he was unable to resolve. His behaviour included having temper tantrums, lying in bed for days on end, and then joining a hippy cult. She had chosen as her second husband a man who was ambitious, competitive and keen to please, completely the opposite in character to her first. The reconstituted family consisted of Mr and Mrs R, Christine 10, and Sean 8. Christine had been referred because of a long history of defiance, rudeness and temper tantrums, particularly in relation to her stepfather. Mr R was wary of showing his feelings for fear of being compared with Christine's father. Supported in this by his wife, he failed to express any of his own distress or anger at the situation. In addition, Mrs R discouraged him from taking disciplinary action against Christine, feeling that as her mother she was the only person who should do this. Mr R had a heart-attack within three months of their marriage.

Individual, analytically-orientated psychotherapy, aimed at helping Christine see that through her behaviour she was both expressing her identification with her real father and displacing her anger and hurt feelings from him to her stepfather, had little effect. Mr and Mrs R asked for further help. The therapist insisted on family meetings, which were dominated by Christine's rude and defiant behaviour. When Mr R made unconvincing and unsuccessful attempts to control Christine, his wife would protect her, but when this was pointed out, both parents rationalized their actions and returned the focus to Christine who happily accepted it.

An important point in the therapy occurred during the third session.

Mrs R: Christine can be really odious at times.
Christine: No I'm not, you two are odious.
Mr R: If only you weren't so rude we would all get on much better and . . .
Mrs R: But you do provoke her by telling her off so much . . .
Christine: [to Mr R] Yes it's your fault, you silly fool.
Mr R: You see you're doing it again.
Therapist: I think you're all doing it again: you, Mrs R, make a comment about Christine; Christine responds aggressively; you, Mr R, attack Christine; and you, Mrs R, then defend her.

Mrs R: Yes that's right, she gets between us, what can we do?

Christine: Go off and stuff yourselves.

Sean: Christine gets all the attention, you never talk about me.

Mr R: Yes well let's talk about you. Why don't you do your homework?

Sean: I do.

Mr R: No you don't, you sit around watching television and finding all sorts of excuses for not doing it.

Mrs R: But he's only 8, you can't expect him to do much homework.

Therapist: It seems like Sean comes between you as well.

Mrs R: Well I have to protect Sean from David's criticism; he does go on at him a lot.

Mr R: I don't think protect is the right word, it's more like seeing his point of view.

Therapist: Hold it . . . the same thing's happening now with Sean. Either Sean or Christine is the focus of attention, the two of you as parents disagree, and you Mrs R side with one of them, I point this out, and you then philosophize about it: "protect" or "point of view". I think you're avoiding something between the two of you, some sort of conflict.

Mr R: No you've got it wrong—we don't have any conflict, sometimes we disagree, and other times we . . .

Therapist: Okay, not a conflict. Sometimes you have a problem working effectively as a couple.

Mr R: Yes that's right. I feel like an undermined policeman. I'm expected to control the children, but when I tell them off, I get told off myself.

Mrs R: But it's when you pick on them, especially Christine. You're always picking on her, and I know you don't like her, but I just don't know what to do about that.

Therapist: There are times when you feel really angry with each other, like now, but it never gets sorted out.

Mrs R: But I don't know what will happen if I have it out with David. I don't know if he'll get upset and feel hurt, or go quiet and sulky, or take it out on the children more, or what.

Therapist: Or even have another heart-attack.

Mrs R: Yes . . . [cries]

Therapist: You can't really have it out with David because you're frightened he'll have another heart-attack, so you snipe at him instead, through the children, and things never get sorted out.

Mrs R: That makes sense.

Mr R: So what do we do?

The therapist's offer of a couple of sessions just for the parents was eagerly accepted.

They started the next session by saying they did not need marital therapy, did not think Christine was caught up in any disagreement, and they simply wanted advice on management. The therapist asked for an example of an incident over which they had had difficulty, and the parents gave a perfect description of how they had disagreed over management. Christine had defied her stepfather's request to do something and had sworn at him. Mrs R, feeling angry with her husband for making an unreasonable demand but not wishing to hurt him by expressing this, had invited Christine to join him doing something else.

The therapist encouraged Mr and Mrs R to work out an alternative response for a similar situation, and in so doing, considerable pent-up feeling was expressed. Afterwards Mr R said to his wife "and you needn't worry. I haven't got angina". In succeeding sessions, they shared their previously covert fears of further serious illness. Gradually they learned to confront and support each other. This model of discussing and resolving disagreement helped Christine find a more acceptable way of expressing her own feelings, and Mr R remained well himself.

In this example, there was a circular interaction between an inability to cope with conflict, a serious illness, and fear of recurrence of the illness. The successful intervention was based on an understanding of this interaction, after an attempt to help one individual with her intrapsychic distress had failed.

X. CONCLUSIONS

Weakland (1976) has commented in a paper entitled *Family Somatics — A Neglected Edge* that the relationship between the family interaction viewpoint and illness and disease has received some consideration, but deserves a much more extensive examination and research effort.

As Grolnick (1972) has stated with reference to psychosomatic illness

> there is no priori reason to assume a causal relationship between any aspect of the family system and a psychosomatic illness any more than such a relationship exists between a psychosomatic illness and a particular intrapsychic conflict.

Several years later, there is some limited evidence that a particular family constellation may predispose an already vulnerable child to psychophysiological changes. There is general agreement that physical illness can have a prolonged and powerful effect on the family, and that the effect may itself influence the illness.

Despite enthusiastic pleas for the use of family therapy in the treatment of many conditions, there is only limited evidence as to its usefulness. Devotees of family therapy are in danger of travelling the same overenthusiastic and uncritical path as that taken by their psychoanalytic colleagues, in terms of causal relationship, specificity and the value of therapy. There is an outstanding need for carefully-designed studies to test clearly defined hypotheses with proper scientific precautions against error. Some of the massive effort currently being put into therapy should be transferred to process and outcome research.

REFERENCES

Alexander, F. (1961). "The Scope of Psychoanalysis", Basic Books, New York.
Alexander, F., French, T. and Pollock, G. (1968). "Psychosomatic Specificity", University of Chicago Press, Chicago.
Apley, J., McKeith, R. and Meadow, R. (1978). "The Child and His Symptoms", Third edition. Blackwell, London.
Bastiaans, J. and Groen, J. (1955). Psychogenesis and Psychotherapy of Bronchial Asthma. In "Modern Trends in Psychosomatic Medicine", (D. O'Neill, ed.), Hoeber, New York.
Bingley, L., Leonard, J., Hensman, S., Lask, B. and Wolff, O. (1980). "The comprehensive management of children on a paediatric ward — a family approach", Arch. Dis. Childhood., 55, 555-561.
Block, J. (1969). Parents of schizophrenic, neurotic, asthmatic and congenitally ill children. Arch. Gen. Psych., 20, 650-674.
Carey, W. and Sibinga, M. (1972). Avoiding paediatric pathogenesis in the management of acute minor illness. Paediatrics, 49, 553-562.
Cobb, S. (1972). "The intrafamilial transmission of rheumatoid arthritis", J. Chronic Diseases, 25, 193-225.
Crain, A., Sussman, M. and Weill, W. (1966). Family interaction, diabetes and sibling relationships. Int. J. Soc. Psychiatry, 11, 35-43.
Dunbar, H. (1954). "Emotions and Bodily Changes", Fourth edition. Columbia University Press, New York.
Finch, S. and Hess, J. (1962). Ulcerative colitis in children. Amer. J. Psychiatry, 118, 819-826.
Fitzelle, G. (1959). Personality factors and certain attitudes towards child rearing practises among parents of asthmatic children. Psychosomatic Medicine, 28, 323-332.
Friedman, M. and Rosenman, R. (1974). "Type A Behaviour and your Heart", Alfred A. Knopf, New York.
Freud, S. (1905). "Fragment of a Case of Hysteria", (Standard edition 7:41) Hogarth Press 1953, London.
Gath, A. (1978). "Down's Syndrome and the Family: The Early Years", Academic Press, London and New York.
Gehre, S. and Kirschenbaum, M. (1967). Survival patterns in conjoint family therapy. Fam. Proc., 6, 65-80.
Goldberg, E. (1958). "Family Influences and Psychosomatic Illness", Tavistock Publications, London.
Grolnick, L. (1972). "A family perspective of psychosomatic factors in illness", Fam. Proc., 11, 457-486.
Hoebel, F. (1977). Coronary Artery Disease and Family Interaction: A Study of Risk Factor Modification. In "The Interactional View", (P. Watzlawick and J. Weakland, eds), Norton Press, New York.
Hopkins, P. (1959). Health, happiness and the family. Brit. J. Clin. Practice, 13, 311-313.
Hughes, M. and Zimin, R. (1978). Children with psychogenic abdominal pain and their families. Clinical Paediatrics, 17, 560-573.
Jackson, D. and Yalom, I. (1966). Family research on the problems of ulcerative colitis. Arch. Gen. Psych., 15, 410-418.
Johnson, A., Shapiro, L. and Alexander, F. (1947). Study of rheumatoid arthritis. Psychosomatic Medicine, 9, 295-304.
Kellner, R. (1963). "An Investigation in General Practice", Tavistock Publications, London.

Kreitman, N. (1964). The patient's spouse. *Brit. J. Psychiatry*, **110**, 159-170.

Langner, T. and Michael, S. (1963). "The Mid-Town Manhattan Study: Life Stress and Mental Health", Vol. 2. McGraw Hill, New York.

Lask, B. (1980). Illness in the Family: A Conceptual Model. *In* "Family Therapy: Collected Papers", (S. Walrond-Skinner, ed.), Routledge & Kegan Paul, London.

Lask, B. and Matthew, D. (1979). Childhood asthma: a controlled trial of family psychotherapy. *Arch. Dis. Childhood*, **54**, 116-119.

Lavigne, J. and Ryan, M. (1979). Psychological adjustment of siblings of children with chronic illness. *Paediatrics*, **63**, 616-627.

Liebman, R., Honig, P. and Berger, H. (1976). An integrated treatment programme for psychogenic abdominal pain. *Family Process*, **15**, 397-406.

Liebman, R., Minuchin, S. and Baker, L. (1974a). The use of structural family therapy in the treatment of intractable asthma. *Amer. J. Psychiatry*, **131**, 432-436.

Liebman, R., Minuchin, S. and Baker, L. (1974b). The role of the family in the treatment of anorexia nervosa. *Amer. J. Acad. Child Psychiatry*, **13**, 264-274.

Lipowski, L. (1968). Review of consultation psychiatry and psychosomatic medicine. *Psychosomatic Medicine*, **30**, 395-422.

Lipowski, Z., Lipsitt, D. and Whybrow, P. (1977). (eds), "Psychosomatic Medicine — Current Trends and Clinical Application", Oxford University Press, New York.

Lowy, F. (1977). Management of the Persistent Somatiser. *In* "Psychosomatic Medicine", (Z. Lipowski, D. Lipsitt and P. Whybrow, eds), Oxford University Press, New York.

Mechanic, D. (1977). Illness behaviour, adaptation and illness. *J. Nerv. and Mental Disease*, **165**, 83.

Meissner, W. (1966). Family dynamics and psychosomatic process. *Family Process*, **5**, 142-161.

Meyer, R. and Zaggerty, R. (1962). Streptococcal infections in families. *Paediatrics*, 539-549.

Minuchin, S., Rosman, B. and Baker, L. (1978). "Psychosomatic Families", Harvard Press, London.

Nemiah, J. and Sifneos, P. (1970). Affect and Fantasy in Patients with Psychosomatic Disorders. *In* "Modern Trends in Psychosomatic Medicine", Vol. 2. (O. W. Hill, ed.), Butterworth, London.

Paulley, J. (1976, 1977). Psychological management of multiple sclerosis. *Psychotherapy and Psychosomatics*, **27**, 26-40.

Peachey, R. (1963). Family patterns of stress. *General Practitioner*, **27**, 82-87.

Perrin, G. and Pierce, I. (1959). Psychosomatic aspects of cancer — a review. *Psychosomatic Medicine*, **21**, 397-421.

Pincus, L. and Dare, C. (1978). "Secrets in the Family", Faber and Faber, London.

Pinkerton, P. (1967). Correlating physiologic with psychodynamic data in the study and management of childhood asthma. *Journal of Psychosomatic Research*, **11**, 11-25.

Pless, I. and Pinkerton, P. (1975). "Chronic Childhood Disorders", Kimpton Publications, London.

Rachman, J. and Phillips, C. (1978). "Psychology and Medicine", Penguin, London.

Reddihough, D., Landau, L., Jones, J. and Richards, W. (1977). Family anxieties in childhood asthma. *Australian Paediatric Journal*, **13**, 295-298.

Rees, L. (1963). The significance of parental attitudes in asthma. *Journal of Psychosomatic Research*, **7**, 181-190.

Richardson, H. (1948). "Patients Have Families", Commonwealth Fund, New York.

Satir, V. (1964). "Conjoint Family Therapy", Science and Behavior Books, Palo Alto, California.

Shellack, D. (1957). Neurosenpsychologischke Faktoren in der Aetiologie und Pathogenese der Tonsillitis. I. *Z. Psychosoma. Med.* **3**, 265-276.

Schonfeld, W. (1966). Body image disturbances in adolescence. *Arch. Gen. Psych.* **15**, 16-23.

Senn, M. and Solnit, A. (1968). "Problems in Child Behaviour and Development", Philadelphia Press, Philadelphia.

Stewart, L. (1962). Social and Emotional Adjustment during Adolescence as related to Development of Psychosomatic Illness in Adulthood. *Psychol. Monogr.,* **65**, 175-215.

Stein, S. and Charles, E. (1971). Emotional factors in juvenile diabetes mellitus. *Amer. J. Psychiat.,* **128**, 56-60.

Tal, A. and Miklich, D. (1976). Emotional induced decreases in peak flow rate in asthmatic children. *Psychosomatic Medicine,* **38**, 190-200.

Titchener, J., Riskin, J. and Emerson, R. (1960). The family in psychosomatic process. *Psychosomatic Medicine,* **22**, 127-142.

Tomm, C., McArthur, R. and Leahey, M. (1977). Psychologic management of children with diabetes mellitus. *Clinical Paediatrics.* **16**, 1151-55.

Wikran, R., Faleide, A. and Blakar, R. (1978). Communication in the family of the asthmatic child. *Acta. Psychiat. Scand.* **57**, 11-26.

Williams, J. (1975). Aspects of dependence-independence conflict in children with asthma. *J. Child Psychol. and Psychiat.* **16**, 199-218.

Witkin, H. (1965). Psychological differentiation and forms of pathology. *J. Abnormal Psychology.,* **70**, 317-324.

Part VI

Family Therapy and the Setting

Chapter 24

Family Therapy in Paediatric Settings

B. Lask

I. INTRODUCTION

See the whole family? — What on earth for? (Anon.)

The Department of Child Psychiatry has only one room, and shares its premises
with the chapel, so families attending for therapy join those seeing the Chaplain,
and wait in the main hospital corridor. (H. Behr — Personal communication about
family therapy in a general hospital setting)

A multi-disciplinary team approach, based on the principles of family therapy is
described for the comprehensive management of all children on a paediatric ward.
(Bingley et al., 1980)

I have selected (not completely at random) these statements to illustrate the wide
range of attitudes to family therapy in children's hospitals and child psychiatry
departments in Britain. In some units, the paediatricians and child psychiatrists
practising family therapy have no communication, whereas in others, complex
joint research projects have been completed (e.g. Lask and Matthew, 1979;
Richman, in preparation).

In North America, collaborative work between paediatricians and family
therapists seems commonplace. Carey and Sibinga (1972) consider the illness,
the child, the family and the paediatrician as separate-but-interacting participants. Sack (1978), having analysed the child psychiatry consultations in a
paediatric hospital concludes that paediatric hospitals can serve as a disguised
mental health facility for a sizeable number of children and their families.
Schneidermann et al. (1976) always assess the families of children with fatal
lipid-storage disease. Tomm et al. (1977) have described the treatment of juvenile
diabetes using family therapy, as have Hughes and Zimin (1978) for childhood
abdominal pain. Minuchin et al. (1978) and Minuchin and Fishman (1979) have
outlined the family approach to the treatment of a number of psychosomatic
disorders. Russak and Friedman (1970) consider the involvement of the
paediatric resident in family interviewing to be an essential part of his training.
Allmond et al., paediatricians in California, have described their own use of
family therapy in their practice (1979).

It is not all sweetness and light, however, in North America. Bolian (1971) has
described situations where parents initiated and demanded psychiatric consultations over the objections of the attending physician, and others where

he has been asked to see a child surreptitiously so that the objecting parents would not know.

Paediatricians in Britain have long preceded child psychiatrists in calling for a family approach to childhood illness. They have commented on the complex interplay of family and illness (Miller *et al.*, 1970), and the relationship between family patterning and childhood disorder (Apley, 1963). This attitude is best summarized by another paediatrician, Weller (1975), who, when referring to childhood illness, stated:

> By failing to see the whole family as a collective patient, we run the risk of adding to the burden on the community. Not only may the child have to be re-admitted, but the damage to the family may mean more calls on the general practitioner and the social services, both now and in the future, as the stresses wreak havoc on the personalities of the next generation.

The problems of linking the practice of family therapy to the organization and philosophy of a paediatric or general hospital can be enormous. Clearly, there will be many differences between in- and outpatient work. Working in the latter, more self-contained setting, the therapist not only has to contend with structural problems such as space and time, but is aware also that the attitudes of the referring paediatrician as well as the family are often influential. Churven (1978) has investigated the attitudes of families referred to a Child Psychiatry Department of a general hospital to the idea of family assessment and treatment and on the whole found them to be favourable.

II.   CHILD PSYCHIATRY INPATIENT UNITS

More problems may arise on a child psychiatric inpatient unit. The unit is likely to have a different philosophy from that of other units within the hospital, and its separateness may hinder communication and consequently clarification of its purpose. Furthermore although the staff are likely to be "psychologically-orientated", the concept of family therapy may be quite new to them. Such issues as control and dependence may prove central. The admission of a child to hospital implies that the family are handing over responsibility to the staff during the admission. Nursing and medical staff are trained to take responsibility and exercise considerable authority.

Yet central to family therapy are the facts that the family must take responsibility for itself, and that change arises from within the family. This apparent contradiction of expectations needs to be resolved both early in the evolution of the unit, and early in the contact between the unit and the family. Hildebrand and her colleagues (1981) have described the introduction of a full-family orientation on a child psychiatry inpatient unit, and have discussed in detail some of the associated problems. Bruggen (1976) has described a similar setting for adolescents. In both units, the commitment of the family to involvement in therapy is a prerequisite to admitting the child. Hildebrand and her colleagues make use of a signed therapeutic contract. Bruggen uses the reason for requesting admission as the focus of work. Although it is a child or adolescent who is admitted the unit can be so structured as to help the family improve its communication and effectiveness and to learn new ways of resolving problems.

III. FAMILY THERAPY ON A PAEDIATRIC WARD

The setting where most problems for the family therapist are likely to arise is the paediatric ward. This section is devoted to a discussion of the relevant issues, but undoubtedly many of the points are applicable to family therapy in *any* setting.

A. The Role of the Multi-disciplinary Team

A *sine qua non* for the successful use of family therapy in a paediatric setting is a multi-disciplinary team. The joint philosophies of such combined team-work, and the family approach have to be integrated into those of the ward. Successful therapy is dependent upon a mutually trusting relationship in which the family therapist, whatever his or her professional training, is considered an equal with a specific contribution to make to the welfare of the child and his family. Such a relationship can only be built up over a period of time in the context of frequent, regular meetings in which there is an open sharing of views between the family therapist and the medical and nursing staff.

Introducing the theory and practice of family therapy to the philosophy of a paediatric ward involves a conceptual shift for the ward staff. The complex changes of focus which must occur are from an organic to a psychological perspective, from an individual to a family view, and from a didactic to an interactional model of treatment. Once more considerable time may be required to explain the rationale of this approach, and the family therapist must be sensitive to misunderstanding and resistance among the staff.

Similar conceptual changes have to be made by the family. Chassin *et al.* (1974) have described three different types of parental perception of the focus of responsibility for their children's problems.
(1) The first group view the child as a helpless victim, and they tend to take the blame upon themselves for causing the child's symptoms.
(2) The second group see the child's problems as an interactive one which involves the whole family.
(3) The third group, the resistant type, view their child as damaged or emotionally disturbed.
In a paediatric setting, I have found similar responses. One group can accept the family model of "psychosomatic" and stress-related problems: "We knew all along . . ." A second group understands that family relationships can contribute to childhood disorders, and are willing to explore the possibility, although not necessarily feeling that "that is the case with us." The third group cannot accept any such possibility and will shortly depart to seek a second, third, or fourth opinion.

B. Case Examples

The following three examples illustrate the types of family described.

(1) Jean, ten months old, was the first child of a young Australian couple, living in London for a year during father's sabbatical. She was admitted to hospital for investigation of screaming attacks and a severe sleep disturbance. When the admitting doctor took the history, the parents spontaneously volunteered that they were having difficulties in their relationship. They asked for some marital therapy as they were certain that Jean's symptoms were a result of their problem. The symptoms resolved shortly after admission, and the parents involved themselves enthusiastically in six marital sessions prior to their return to Australia.

(2) Jason, 11, had been admitted for investigation of recurrent and painful ulcers of the mouth and rectum. Physical investigations revealed no organic cause. The psychiatrist interviewed the parents, who denied any family stress. They agreed, however, to a family meeting to explore the possibility. In this meeting, the psychiatrist noticed cross-generational alliances between Jason and his mother, and Robin, 13, and his father. Further discussion uncovered some areas of considerable disharmony between the parents. A short series of family sessions led to a resolution of the presenting physical complaint and an improvement in family relationships.

(3) Beverley, 10, was admitted to hospital for investigation of recurrent abdominal pain, having been referred by her local paediatrician, who had made a diagnosis of psychogenic pain. The parents had been unable to accept this, asking: "How can it be all in the mind when she's doubled-up with it?" Shortly after admission, the psychiatrist and a paediatrician met the parents and explained the concept of psychogenic pain. The parental response was: "Beverley isn't a nutter". Further discussion had no impact on the impasse, and when the psychiatrist asked Beverley's mother, the more resistant of the parents, what *would* convince her that there was no organic cause for the pain, she replied: "Nothing". During the next year, two requests were received from other hospitals for details of our assessment of Beverley.

C. Principles to facilitate a Family Therapy Approach

(1) The early involvement of the family therapist in the management of the case is essential. If the parents know from the first day of the hospital admission that an interest is taken in not just part of the child but the whole child, and not just one member of the family but the whole family, and that this is a normal and natural part of the process, then the required transitions are more easily achieved.

The family therapist should meet the family with a paediatrician within a few days of admission. This meeting may be used both to convey the results of observations and investigations, and to continue the process of helping the family in their transition from perceiving their child as physically ill to understanding that they all have a vital part to play in their child's recovery. When necessary, further explanations are offered of the mechanism by which emotional arousal can precipitate physical symptoms. Exploration of family relationships continues (the paediatrician admitting the child will have already discussed this issue with the parents). The depth of this search will be dependent upon the degree of insight and motivation of the family. Clearly, the pace is even more important at this stage than at later stages.

This phase of assessment and conversion may be brief or prolonged. As soon as possible, however, the therapist should prepare a formulation and decide on the aims of therapy, and who shall be involved in the treatment. There are good reasons for the continuing involvement of the paediatrician during the hospitalization.

(2) The use of the paediatrician as co-therapist provides an important bridge for the families. Within the security of a medical nexus, a family finds it easier to look at the different strands involved in illness. The paediatrician's presence in sessions assists the therapist to cope more effectively with the tendency of families to seek organic explanations. The combination of paediatrician and family therapist can help the family at a symbolic level to appreciate the interaction between physical symptoms and family relationships. The paediatrician may be able to add relevant observations about events affecting the family on the ward between sessions. Finally, he gains from the experience of assessment and treatment of family problems. Although an overall family perspective is retained, other modes of therapy may be incorporated, either as complementary to or an alternative to family therapy.

IV. WHEN SHOULD FAMILY THERAPY BE OFFERED?

In the light of present knowledge, and in the absence of appropriate research, no one can say with any certainty what the indications and contraindications are for family therapy. As views expressed are based almost exclusively on clinical impressions (a grossly under-estimated source of error) it is hardly surprising that there is considerable disagreement in the literature.

A. Indications and Contraindications

In general, I agree with Bloch and La Perrière (1973) who use family therapy for all conditions where some form of psychotherapy is indicated, unless a specific contraindication can be found. It is worth remembering Haley's point (1970) that any form of intervention is an intervention in the family. In the context of this chapter, contraindications include practical considerations such as the refusal or inability of a key member to attend sessions, or problems related to travelling long distances. Even so, I have treated families who travel 200 miles each way once a week for treatment. Such families invariably seem to do well!

The only families I have found unsuitable are those containing severely paranoid individuals. I do not agree with Bloch and La Perrière (1973), Martin (1977) or Elton (1979) who all consider serious illness as a contraindication to family therapy. Satir (1978) recommends family therapy whatever the diagnosis. Stewart and Johansen (1976) use such an approach for end-stage renal disease and Cohen and Wellisch (1978) have described the treatment of families in which one person has cancer. Minuchin, Rosman and Baker (1978) and Lask and Matthew (1979) have described replicable studies which claim to show that family therapy can improve the outcome of serious illness.

B. Particular Indications

I have found family therapy in a paediatric setting to be of particular value for the following problems:

(1) the presenting symptoms are physical, but psychological factors are of major importance in the aetiology and maintenance of the condition,

(2) adjustment to physical illness or handicap,

(3) adjustment to mental retardation and developmental delay,

(4) relationship difficulties between parents and pre-school children as manifested by screaming, tantrums, sleeping and feeding disorders, and failure to thrive,

(5) specific problems arising from such aspects of hospitalization as separation, special investigations, and painful and immobilizing treatments.

V. CRISIS INTERVENTION

Central to the use of family therapy is the element of crisis, created by the hospital admission, i.e. period of disequilibrium overpowering the family's homeostatic mechanisms. The family in such a state of crisis has a unique potential for change, for it is faced with a new problem that requires novel solutions (Spiegel, 1957 p.15). The disturbance brought about by traumatic experience can, if constructively used, bring about the energy and motivation for change. Hospital admission for many children with emotionally-determined physical disorders may be the only way of sufficiently involving the family to enable it to make the changes necessary for recovery.

A. Case Example: Rachel and her Family

Rachel, 5, the eldest of four children, was referred to the psychiatrist and paediatrician jointly by a local psychiatrist who had been unable, on an out-patient basis, to help the family deal with her compulsive over-eating, sullenness and temper-tantrums. On the ward, Rachel was well-behaved and happy, with no over-eating, except at the times her family visited, when she became miserable and demanding. The family meeting was initially chaotic with all the children shouting, crying and making demands. The parents responded inconsistently, and their only predictable response was either to neglect or discipline Rachel. At the next family meeting, the psychiatrist instructed the parents to control the children and divide their attention equally. At the third meeting, Rachel's parents stated, much to the psychiatrist's surprise, that they had been missing Rachel while she was in hospital, felt they had been giving too much attention to the other children, neglecting her and then resenting her reaction (a perfect formulation). During the course of a couple of weekends at home, they seemed to be able to adjust their handling of her, and she lost some weight. At three months' follow-up she had not gained any appreciable weight, and was obviously happier. Her parents said that everything was better.

Such a positive use of hospital admission is also valuable in helping children with chronic or handicapping conditions and their families to adjust their responses to the problem. Similarly, this approach can be used to involve the extended family who so often profoundly affect the nuclear family's reaction to illness, and who can in other situations be significantly inaccessible.

B.   Chloe and her Family

Chloe S, aged 2, was admitted for the investigation of her failure to thrive, severe sleep disturbance and tantrums. Her parents had married against the wishes of their own parents when they were both 17. Chloe's father was unemployed and her mother was studying at a local art college. The maternal grandparents lived in the same area, and the grandmother would visit her daughter every day. She denigrated the attempts of Mr and Mrs S to be parents, and imposed her own views on child-rearing. The young couple were increasingly undermined, and eventually lost any confidence they had. Their inability to cope reinforced Chloe's behaviour problems.

The medical social worker and a paediatrician-in-training arranged a series of meetings, initially for Chloe and all four adults, and later separate sessions for the parents and grandparents. The aims of this treatment were to (a) distinguish between the parental and grandparental roles, (b) increase parental confidence and autonomy, (c) establish and consolidate the appropriate nuclear family, and (d) enhance the relationship between the grandparents to offset the loss of their parenting role.

The nursing staff taught Chloe's parents how to manage her behaviour problems, and particularly her sleep disturbance. They pointedly discouraged the grandparents from usurping and undermining the parents, while encouraging them to play with Chloe and take her for trips to the park.

Chloe gradually improved, and was soon able to go home with her parents for a night at a time, and later for weekends. Six weeks after admission she was discharged, having gained a considerable amount of weight and lost her behaviour problems. The first three aims of treatment had been achieved, but the grandparents continued to need help with their "loss".

An unexpected and additional effect of this treatment was that the paediatrician, impressed with this approach, decided to undertake a training as a child psychiatrist.

VI.   PITFALLS OF FAMILY THERAPY
IN PAEDIATRIC SETTINGS

A.   Pace of Work

It is essential to work at the family's own pace in the development of their understanding of the problem. Such families may not anticipate or accept the relevance
of a family approach to their child's problems. Admission to hospital may imply
considerable difficulties in unravelling the problem in the outpatients' department, or difficulty for the paediatrician in conveying the psychological aspects of
the diagnosis of the child's problem. Often the family have a strong need to
perceive the problem as based in the child's illness. Such high levels of resistance
have sometimes been compounded by previous experiences in which a
psychological explanation might have been offered in a ham-fisted way. Such
families can cling to a medical model with tenacity and determination.

The sometimes lengthy process of involvement and treatment can create
problems. Inexperienced medical and nursing staff may impatiently question
such an intensive involvement without immediately obvious benefits. Demands
for hospital beds can harass the therapist. Resistant and disturbed families can
increase the already numerous stresses experienced by ward staff. Regular team
discussions are essential to support the staff involved and enable them to
continue to work effectively. Without these, there are the risks of unconstructive
overlap and professional rivalry in the contacts with the family.

The father of a 13-year-old girl who had been admitted for investigation of
weight-loss and subsequently diagnosed by the psychiatrist as depressed,
brought in presents for all the nursing and medical staff, but not for the
psychiatrist who had successfully treated the family!

B.   Over-identification with Children and Parents

Less experienced staff need support and advice to avoid over-identification with
or judgment of families. They have to learn to be not only caring and uncritical,
but also able to cope with criticism and hostility from parents. In parent–child
relationship problems especially, often young and immature parents may
themselves require parenting and lessons in new ways of managing their
children. That this may be provided by nurses younger than themselves can
create resentment and bewilderment.

Joan, aged 3, the youngest of three children, had a six-month history of
recurrent vomiting, extensively investigated without success elsewhere. She was
admitted obviously ill and seriously dehydrated. Further assessment confirmed
our initial suspicion that she had cyclical (psychogenic) vomiting. Her parents
reacted to this diagnosis with disbelief and resentment, feeling that their
parenting skills were being questioned. They reminded us that their elder
children had no problems. Their resentment was accentuated by Joan's
improvement in their absence. They embarked upon a systematic campaign of

criticism of and complaint about every aspect of Joan's management. Many nurses were reduced to tears, and one of the doctors to repeated overt expressions of anger at the parents. Several staff meetings were necessary to help everyone understand what had happened, and how to respond.

VII. ILLUSTRATIONS FROM THE T FAMILY

As a way of completing this chapter, I have included a slightly more detailed case-description. This case illustrates the significance of many points made previously, and in particular emphasizes the combined roles of the paediatrician and the family therapist, the problems relating to the necessary conceptual changes both for the family and the staff, the effective use of a crisis, the support necessary for nursing staff, and the use of additional modes of therapy.

A. The Family Constellation

Caroline, 13, had been admitted with a six-month history of anorexia nervosa. Her parents had separated six years previously, and her mother had remarried three years later. The reconstituted family consisted of the stepfather. Mr T, a businessman in his late 40s; Caroline's mother, Mrs T, an ex-secretary in her mid-40s; Pauline, 18; and Andrea, 17; the daughters of Mr T's first marriage; and Marilyn, 17; Caroline, 13; and Fiona, 9, the daughters of Mrs T's first marriage. The stepfather was an overweight intellectualizer, who tended to sit back, puff his pipe and avoid important issues. Mrs T was the opposite, intensively and dramatically involved, highly loquacious. She was receiving treatment for alcoholism, but currently "dry". All the girls were upset and bewildered by what was happening. A series of meetings with the reconstituted family and one with Caroline and her biological parents allowed the following formulation. Caroline played a central role in the family, being caught up in unresolved conflicts between:
  (1) her mother and stepfather,
  (2) her father and stepfather,
  (3) her biological parents
as well as being the person her mother leant on during drinking bouts. The family pointed to her central position by all agreeing that they felt safer when Caroline was at home. There were unclear boundaries between the two families, with much unexpressed and unrecognized anger and sadness, and the three youngest children all felt personally responsible for the disharmony.

B. The Family Therapy Contract

A contract was made for weekly family meetings with the social worker and paediatrician as co-therapists, and a behavioural programme instituted to help Caroline gain weight. For the first month there was no appreciable change, after which Caroline dramatically deteriorated until she was only half her expected weight. In the family meetings much of the conflict had come into the open, the sessions became increasingly distressing, but the family resisted change, persistently denying the severity of their distress, and "covering-up" at the start of each session. The parents particularly insisted that this was a problem within Caroline and not to do with them.

C.   Initial Work

Caroline complained of her humiliation related to the behavioural programme and pleaded for more autonomy. She begged to be allowed a weekend at home where she lost yet more weight. The therapists concerned by her progressive deterioration offered her a choice between stricter behavioural controls and tube-feeding. Despite her mother's plea to the contrary, Caroline chose tube-feeds and accused her mother of wanting her to die, for why else would she oppose tube-feeding? The nursing staff were split in their reactions, some feeling resentful of Caroline's verbal abuse at them, others feeling sorry for her, and angry with the doctors for "force-feeding" her, and so upsetting her in the family meeting.

After two weeks of tube-feeding, Caroline had regained all the weight lost while in hospital. The therapists used this critical period to emphasize the severity of the problem, and challenge some of the defences.

D.   Extract of Session

The following extract illustrates the family's tendency to deny and detour conflict, to accommodate and intellectualize.

Mrs T: I suppose the real problem is that I have always leaned on Caroline especially when I'm drinking. You see I've always felt closest to her, we have an understanding of each other, and a sort of respect. This must be difficult for you to understand though I suppose you might have seen families like us before. No, I don't think that's likely. Anyhow I don't think the rest of the family appreciate how it feels for us and . . .

Therapist: Caroline, can you respond to what your mum's saying?

Caroline: Well, yes, you see I love Mummy so much . . .

Therapist: I wonder why your wife can't lean on you, Mr T.

Mrs T: I lean on everyone, on Richard, on the girls, not just Caroline. You see being an alcoholic is like . . .

Therapist: I asked your husband.

Mr T: I become unsympathetic after a time. I can stand so much, but there's a limit. I attend Al-Anon, and there we're told what makes alcoholics do the things. You see my wife's a special case, and I have to not let her lean on me too much. But anyhow this really hasn't anything to do with Caroline . . .

Mrs T: Oh yes, oh yes it has, Richard. It has everything to do with Caroline. You see so much has happened to both of us even before you came on the scene, and when you get angry we're closer together . . .

Mr T: But don't you think Doctor that the anorexia arises from within Caroline;

it hasn't anything to do with the family and Jean's drinking? In fact I read an article about it and it said that there are all sorts of hormonal changes and that these take away the appetite.

Therapist: Look, I think if we start discussing hormones we'll be avoiding more important issues. I'd like to hear how you react, Mrs T, to your husband's lack of sympathy and his describing you as a case.

Caroline: It's not Daddy's fault, he tries very hard; it's not Mummy's either. It's all my fault because I don't eat. If only I ate everyone would be very happy.

Mrs T: I don't blame Richard or Caroline. Richard's right to get angry with me. I am really impossible . . .

Therapist: Yes but sometimes I guess he could help you.

Mrs T: Only by not shouting and bullying us when . . .

Mr T: Shout? Me? I'm amazingly good-tempered.

Mrs T: Oh, you do, Richard, you do. Just think of this morning when you were ready to leave and Pauline and Marilyn were still in the bathroom, you shouted so loudly Fiona started crying and Caroline slammed out of the door.

Fiona: I didn't cry, I'm used to Daddy shouting.

Caroline: I didn't slam the door.

Therapist: I think Fiona and Caroline are rescuing Mummy and Daddy from having a disagreement.

Mrs T: Yes that's what's happening. Especially Caroline stops us arguing, and since she's been in hospital . . .

Mr T: We don't argue; this is ridiculous. I occasionally raise my voice when we're in a hurry to catch the train and no one's ready, and I get cross when I can't get into the bathroom because there's hordes of women in there, but what on earth this has to do with Caroline's anorexia I can't imagine.

Mrs T: Oh, Richard, you know we're always arguing, we've argued since the day we married. Someone said it was a marriage of convenience and they were right, you just don't want to see it.

Caroline: Oh, shut up.

Mr T: So what's wrong with a marriage of convenience?

Therapist: Why did Caroline say "shut up"?

Caroline: I can't stand Mummy's way of speaking when she speaks like that. It goes right through me. I can't stand it. I wish you'd shut up.

Mrs T: What is it about how I speak?

Therapist: How can we help Caroline and the others not to rescue the two of you when you're trying to work something out between you?

Mrs T: Well we're okay really. The girls understand, and they just go out of the room if Richard and I want to discuss something.

Caroline: Then you shout at us for always going out.

Mr T: No Caroline, only at meal-tmes when you should be eating with us. You see it really all comes back to her not eating [!]

Therapist: I think we'll make more progress if we ban discussion of Caroline's not eating. This may sound odd to you, but Caroline has a life-threatening illness. You've come to us for help, and you're going to have to accept our advice.

E. Response to Work

After several weeks, the conflict between Mr and Mrs T became the central focus. Caroline continued to gain weight both in hospital and at home during weekends, until she was discharged having reached the third percentile. Family therapy continued on a long-term basis after Caroline's discharge. The family continued to use a number of defences but slowly changed. Despite many periods of concern and threats to withdraw from treatment, the situation slowly improved, and Caroline had maintained a most satisfactory weight-gain one year after discharge.

F. The Paediatrician's Role

Throughout Caroline's hospital admission, there was realistic concern about her physical state, which required constant monitoring. At one stage, day-to-day decisions were necessary regarding life-saving measures. The family's understandable concern often intruded upon treatment, but the use of a paediatrician as co-therapist proved particularly opportune in that it was possible for the therapists to deal with anxieties at a factual level at the start of each session. Practical decisions could be made by the paediatrician while the social worker, as the experienced therapist, controlled the rest of the session. In particular, she was able to capitalize upon the crisis induced by Caroline's dramatic decline in weight with subsequent fears for her life. Both therapists had a vital but different role, and the paediatrician gained valuable experience in the treatment of a family in crisis. Weekly group discussions with the nurses were necessary to help them cope with their own strong feelings which replicated much of what was happening within the family.

VII. CONCLUSIONS

The successful application of family therapy in hospital settings is dependent upon the attitudes and co-operation of such staff as paediatricians and nurses. They start from a similar position to that of the client, expecting an organic, didactic and individual approach to childhood psychological and psychosomatic problems. Their bewilderment at a family approach may parallel that experienced by the family therapist who discovers that a colleague whom he expected to treat a family had in fact not seen the parents at all, and had prescribed a tranquillizer for the child.

The family therapist must understand the other's position, put himself into his colleague's conceptual framework and educate from that point. Education, like therapy, is a two-way process, and discussion and explanation are essential components. Repetition of points may be as necessary an education as is the repetitive challenging of rigidity or enmeshment.

The method described by Bingley and her colleagues (1980) would seem to be a useful model. They claim a 66% improvement rate for children with a wide range of severe problems treated on a paediatric ward using a family therapy approach. The essence of such work is the use of a multi-disciplinary team which meets regularly and is able to discuss freely its difference and reach some resolution—just like any functional family.

Acknowledgements to Liza Bingley for teaching me so much about liaison.

REFERENCES

Allmond, B., Buchman, W. and Gofman, H. (1979). "The Family is the Patient", C. V. Mosby Co. London.

Apley, J. (1963). Family patterning and childhood illness. *Lancet* Jan. 12, 67-70.

Bingley, L., Leonard, J., Hensman, S., Lask, B. and Wolff, O. (1980). The comprehensive management of children on a paediatric ward—a family approach. *Arch. Dis. Child.* **55**, 555-561.

Bloch, D. A. and La Perrière, K. (1973). *In* "Techniques of Family Therapy—A Conceptual Framework", (D. A. Bloch, ed.), Grune and Stratton, New York.

Bolian, G. (1971). Psychiatric consultation within a community of sick children. *J. Amer. Acad. Child Psych.* **10**, 2, 293-307.

Bruggen, P. (1976). *In* "Mental Health in Children", **3**, 731-742.

Carey, W. and Sibinga, M. (1972). Avoiding paediatric pathogenisis in the management of acute minor illness. *Paediatrics* **49**, 4, 553-562.

Chassin, L., Perelman, M. and Weinberger, G. (1974). Psychotherapy: theory. *Research and Practice* **11**, 4, 387-399.

Churven, P. (1978). Families: parental attitudes to family assessment in a child psychiatry setting. *Journal of Child Psychol. and Psychiat.* **19**, 1, 33-42.

Cohen, M. and Wellisch, D. (1978). Living in Limbo—psychosocial interventions in families with a cancer patient. *Amer. J. of Psychotherapy* **32**, 4, 561-571.

Elton, A. (1979). Indications for selecting family or individual therapy. *J. of Family Therapy*, **I**, 193-201.

Haley, J. (1970). Family Therapy. *International Journal of Psychiatry* **9**, 233-242.

Harkin, H. (1979). A family-orientated psychiatric in-patient unit. *Family Process* **18**, 3, 281-292.

Hildebrand, J., Jenkins, J., Carter, D. and Lask, B. (1981). The introduction of a full family orientation in a child psychiatry in-patient unit. *J. of Family Therapy* **3**, 139-152.

Hughes, M. and Zimin, R. (1978). Children with psychogenic abdominal pain and their families. *Clinical Paediatrics* **17**, 7, 569-573.

Lask, B. and Matthew, D. (1979). Childhood asthma—a controlled trial of family psychotherapy. *Arch. Dis. Childhood* **54**, 2, 116-119.

Liebman, R., Honig, P. and Berger, H. (1976). An integrated treatment programme for psychogenic abdominal pain. *Family Process* **15**, 4, 397-406.

Martin, F. (1977). Some implications from the theory and practice of family therapy for individual therapy and vice-versa. *British J. of Medical Psychology* **50**, 53-64.

Miller, F., Court, S., Walton, W. and Knox, E. (1960). "Growing Up in Newcastle-upon-Tyne", Oxford University Press, London.

Minuchin, S., Rosman, B. and Baker, L. (1978). "Psychosomatic Families", Harvard Press, New York.

Minuchin, S. and Fishman, H. (1979). The psychosomatic family in child psychiatry. *J. of Amer. Acad. of Child Psychiatry* **18**, 1, 76-90.

Russak, S. and Friedman, D. (1970). Family interviewing and paediatric training. *Clinical Paediatrics,* **9**, 10, 594-598.

Sack, W. (1978). Making the second diagnosis. *Clinical Paediatrics* **17**, 7, 548-550.

Satir, V. (1978). "Conjoint Family Therapy", Souvenir Press, London.

Schneidermann, G., Lowden, J. and Rae-Grant, Q. (1976). Family reactions, physician responses and management issues in fatal lipid storage diseases. *Clinical Paediatrics* **15**, 10, 887-790.

Spiegel, J. (1957). The resolution of role conflict within the family. *Psychiatry* **20**, 1-15.

Stewart, S. and Johansen, R. (1976). *Psychotherapy and Psychosomatics* **27**, 86-92.

Tomm, K., McArthur, R. and Leahey, M. (1977). Psychologic management of children with diabetes mellitus. *Clinical Paediatrics* **16**, 12, 1151-1155.

Weller, S. (1975). The patient is the family. *World Medicine.* Nov. 19, 36-38.

Chapter 25

Family Therapy in Child Guidance Clinics

D. Black

I. INTRODUCTION

Childhood as a concept is only 100 years old. It came into being in 1870 with the introduction of compulsory schooling in England. Before that children were exploited at all levels of society (from pit workers to castrati), but with their entry into schools they became "visible", and the numbers of unfit children who emerged jolted the Victorian middle class out of their complacency.

Medical and psychological services were developed to help those prevented by disability from benefitting by normal education, and special schools for the subnormal were established by the beginning of the First World War.

Child Guidance Clinics started in the USA in 1922 out of a concern with increased juvenile delinquency

> to develop the psychiatric study of difficult pre-delinquent and delinquent children in schools and juvenile courts and to develop sound methods of treatment based on such study (Underwood, 1955)

The first clinic in Great Britain was started in 1927 by the Jewish Health Organisation under the direction of Dr Emanuel Miller and staffed by a team of psychiatrists, a psychologist and a psychiatric social worker. Their early realization that children's problems were multi-faceted and that the family and the network must be involved in treatment is documented (Renton, 1978), but may have got lost in the enthusiasm for the new technique of child psychotherapy that was being developed by Anna Freud and Melanie Klein, brought here in the 30s. The numbers of clinics grew, slowly at first, but more rapidly after the 1944 Education Act and the establishment of the National Health Service in 1946, and most areas are now served by clinics or centres funded by public money. The growth of services was uneven and haphazard, governed more by local interest, enthusiasm and needs than by planning, so that a description of the functioning of one child guidance clinic cannot reflect the variations up and down the country.

II. PATTERNS OF ORGANIZATION
OF CHILD GUIDANCE CLINICS

At the time of writing, there are two major patterns of organization:

A. National Health Service Administered

One pattern is a child and family psychiatric service wholly N.H.S. funded and administered, housed either in hospital premises or separate premises and headed by a consultant child psychiatrist, with a multidisciplinary team employed by Health, Education and Social Services.

A separate school psychological service is funded and administered by the local education authority, usually but not always in separate premises.

B. Education Service Administered

Another pattern is a child guidance service funded and administered by the local educational authority, again with a multidisciplinary team employed by different authorities. There may also be a separate school psychological service or it may be integrated. Until recently all child guidance services had a medical director, but this is often no longer so, and issues of leadership arise which have not been satisfactorily solved.

In this chapter we will describe current practice and especially examine the growth of family therapy in child guidance clinics and its practice there, looking at the advantages and the constraints to practice which the setting imposes, the sources and nature of referrals and the services offered from clinics to families and those caring for children and families.

III. THE CHILD GUIDANCE TEAM AND ITS WORK

A. Professionals Involved

The association of the core team of professionals (the child and adolescent psychiatrist, psychologist and social worker) working regularly together from the same premises, and assessing and treating disturbed children and their families constitutes a child guidance team. There may be other staff involved (child psychotherapists, psychiatric nurses, occupational therapists, remedial teachers), and other services offered (inpatient treatment, day hospital unit treatment, consultation to other agencies and individuals concerned with children, tuition units, post-graduate education, domiciliary assessment and treatment, etc.), but central to the concept of child guidance are the multidisciplinary approach, and the provision of treatment. The same team members operate in other settings (e.g. Assessment Units run by Social Services departments, special residential and day schools for maladjusted children, etc.), but are more likely to be concerned with assessment and recommendations to the head of the unit, than with undertaking treatment themselves. These distinctions are blurring somewhat as the concept of offering a comprehensive psychiatric service to the disturbed children and families in a district or area is replacing the more limited concept of a service which responds to demands and treats referred patients, but currently treatment services by the multidisciplinary team are mainly concentrated in hospital departments of child psychiatry and in child guidance clinics. The work of these two services is often similar, with different emphases arising from the settings and referral sources. The work of hospital departments of child psychiatry is dealt with in Chapter 24.

B. Developments and Disadvantages of Child Guidance Approaches

Child guidance expanded largely in response to the needs of schools for help with learning and behaviour problems in children. The model for practice which we imported from the USA was a pioneering one for its time. The team of psychiatrist, psychologist and social worker was seen as necessary to do full justice to the biological and psychosocial complexity of the child. But the establishment of the clinics had other less desirable effects. Sited in homely surroundings, linked more with education than with health services, they led to the alienation of child psychiatrists from their roots in biology, medicine and adult psychiatry, the alienation of educational psychologists from their clinical psychology colleagues and from their roots in scientific method and the evaluative research which might have hastened the abandonment of ineffective treatment techniques. Clinic social workers too found themselves isolated from their colleagues in local authorities and hospitals, and while the specialized training of psychiatric social workers was regarded as excellent, it may have fossilized an approach to childhood disturbances which has taken some time to change. This was based on the practice of casework with individual parents while the doctor treated the child with "play" therapy. Treatment was weekly for years. This treatment approach was based on psychoanalytic theory and was, in the first twenty years of child guidance, the most fruitful treatment available. It was an effective technique for relieving neurotic disorders, but as we now know from long-term follow-up studies (Robins, 1966), it was totally ineffective for the large numbers of children with conduct disorders.

C. Re-evaluation of Roles and Tasks

The pioneering epidemiological studies of Rutter and his colleagues (Rutter et al., 1970, 1975, 1976) forced child guidance practitioners to recognize that clinics had only been scratching the surface of an enormous problem of child and family misery. Only ½ to 1% of the child population were receiving help from the child guidance clinics (Kolvin, 1973) yet 7-20% were identified as suffering from a definite and functionally handicapping child psychiatric disorder.

Even before these studies forced clinics to re-examine their practice, some workers were unhappy with the use of slender resources to treat so few children, with the resultant long waiting lists and the virtual exclusion of those unable to respond to a treatment which required qualities of perseverence and verbal ability usually absent in the patients and families who most needed help. Many children lapsed in attendance before completing treatment. The appearance of a new profession, the non-medical child psychotherapist (see Daws and Boston, 1977) in child guidance clinics, may have improved the quality of some individual child psychotherapy, but produced a new procrustean bed for children to fit: "suitable for treatment". Skynner (1976) has suggested that the label "not suitable" might better be applied to those *therapists* who are unwilling to find other more suitable techniques for helping their patients.

Apart from the pitifully small effect the therapeutic efforts of clinicians in child guidance clinics were having, very little impact was being made on harmful child-care practices in hospitals, especially long-stay ones for the mentally handicapped, childrens homes, day and residential nurseries and residential schools, in spite of our increasing knowledge as a result of research (see Rutter and Hersov, 1976). Further, as Eisenberg (1969) put it, "the promisory note of prevention issued by the mental hygienists (at the turn of the century) has not been able to be redeemed". We could not, as our predecessors had hoped, prevent adult mental illness by treating troubled children (Rutter, 1966), even though the justification for psychiatric services for children, as for adults, does not depend only on our capacity to cure. Nevertheless, the "holy trinity" as Kanner calls it, of the psychologist, social worker and psychiatrist, has eaten up "countless extra hours in interdisciplinary communication in situations where one qualified professional could more effectively manage the problem without ending up talking to himself" (Eisenberg, 1969).

D. Introduction of Family Approaches to Child Guidance Clinics

Impelled by these considerations, Minuchin and his colleagues in the Philadelphia Child Guidance Clinic (Minuchin *et al.*, 1967) and in this country, Skynner and his colleagues at Woodberry Down Child Guidance Clinic in North London (Skynner, 1969; Roberts, 1968; Gorell Barnes, 1973) changed their practice by beginning to view the child's problem as a symptom of family dysfunction. The whole family, including fathers and siblings, were invited to attend the clinic, and by (if necessary) accommodating to the family's work and school pattern with out-of-hours appointments together with an approach which clearly valued the presence of the other family members, a high rate of whole family attendance was achieved. Other clinics were influenced by the possibilities that this approach opened up of more effective, briefer treatment for a wider range of problems so that by 1976, Graham in a review article on recent trends in child psychiatry, could report that among other changes in the practice in child psychiatric departments and child guidance clinics, there was widespread and increasing use of therapeutic techniques involving the whole family, and a greater emphasis on brief, focussed methods of therapy (Graham, 1976).

Unfortunately, evaluation of these changes has lagged behind the enthusiasm for change (see Wells *et al.*, 1972 and Lask, 1979 for reviews of outcome studies in family therapy) and as Gale (1979) has pointed out, the practice of family therapy is not uniform enough or rigorously scientific enough to enable useful evaluation to occur yet. Gurman and Kniskern (1978), in a thorough and exhaustive review of research studies in family and marital therapy, have however ventured tentatively to suggest that the outcome seems at least as good as in individual therapy and that systems therapies should be the treatment of choice for certain problems, for example anorexia, childhood behaviour problems and juvenile delinquency. It is probable that consumer satisfaction too, as measured by attendance rates and follow-up studies, is higher with family therapy than with individual therapy and casework (see Burck, 1978 for a review of the literature on child guidance clinic attendance), although the public's knowledge of what to expect from a child guidance clinic is very confused and inadequate (Whitmore, 1974). Several papers in the USA have documented the transformation of clinics from a traditional approach to one based on brief therapy by a single therapist with a family orientation where consumer satisfaction and attendances have improved (Leventhal and Weinberger, 1975; Sands and Young, 1973; Hetznecker and Forman, 1974).

The other major changes in child guidance practice will only be briefly summarized as they are less pertinent to the theme of this chapter. There has been more emphasis on the use of professional time for consultation with other people caring for children rather than working with children and their families directly (Black *et al.*, 1974; Mannino and Shore, 1975); the use of a wide variety of treatment techniques including behaviour therapy, drugs and day and residential placements of various kinds (Graham, 1976), the greater use of paraprofessionals (Hetznecker and Forman, 1974; Sands and Young, 1973) and finally an interest in the possibility of altering the organization of institutions for children to increase their therapeutic effectiveness (Rutter *et al.*, 1979; Tizard *et al.*, 1975).

IV. CURRENT PRACTICE IN CHILD GUIDANCE CLINICS

A. Sources of Referral in Child Guidance Clinics

The majority of referrals to child guidance clinics come directly or indirectly (through school doctors, welfare officers and educational psychologists) from the schools. Table I shows the sources of referrals from two clinics. The Burnt Oak Child Guidance Clinic receives few referrals from the neighbouring District General Hospital as there is a child psychiatric service there which deals with most internal referrals. Referrals from family doctors go to the clinic rather than the hospital, although the presence of several large teaching hospitals and clinics within a few miles means that these figures do not reflect the total referrals for child psychiatric help within the area served. At both clinics, the single largest referral source is the school. At Burnt Oak, the educational psychologists in the school psychological service deal with most learning problems, and the milder behaviour problems directly and only refer on those which require the skills of the psychiatric team.

Table I. Sources of referral to full clinic teams at two child guidance clinics.

Source	Isle of Wight 1965 (Rutter et al., 1970)		Burnt Oak (London Borough of Barnet, 1978)	
	Number	%	Number	%
(1) Education				
(a) Teachers, educational psychologists, educational welfare officers	10 ⎤	11 ⎤	69 ⎤	31 ⎤
	⎬ 36	⎬ 39	⎬ 109	⎬ 49
(b) School medical officer or speech therapist	26 ⎦	28 ⎦	40 ⎦	18 ⎦
(2) Other doctors				
(a) G.P.	33 ⎤	36 ⎤	43 ⎤	20 ⎤
(b) Hospital	5 ⎦ 38	5 ⎦ 41	9 ⎦ 52	4 ⎦ 24
(3) Health Visitors	3	3	8	4
(4) Social Services including Probation	7	8	24	11
(5) Parents	8	9	27	12
Total	92	100	220	100

B. Types of Referral

The commonest problems for which help is sought by schools are those of school attendance, difficulties in learning not due to low intelligence and disruptive, aggressive or other antisocial behaviours. Schools also increasingly refer children with problems in relating to peers, or who appear abnormally withdrawn, or anxious in the school setting. Primary schools, with their more intimate and continuous teacher-pupil contact, are also able to detect and refer for help, children who are rejected or abused at home, or whose home circumstances are so adverse that placement away from home might facilitate their development.

Medical and health visitor referrals are more likely to be made because of parental concern, but there is considerable overlap with school referrals. Children whose school refusal presents as somatic symptoms (abdominal pain, headache, nausea and vomiting, etc.); children with anorexia, depression, developmental and habit disorders, such as sleep problems, and enuresis and encopresis are more likely to come via the G.P. Hospital doctors (paediatricians, neurologists, ophthalmologists, etc.) refer children whose behaviour on the ward is unmanageable as well as others.

Social workers in local authority departments and probation officers will refer delinquent adolescents, families who neglect or abuse their children, and problems of access and custody in divorced parents. Children in Care are among the most disturbed group, and often receive the least skilled treatment (Wolkind and Rutter, 1973).

Parents and occasionally adolescents will refer themselves with a wide variety of problems of conduct, emotions and learning. They can be rewarding to help as their motivation is usually high. Table II shows the reasons for referral to two clinics. The large number of enuretics referred to the Isle of Wight clinic are more likely to be dealt with by paediatricians or enuresis clinics now. Fifty per cent of the cases are problems of behaviour which also include other school attendance problems such as truancy. Increasingly, referers are asking us to see whole families with relationship problems rather than symptomatic individuals.

Table II.   Reasons for referral.

	I.O.W. (1965) number	%	Burnt Oak C.G.C. (1978) number	%
Behaviour problems	34	37%	111	50%
Emotional and psychosomatic problems	28	30%	41	19%
Habit disorders (enuresis, encopresis etc.)	25	27%	8	4%
Learning problems	1	1%	8	4%
Difficulties in school attendance	2	2%	10	5%
Psychotic	—	—	6	3%
Family relationship problems	—	—	11	5%
Others	2	2%	25	11%
Total	92		220	

V.   FAMILY THERAPY PRACTICE

There are three aspects of the changes in child guidance practice which relate to families: family assessment, conjoint family therapy, and a family centred approach while utilizing other forms of treatment.

A.   Family Assessment

Many child guidance clinics now prefer to invite the whole family to the first assessment interview which may involve one or more of the child guidance professionals as appropriate, although subsequently, treatment may be offered to only one of the family subsystems (e.g. individual therapy, marital therapy, remedial teaching etc.). The aims of assessing the whole family when one of the children has been nominated as the patient have been set out by Bentovim (1978) as follows:

(1) to understand that problem in terms of the individual presenting it,
(2) to understand the origins of the problem in that individual and the role that his family plays in both its genesis and its maintenance,
(3) to determine which aspect of that individual and his family needs to change for amelioration of symptoms and improvement of family life,
(4) to engage and motivate the family to accept a need for change and to enter into a contract with the therapist to achieve it.

Therapy begins at the first session, and it is important to negotiate a contract before it ends. Engaging the family, who may be resistant to the idea that a child's symptom might be helped by family attendance, is the most skilful part of treatment. Recently, the acquisition of these skills has been improved by the use of one-way screens, peer group supervision and videotape recordings. (See Roberts, Chapter 7; Gorell Barnes, Chapter 8)

Sometimes parents are reluctant to attend a family assessment, and they will need to speak to the therapist first who can reassure them that they need not speak about private matters, but can also point out that many so-called secrets are known to children who sense their parents' reluctance to discuss them, and that this may be part of the problem. Engaging families is further discussed by Bentovim (1978).

B.   Engaging Difficult Families

The following case illustrates some of the problems of engaging difficult families.

(1) Susan and her Family: Presentation
Susan (8 years) was referred by the clinical medical officer. She had wanted to refer her 3 years earlier, but the parents were reluctant to come. There was a longstanding problem of difficulty in going to school. Although attendance was good, she cried and was sick every morning. The school doctor saw the problem as a difficulty in the mother/child relationship. Mother complained of being intruded upon by Susan, who nagged her and talked to her incessantly, bossed her and James, her 5-year-old brother, and had fierce and frightening temper tantrums. At school, however, she was fearful, cringing and non-communicative, and was thought to be of average intelligence. The school thought that mother was browbeaten by her daughter, and had an exaggerated view of her abilities. Father seemed a shadowy figure whom no one had seen, and there was a hint of marital disagreements and previous psychiatric treatment for mother.

Invited to come as a family, mother wrote saying that she couldn't accept a family interview, in which Susan's behaviour difficulties were discussed; indeed she did not wish to tell Susan she was going to see a psychiatrist because she would be tormented by the girl about it. She wanted to tell her that "various doctors were gathering information on family life for a book, and that we have volunteered to be one of the families".

(2) Seeing the Parents First

I asked the parents to come alone for the first interview, after discussion with the referring doctor, who was most anxious that I engage the family given their long history of difficulties and their reluctance to come. Significant factors which emerged were the death of maternal grandmother when mother was the age Susan had now reached, and the description of Susan by mother: "the minute she was born and opened her eyes there was a glint of perception. She was always an adult: shrewd, streets ahead, very understanding". Mother clearly both admired and feared Susan, and the parents were at odds over child-rearing. Mother felt she shouldn't frustrate Susan's demands; father felt she was too soft, but also felt powerless to intervene and had opted out of the battle. Mother insisted that we must maintain the fiction she had devised, and because I felt that she needed help and that otherwise I would not be allowed in, I agreed with the proviso that I could shift the interview in a therapeutic direction if it seemed possible. Since I usually introduce myself as a doctor who is interested in families and their problems, I did not in fact change my behaviour at all in the first full family interview.

Susan was an attractive, intelligent, lively chatterbox who enjoyed and dominated the session. I invited each of them to use one word to describe the other members of the family. Susan described her mother as a "giver-in". Her mother was amazed and asked Susan to expand. The situations Susan described were all ones in which mother felt she had been persuaded by Susan that she was being unreasonable to withhold. Rapidly it was established that Susan's separation anxiety and the intolerable screaming were attempts to get her mother to set limits but as Susan pushed, mother bent backwards.

(3) Further Exploration with the Family

Sculpting (see Byng-Hall, Chapter 5) was used to explore this further. At my request, Susan physically pushed her mother backwards and father was asked to represent what he usually did, without the use of words. He tried to get between them and push Susan back, but this was extremely hard to do as she resisted him or returned to the attack. He got more angry, amusing Susan at first, but eventually frightening her, and she started to cry. He turned to mother to try to support her into standing firm, but she couldn't maintain the posture and he hurt her. This frightened him and he withdrew from the arena. Repeating this ballet on several occasions made them realize that mother was still the centre of the family conflict, and that her inability to withstand Susan's pressure because of her own childhood experiences was adversely affecting family functioning. By experiencing this process kinaesthetically rather than learning about it intellectually, the family were motivated to look for change, and Susan was the first to agree to a therapeutic contract. Subsequent sessions used similar techniques to explore the other options open until they discovered that by taking a united and combined stand, Susan could not push; she then turned away to James and they began to play. The individual members of the family were invited to describe their feelings in each of the sculpts and mother was surprised and relieved to discover that Susan felt most comfortable when able to play with her brother and be a child.

Sculpting (Duhl *et al.*, 1973) is a very useful technique for engaging children, and for preventing over-intellectualization and verbal obfuscation in adults. In this case, it engaged the two resistant members of the family, Susan and father, and enabled a successful piece of work to be done.

C. A Family Approach to Treatment where Conjoint Family Therapy is Inapplicable

A family view is essential to good work in a child guidance setting, even when other treatments (drugs, behaviour therapy, social skills training, residential placement) appear indicated. All these can be more effectively used working with the whole family, as can individual therapy in some cases (Black, 1979). Even when placement of the child away from home is essential for his physical and mental well-being, it is possible by insisting on meeting the whole family to help the family to accept the recommendation. By the therapist's attitude to the family, he can convey his respect for their ability to take a painful but mature decision for the sake of the child's well-being, and thus prepare the way for an eventual return.

(1) Case Example: Brian and his Family
Brian, aged 10, was referred by his headmistress because he kept running away from school and home, and staying out for several days. The head had a good relationship with him, and he had confided how he had often been beaten by his stepfather. The family had agreed to the referral when she discussed it with them, but failed the first appointment. A home visit in the evening was offered and accepted. Mother was a harrassed young woman with four children younger than Brian. Her husband had abandoned them, and she was cohabiting with a man who was 20 years older who had brought up one family, not very success-fully. Three of his children had been in care or on probation for delinquencies. He had chronic bronchitis and looked very ill. He had been unemployed for long periods and could not work at his trade as a van driver as he had lost his driving licence because of drunkenness.

(2) Family Attitudes and Management
Both the parents were implacable in their hostility towards Brian, and he was clearly a rejected child. They reeled off a long list of bad behaviours, and felt he was already doomed to end up like his stepbrothers, and his father, who was in jail. They were not interested in looking at the family's part in Brian's behaviour, and both parents had a long history of deprivation, which made it difficult for them to give adequate care to so many children on so little money in the face of overcrowding and ill-health. Brian, in a healthy way, was voting with his feet to go away. I said I knew a school where Brian could go where they would teach him to behave, but I thought it was important that the parents visited it first and made sure it was the right place for Brian. He could not go without their agreement. I told Brian that it was clear to me that his parents were asking for help in ensuring that he would grow up to be a healthy and successful

adult, and they were worried that he was not getting the education and discipline needed to ensure this. I wanted to help them to find a place that could do both. I had in mind a boarding school which was run using a token economy system, but where the staff were caring and which had had great success in helping maladjusted children from chaotic families. The cost to the community of two years at this school would be less than taking him into care, or a period in Borstal later on, and might at the same time give him the loving control he so patently could not get at home. With the enthusiastic agreement of his school and the educational psychologist, and the approval of his parents whose inclusion in the decision-making process was the first stage in the therapeutic plan, Brian spent 2 years at the residential school (with long holidays, half-terms and weekends at home). The parents were loud in their praise of the structured regime: "he needs that strictness", and began to apply the school's principles to the other children who also benefitted. Brian flourished with a warmer more accepting environment, and could cope better with his parents' harshness, which in its turn gave way before his lessening demands so that they found a way of living together which made it possible for him to start secondary schooling at a day school. Brian never needed the behavioural programmes offered by the school as his behaviour was never a problem there. He became a valued member of the school and returns there every summer "to help with the little ones". He plans to become a house-parent there when he grows up.

(3)   Re-uniting the Family
The placement of Brian at a special residential school enabled the parents to retain and increase their parenting role, which alternative placements would have diminished. The therapist was able to convey respect for the part of them that *wanted* (but was unable) to care for their children better than their own parents had cared for them. By maintaining and increasing their self-respect, they were able to establish a better relationship with Brian and improve their parenting behaviour with the other children: a family-centred therapeutic approach facilitated by the setting of the child guidance clinic able to call on educational resources.

D.   Role in Custody and Access Disputes
(see Bentovim, Chapter 28)

A family-centred approach has also been found helpful in custody and access dispute cases.

(1)   Case Example: Lorraine and her Family: Presentation
Lorraine, aged 3½, was referred by her social worker because of the recent onset of nightmares and nocturnal enuresis (after one year of dry nights). She had come into care at her mother's request at 10 months and was placed with foster parents where she had remained. The original reasons for the reception into care were obscure as all concerned with the case had left and note-keeping was poor. It was thought that the mother had been mentally ill, and the parents had separated.

The father had kept in touch with the foster parents, but had not visited the child. The mother who had not kept in touch then applied for the child's return to her. She had remarried and her husband had pressed for the child's return as they could not have children. The social services department had opposed the return on the grounds that the best interests of the child were served by staying with the foster parents to whom the child was firmly attached and who regarded her as their child, but the judge had overruled this, insisting that a programme be worked out for her gradual return to her mother. The symptoms had arisen after she had stayed with her mother and stepfather for a week.

(2) Meeting with the Total System
The therapist, by meeting all concerned, found it possible to work with the mother and stepfather towards an acceptance that Lorraine's happiness depended on not disrupting a bond with her foster parents. It was clear that Lorraine's security had been undermined by her week away from her foster parents, and she was reacting angrily to them for having sent her away. It was probable that the mother was suffering from chronic simple schizophrenia; she was passive and indifferent to the child. It was her husband who was keen to have the child; he could also respond to the authoritative statement of where Lorraine's best interests lay, painful though it was for him, when it was clear that the therapist could empathize with the pain and respect his clear affection and concern for the child. The case was not pursued, and Lorraine was freed for adoption by her foster parents.

In the cases of Brian and Lorraine, the family therapist sought to change the system using carefully worked out strategies which bring pressure to bear on part of the system. Brian's parents' rejecting behaviour was reframed as a laudable concern for his well-being. This enabled them to mobilize the healthier aspects of their parental functioning so that they in fact became what we said they were: concerned parents and not rejecting ones. Lorraine's stepfather could relinquish his claims on her when his litigious behaviour was reconstrued as that of a loving parent who wants the best for his child. This reframing forced him to act as the adult who can make painful decisions, rather than the child who looks to parents (the judge) to solve his disputes, by an exercise of justice.

E.   Conjoint Family Therapy in Child Guidance Clinic

The presence of a psychiatrically trained doctor in the child guidance team makes it possible to work with families containing mentally ill members, which may release the children from nursing sick parents, or being scapegoated, so that they can continue their development.

(1) Case Example: Donald and his Family: Presentation
Donald, aged 15, was referred by the Court for a psychiatric report. He had severely stabbed a school-mate and endangered his life. Both boys had been sniffing glue.

Donald had been referred to the clinic a few months earlier by his G.P. who had had to deal with a bout of acute intoxication from a previous incident of glue sniffing, but the parents had been reluctant to attend, hoping that Donald had learned his lesson. There were six children ranging from 10 to 21. Donald and his sister, Jane, were the middle children and although the older and younger children seemed problem-free, Jane (17 years) had been admitted on two occasions to the local hospital for terminations of pregnancy. She had now left home and was living with her boy-friend. Both the parents had responsible jobs (father managing a shop and mother running a factory canteen), but had come from poor backgrounds and equated love with material goods. It was probable that the middle children had missed out most on the limited emotional supplies available because of their position in the family. The crisis of Donald's Court appearance enabled a family therapy contact to be negotiated under the umbrella of a probation order.

(2) Family Pattern
The dominating feature of the first session was the way in which Donald invited scapegoating from his older brothers and father, who viewed him as someone who had disgraced the family. Donald both accepted this position and by various actions (staying out late, cutting his home tuition, turning up late for family therapy sessions, choosing a seat as far removed as possible from the rest of the family, etc.) provoked continued attacks from the family. A repetitive pattern emerged: father would attack Donald, mother would cajole Donald to be more part of the family, father would turn on mother; older brother would attack Donald for causing marital friction, and Donald would do something to draw father's fire again. The therapist's problem was to work out a strategy which would interrupt this repetitive circular sequence which pushed Donald out of the family, and forced him into antisocial behaviour and drug-taking, thus providing the justification for father's attacks and detouring the marital conflict. Various straightforward tactics failed, and the family became more hostile to the therapists who became discouraged and thought that perhaps Donald should have individual treatment as they didn't seem to be making any impact.

(3) Use of Paradoxical Injunction
Eventually a paradoxical injunction (Palazzoli *et al.*, 1978; Cade, 1979; Gorell Barnes, Chapter 8; Cooklin, Chapter 4) was given. Donald was congratulated on his ability to be the victim in his family. Someone clearly had to be the scapegoat, he was told; Jane had taken this role until she left, and now he had manfully and bravely shouldered it. He was told that it was essential for the well-being of everyone else in the family that he continue to be the "fall-guy", and that he should be careful to ensure that he did something every day that he would be criticized for. Donald was very shocked by this instruction and the parents very angry. At the next meeting, however, it was learned that following the previous session Donald had got a job, was coming home at the stipulated time and had not sniffed any glue. He told the therapists that he had decided that he had to make his own decisions about his future and not be "put upon" by other people.

(4)   From Family to Marital Work
The rest of the family therapy sessions were spent, at the parents' request, in marital therapy. In exploring their own problems, the parents recognized that they were following a pattern which their own parents had taught them. Both Jane's terminations of pregnancy had been kept a secret from her father. Mother had assumed that he would be angry and rejecting, as her father had been when she became illegitimately pregnant. The pattern of protecting the father from family tensions was common in both their families of origin. For the first time, this couple began to talk to each other about what they wanted from marriage and family life, which was different from what each of them assumed the other wanted.

Donald committed no more offences; he made some restitution to the boy he injured, and started an apprenticeship. Unlike his sister he did not have to leave home, although he began to go out with a girl. His parents were able to manage family life in a more satisfactory way.

Although it is not possible to be sure what would have happened without family therapy, it is likely that at worst, Donald's need to detour the marital conflict would have led him to continue his damaging delinquent behaviour. At best he would have had to leave home, before he was really ready to cope on his own, and would have contracted a marriage or a liaison which would have perpetuated the family history. Family therapy may have enabled him to complete more of his development at home, and perhaps more importantly enabled his younger siblings and his parents to interact in a potentially less pathogenic way.

F.   Behavioural Approaches to Family Therapy

Given the preponderance of behavioural problems referred to child guidance clinics, and the clinics' previous poor record for influencing adverse outcome in these cases, there seems to be some prospect of a higher success rate using family therapy with behaviour therapy.

There is little doubt that if parents cannot find an effective way of controlling their children, they feel failures as parents, and may reject the child that makes them feel so. It is essential early on in therapy to give parents a taste of success, and this can be easily done using behavioural techniques within family therapy (e.g. Alexander and Parsons, 1973).

(1)   Case Example: Andrew and his Family: Presentation
Andrew, 10 years, was referred by his school because of tormenting behaviour towards his peers. His parents complained that he was the same with his younger sister and was very disobedient. He had few friends, and was also backward in reading and writing. What was striking at the initial family interview, was that Andrew's attitude towards his sister was that of a parental child, and that this behaviour was approved of by his parents. Psychological assessment had revealed a specific reading and writing disorder in this boy of average ability, for which remedial teaching was arranged. The family session had revealed that

mother had already had one failure in a parental role, with disastrous results, which was affecting her attitude to Andrew. Maternal grandmother had died after a long illness, when mother was 16 and she had reared her younger brother ten years her junior. He had been very disturbed: she had hated the task and had felt a failure, when with sighs of relief he had gone to boarding school.

He was now an unsociable, morose bachelor. Any signs of similar traits in Andrew, evoked in mother all these feelings of failure. Father, freer from the experience of parental failure, enjoyed Andrew's boyish behaviour, but then felt pulled between his wife and Andrew. His solution was to elevate Andrew to the parental subsystem, but this then distorted the generational boundaries and pushed his wife down into the child subsystem. She developed back trouble and took to her bed, so that he had to look after her.

(2)   Behavioural Intervention
It seemed essential to restore the boundaries and give mother a taste of success so a star chart was introduced which rewarded the children for specific behaviours, decided by mother, one of which was that Andrew was not to tell his sister what to do, but to leave it to mother. Using back-up rewards from father, such a simple operant conditioning programme was rapidly successful in boundary making, and family life became happier. If one can give parents some experiences of success, the ensuing family harmony is so rewarding that it may not be necessary to do any more. In this case, mother was able to recognize that Andrew's experiences were different from her brother's, and she need no longer act in a way which made her fears self-fulfilling. In this she had the enthusiastic support of her husband who had felt helpless before and had tended to opt out by staying longer at the office.

VI.   STRENGTHS AND LIMITATIONS OF THE CHILD GUIDANCE SETTING

A.   The Conflict between "Child" Guidance and Family Therapy

The shift in conceptual thinking brought about by a systems approach to troubled or troubling children has been one of the main disruptive influences on child guidance organization. Family therapists have felt increasingly unhappy at working in clinics whose very name implies an individual focus rather than a family systems one. Attempts at compromises with individually-orientated therapists lead to the clinic appearing like "a football team in which a few of the members decided to play baseball during the game" (Haley, 1975). Brunel University's studies of organization in child guidance clinics (B.I.O.S.S., 1976, 1978) revealed that the organizational structure of the clinics was muddled, and relied overmuch on good personal relationships for their functioning. These relationships are being sustained by several factors (see "Multidisciplinary Work in Child Guidance" published by the Child Guidance Trust, 1982, a report of the four professional organizations concerned with child guidance), including the difficulty of defining leadership and goals at a time of rapid change.

Family Therapists can be from any of the child guidance professions, and the practice of family therapy tends to blur boundaries and to lead therapists to draw less on the distinctive knowledge bases and skills learned in their primary professional training.

In order to overcome the problems then posed by salary, status and career differences stemming from the fact that originally they come from different professions, mental health professionals will have to, in Querido's words, become a metaprofession in which people from a number of different backgrounds, psychology, psychiatry, social work and others could come together and find a new professional identity (quoted in Jones, 1978).

B.   Can Family Therapy disrupt Child Guidance or strengthen it?

The problem is that it is difficult, if not impossible to focus both on the individual and the family system. One approach excludes the other. Child guidance personnel therefore can no longer sit in their clinics, but have to link with adult psychiatric services, social services, schools, hospitals and other institutions. Haley (1975) in a paper which outlines the problems which hit a clinic which attempts to introduce family therapy concludes, not entirely ironically, by suggesting that mental health clinics must avoid family therapy if they are to survive, because the introduction of family therapy will produce

> disorientation of the staff, radically changed administrative procedures, less har-
> mony among the professions and confusion in the administrative hierarchy.
> Staff members will find themselves asked to think in terms of a theory in which
> they were not trained and to diagnose social rather than individual problems. The
> staff will also be expected to intervene actively in human dilemas, to work with
> poor people, to do therapy under observation where all errors are visible, and quite
> possibly to have the results of their therapy evaluated. In exchange for the con-
> fusion in the clinic the clinic receives a relatively small return. There will be service
> to larger numbers of people, less of a waiting list, more time devoted to therapy and
> less to other activities and better treatment outcome. Obviously this is not a
> sufficient return for a mental health clinic to undertake this adventure irresponsibly.

Can child guidance clinics survive into the 80s? For them to do so they themselves must change like the dysfunctional families they treat. First, the name itself must go, to be replaced by one which embodies the concept of the family as the unit of treatment. They must accelerate their rate of change from responders to demands towards initiators of new ways of helping the large number of suffering children and their families which Rutter and his colleagues have identified (Rutter *et al.*, 1970, 1975, 1976). They must evaluate their work and be more flexible in their training and use of staff. What is certain is that unless the family of professionals in child guidance can solve their problems of rivalry, hierarchy, autonomy and leadership, they will not be able to heal the families in trouble who come to them for help.

REFERENCES

Alexander, J. and Parsons, B. (1973). Short-term behavioural intervention with delinquent families. *J.Abn.Psychol.* **85**, 219-225.

Bentovim, A. (1978). Family therapy when the child is the referred patient. *In* "An Introduction to the Psychotherapies", (S. Bloch, ed.), Oxford University Press, London.

B.I.O.S.S. (1976). "Future Organization in child guidance and allied work", Brunel University, Uxbridge.

B.I.O.S.S. (1978). "Organization of Services for the Mentally Ill", by R. Rowbottom and A. Hey, Brunel University, Uxbridge.

Black, D., Black, M. and Martin, F. (1974). A pilot study on the use of consultant time in child psychiatry. *Brit.J.Psychiat. Supplement.* September pp.3-5.

Black, D. (1975). Family therapy as a setting for other treatment modalities. *J.Fam.Ther.* **1**, 183-192.

Burck, C. (1978). A study of families' expectations and experiences of a child guidance clinic. *British Journal of Social Work* **8**, 145-159.

Cade, B. (1979). The use of paradox in therapy. *In* "Family and Marital Psychotherapy: A Critical Approach", (S. Walrond-Skinner, ed.), Routledge & Kegan Paul, London.

Daws, D. and Boston, M. (1977). "The Child Psychotherapist and the Problems of Young People", Wildwood House, London.

Duhl, F. J. and Duhl, B. S. (1973). Learning Space and Action in Family Therapy: a primer of sculpture. *In* "Techniques of Family Psychotherapy, a Primer", (D. A. Bloch, ed.), Grune & Stratton, New York and London.

Eisenberg, L. (1969). The Past quarter century. *Amer.J.Orthopsychiat.* **39**, 389-401.

Gale, A. (1979). Problems of outcome research in family therapy. *In* "Family and Marital Psychotherapy. A critical Approach", (S. Walrond-Skinner, ed.), Routledge & Kegan Paul, London.

Gurman, A. S. and Kniskern, D. P. (1978). Research on marital and Family Therapy: progress perspective and prospect. *In* "Handbook of Psychotherapy and behaviour change", (S. L. Garfield and A. E. Bergin, eds), Wiley, New York.

Gorell Barnes, G. (1973). Working with the family group. *Social Work Today*, **4**, 65-68.

Graham, P. (1976). Management in Child Psychiatry: Recent Trends. *Brit.J.Psychiat.* **129**, 97-108.

Haley, J. (1975). Why a mental health clinic should avoid family therapy. *J. Marriage & Family Counselling*, **3**, 13-20.

Hetznecker, W. and Forman, M. A. (1974). "On Behalf of Children", Grune & Stratton, New York.

Jones, K. (1978). Society Looks at the Psychiatrist. *Brit.J.Psychiat.* **132**, 321-332.

Kolvin, I. (1973). Evaluation of Psychiatric Services for children in England & Wales. *In* "Roots of Evaluation", (J. K. Wing and J. Häfner, eds), Oxford University Press, Oxford.

Lask, B. (1979). Family Therapy outcome research. 1972-1978. *J.Fam.Ther.* **1**, 87-91.

Leventhal, T. and Weinberger, G. (1975). Evaluation of a large scale brief therapy program for children. *Amer.J.Orthopsychiat.* **45**, 119-133.

Mannino, F. V. and Shore, M. F. (1975). The effects of consultation: a review of empirical studies. *Amer.J.Comm.Psychol.* **3**, 1-21.

Minuchin, S., Montalvo, B., Guerney, B. G., Rosman, B. L. and Shumer, F. (1967). "Families of the Slums", Basic Books, New York and London.

Palazzoli, M. S., Cecchin, G., Prata, G. and Boscolo, L. (1978). "Paradox & Counter-Paradox", Aronson, New York and London.

Renton, G. (1978). The East London Child Guidance Clinic. *J.Child Psychol. Psychiat.* **19**, 309-312.

Roberts, W. L. (1968). Working with the family group in a child guidance clinic. *Br.J.Psychiat. Social Work,* **9**, 4.

Robins, L. (1966). "Deviant Children Grown Up", Williams & Wilkins, Baltimore.

Rutter, M. (1966). "Children of Sick Parents", Maudsley Monograph 16. Oxford Univ. Press, London.

Rutter, M., Tizard, J. and Whitmore, K. (1970). "Education, Health & Behaviour", Longman, London.

Rutter, M., Cox, C., Tupling, C., Berger, M. and Yule, W. (1975). Attainment & Adjustment in Two Geographical Areas, I. *Brit.J.Psychiat.* **126**, 493-509.

Rutter, M., Graham, P., Chadwick, O. F. D. and Yule, W. (1976). Adolescent Turmoil: Fact or Fiction. *J.Child Psychol.Psychiat.* **17**, 35-56.

Rutter, M. and Hersov, L. (eds) (1976). "Child Psychiatry: Modern Approaches", Blackwell Scientific, Oxford.

Rutter, M., Maughan, B., Mortimore, P. and Ouston, J. (1979). "Fifteen Thousand Hours. Secondary Schools & their effects on children", Open Books, London.

Sands, R. M. and Young, A. K. (1973). The retooling of a child guidance center. *Amer.J.Orthopsychiat.* **43**, 65-72.

Skynner, A. C. R. (1969). A Group Analytic Approach to Conjoint Family Therapy. *J.Child Psychol.Psychiat.* **10**, 81-106.

Skynner, A. C. R. (1976). "One Flesh, Separate Persons. Principles of Family & Marital Psychotherapy", Constable, London.

Tizard, J., Sinclair, I., Clarke, R. V. G. (eds) (1975). "Varieties of Residential Experience", Routledge & Kegan Paul, London.

Underwood, J. E. A. (1955). "Report of the Committee on Maladjusted Children", Ministry of Education H.M.S.O. London.

Wells, R., Dilkes, T. and Trivelli, N. (1972). The results of family therapy: a critical review of the literature. *Fam.Proc.* **11**, 189-207.

Whitmore, K. (1974). "The contribution of child guidance to the community", MIND occasional paper 2.

Wolkind, S. and Rutter, M. (1973). Children who have been "in care"; an epidemiological study. *J.Child Psychol.Psychiat.* **14**, 95-105.

Chapter 26

Family Work in a Secure Unit

T. Bruce

I. INTRODUCTION

The following is an account of my work and that of my colleagues with families in a Youth Treatment Centre (St. Charles at Brentwood). St. Charles was the first of two Youth Treatment Centres (the second, Glenthorn, was opened in 1977 in Birmingham), and was set-up by the Department of Health and Social Security (DHSS) in 1971 to provide care, control and treatment in conditions of security for children between the ages of 13 and 19. These were children who had been found uncontainable (usually because of violent behaviour) in other institutions (such as community homes, observation and assessment centres and adolescent psychiatric units). Some of the St. Charles children attend under Section 53 of the 1933 Children and Young Persons Act. These are children who have committed a crime such as murder or arson, and who are either detained during Her Majesty's Pleasure or given a definite sentence of imprisonment. Although most of the children at St. Charles are the responsibility of the DHSS, the Section 53 children remain under the care of the Home Office.

The Centre does not have perimeter security. It is divided into three houses, one of which is especially secure, and it is to this house that children usually go for the first 10 months of their stay in St. Charles. As a rule, they usually then transfer to either House 2 or House 3 where they are given what, in the Centre, is called "extra mobility". On average, the children stay in the Centre for between two to three years. Following their stay, a few return to their own homes, a few set up their own homes, but the majority go either into "living in" work, or into local authority hostels. The Centre is staffed by "group workers" who share the tasks of teaching, care and treatment of the children. The group workers are in the main recruited from the social work, teaching and nursing professions. There is a supporting staff consisting of a Psychiatrist, a Social Worker and a Clinical Psychologist.

II. WORK WITH FAMILIES OF ORIGIN

Systematic work with families at St. Charles started in 1976. It is worth saying at the outset that the results of three years of work suggest that the majority of the children who come to St. Charles are the products of family systems which are so disturbed or disrupted that there is little hope of mending them. One of the main tasks for the St. Charles staff is therefore to provide substitute parenting for the children in their care. If this substitute parenting is good enough, it enables the child to give up fantasies (both good and bad) which he has of his family and which are interfering with his adjustment to reality. The St. Charles experience is that process can occur most rapidly and thoroughly if, while receiving substitute parenting, the child is kept in contact with his family of origin (or put into contact with it where contact has been lost). Our experience is in line with that of Colon (1978), who, writing from personal experience and from professional experience with the children of divorced parents, has written:

> Persons who experience emotional cut-offs from significant others are persons at higher risk emotionally and psychologically than those who have resolved such cut-offs . . . A determined effort must be made to connect the child to an absent parent . . . Even if unsuccessful—the fact of the attempt is meaningful.

Colon's work on divorced parents is particularly relevant to the St. Charles system, not only because most of the St. Charles children are the products of broken families, but also because the St. Charles staff in their role as substitute parents tend in many ways to function like the parent of a divorced couple who has custody. Using Weisfeld and Laser's terminology (1977), they are the "in-parents", while the family of origin becomes the parent without custody, the "out-parent".

A.   The Roles of "In-parents" and "Out-parents"

As an example of the "in-parent"/"out-parent" phenomenon in St. Charles, I have chosen the case of a boy, Brian, aged 14, who came to the centre because of several offences involving arson. In his fire-raising (he had burnt down his school, and had also tried to set fire to the approved school he was in before coming to St. Charles), he had displayed what appeared to be a totally ruthless disregard for other people's life and property. He had been adopted at the age of two by a childless couple. They were hard working professional people who had taken Brian on even though the first two years of his life had been spent in children's homes and in hospital because of an intestinal complaint. One of his adoptive mother's earliest memories of him was of his stepping over the Christmas presents they had put outside his bedroom door without giving them so much as a glance. The parents had been excitedly waiting and watching to see his reaction. There were some quite serious sexual difficulties between the parents, but on the whole they got on well enough together.

Brian treated them with total contempt. On one occasion when he ran away from the centre with two other boys, he broke into his parents' house and did a certain amount of damage, including defaecating on the sitting-room carpet. After many initial difficulties in the centre, Brian settled down to a considerable degree, and became very attached to his host worker, Ian. It was felt however that the split between Ian as the "in-parent", and Brian's own parents as "out-parents", was a problem which had to be worked on, and Ian, Brian and his parents were seen for a series of family sessions. At first Brian's mother presented as hard and embittered. As the sessions advanced she became more relaxed, until eventually in one session (a session which in retrospect had a profound effect on Brian), she was able to weep, and to talk about her feelings of guilt and failure.

Following this session Brian was able to begin to return for weekends to his family, and at the time of writing this chapter, he has been discharged from the centre, and is living at home.

I think it should be emphasized that family work on its own would not have been enough to have altered Brian's behaviour. He was able to forgive his adoptive mother only because he had had a good enough experience in relation to his "in-parent", Ian.

The St. Charles view follows that of Colon, and is in contrast to that of Goldstein *et al.* (1980), who have written of the children of divorced couples:

> A visiting parent has little chance to serve as a true object for love, trust and identification since this role is based on his being available on an uninterrupted day to day basis.

Our experience has been that a child cannot become free to love, trust and form satisfactory identifications with the St. Charles staff unless the visiting parent is kept in the picture. If the parent, however unsatisfactory, is not kept in contact, the child is forever (in fantasy and, frequently, in fact) chasing after his family of origin. Even if a parent is in prison or in mental hospital, or thoroughly unreliable or malicious, it has been our experience that the child is better off having contact, although of course under controlled conditions, than not. Cutting a child off from the pain of relating to unsatisfactory parents may in Colon's words: "give temporary relief from conflict but only at the cost of burying that conflict".

B. "In-parents" and "Out-parents": how they relate

It is impossible to generalize about the families of the children in St. Charles. They present as wide a variation of dynamics and pathology as families encountered in day to day child guidance work. These families do, however, have one feature in common, a profound suspicion of, and at worst a hatred of, authority as represented by the St. Charles staff, whom the families perceive as not only having taken over parental rights, but also as having consigned their child to virtual imprisonment. Even those families which start off by being non-resentful of authority become so following the massive intervention in their family life which the commitment of one of their children to a Youth Treatment Centre involves. There is no way that the St. Charles staff can duck the authority which society has invested in them. The great disadvantage to being perceived as a revenging authority is that the child can be manipulated often quite unconsciously by the family to undermine the authority of the St. Charles staff. One boy, for example, with a history of performing reckless electrical and chemical experiments was allowed by his parents (after a weekend at home) to return to the Centre with a chemical fertilizer which he very nearly succeeded in incorporating into an explosive device before being discovered.

Another example is that of Diana who was aged thirteen when she came to the centre. She had been utterly out of the control of her mother and stepfather, and was consorting with such unsavoury people that her life was feared for. On several occasions, Diana ran away from the centre and was harboured by a man with whom her mother had lived for a number of years and who had to some extent been like a father to Diana. There was some discussion whether to prosecute this man for failing to inform the centre and the police about Diana's whereabouts, but it was decided to try to involve him in family work instead. He had seen the centre as treating Diana very badly, and he was angry with Diana's mother for having, as he saw it, acquiesced to her being placed there. Once he had been included in the family work, he came to identify with the aims of the centre, and Diana also felt happier and more safely contained. Since then, she has done quite well for herself in the pop music industry. One of the great advantages of family work is that it can cut down the incidence of such acting out on the part of parents and relations.

III. DIFFICULTIES IN SETTING UP FAMILY THERAPY IN AN INSTITUTION

A. Liaison with Network

Although provision was made in the setting up of St. Charles for work to be done with families, and a full-time social worker was employed for this purpose, it was envisaged that the social worker's main function would be to act as liaison between the Centre and the local authority social workers. It was imagined that the latter would carry out most of the family work because most of the children would be coming from places far distant from Brentwood. This system did not work well for the following reasons:

(1) Once the child, who had been a thorn in the flesh of the local authority social work department, had gained admission to St. Charles, there was a tendency for the local authority social worker to withdraw interest from the case. Most local authority social workers found that other commitments made it very difficult for them to visit the child in the Centre more frequently than the quarterly reviews. In addition, the two-to-three year stay for most children in St. Charles usually meant that the social worker who had arranged their admission had moved on within a year or so. It was difficult for another social worker taking over the case to feel the same urgency once the family crisis centring around the admission of the child to St. Charles had passed.

(2) Because most of the St. Charles families live at some distance from the Centre, a great deal of fetching and carrying, either of the family to the Centre or of the child to the home, is necessary if family work is to take place. Few local authority social workers had the motivation to initiate such a programme.

(3) Local authority social workers vary very much in their training, overall experience, and in particular in their experience of family therapy.

(4) It is quite common for families to try to play the local authority social workers off against the Centre.

Because of the above difficulties, what is needed is a therapist who is in a position to work with a system which includes the local authority social worker. The "minimal sufficient network" (Skynner, 1971) consists of the St. Charles child (the designated patient), his host worker, his parents, his siblings (depending upon their availability), and the local authority social worker. At St. Charles, the only people who are in a position to act as therapists to this network are the Centre Social Worker, the Clinical Psychologist, and the Consultant Psychiatrist. For the Consultant Psychiatrist and the Clinical Psychologist, there were technical difficulties in adopting this role because it blurred with other roles. The Consultant Psychiatrist led staff support groups, while the Clinical Psychologist was responsible for staff training. By far the best-placed person to undertake the role of family therapist was the Centre Social Worker. To provide a service for thirty families, our experience was that a minimum of three social workers would be needed.

B.   Institutional Difficulties

In general, difficulties in setting up family therapy in an institution like St. Charles stem from two main sources.

(1)   General Resistance to Change
The first of these is the general resistance of any institution to change. This is particularly true of an institution which has to design its institutional structures to cope with frightening situations (Menzies, 1960). Hospitals, prisons and the armed forces have in common a relatively rigid hierarchy in which everyone knows his or her place and function. Such a system enables the institution to keep going when staff anxiety is high and when everybody is under pressure. At times of course this clarity of role can become rigidified, and the maintenance of a hierarchy becomes an end in itself. Using Schon's terminology (1973), the "Theory" of the institution then takes over from its function, as for example, in the last war in the United States Navy, where the introduction of a more efficient gun was held up because it would make particular naval gunnery ranks redundant. The staff in St. Charles, like those in hospitals, prisons and the armed forces, have to have clearly defined roles and lines of responsibility if the institution is to survive when under threat from very violent young people. Family therapy, however, to some extent cuts across hierarchical lines, and may be resisted because it does so. Haley has described similar resistance in a Mental Health Clinic (Haley, 1975).

Problems of cutting across an established hierarchy may be lessened (and this happened at St. Charles) by providing staff with some training in family therapy, and by helping them to get in touch with the difficulties which they bring from their own family of origin, using such techniques as sculpting and the geneogram. It is wise to include the director of an institution in such a programme if family therapy is to become firmly rooted. In our experience, it was particularly important to convey to staff the notion of complementarity in family systems. It is easy for staff, and indeed with very great justification, to see the St.

Charles type of child as a victim of appalling parental behaviour, and to feel extremely critical of the family of origin (Ekstein *et al.*, 1969). It can be a considerable wrench for staff to have to see, instead, the role which the child and his behaviour have in the overall structure and dynamics of his family, a system in which everyone may be the victim.

(2) Difficulties with Substitute Parenting Functions

The second difficulty in introducing family therapy to an institution is related to the first, and concerns the substitute parenting function of the staff in an institution like St. Charles. Inevitably, this function introduces an element of rivalry between the natural parents and the staff which the children may be quick to exploit. Once family therapy is established, it is easier for these rivalries to be looked at, but it means that staff have to be prepared to look at their own feelings about neglectful parents. A few residential staff quite specifically come into such work because of their own experience of an unhappy childhood, and it can be especially painful and difficult for them to take part in network meetings with the parents of the child in their care.

IV.   THE SYSTEM OF FAMILY WORK
IN USE AT ST. CHARLES

A.   A System of "Family Care"

Before talking in more detail about family therapy at St. Charles, it is first necessary to say something about the overall system of care and treatment in use in the Centre.

(1) Admissions and Early Phases

Admissions to St. Charles Youth Treatment Centre are decided by an admissions panel which meets at the DHSS and which is attended by the Director of the Centre. Approximately 20% of the children referred are admitted. Once a child has been selected for admission, a visit is arranged to the institution where the child is being held (most commonly a closed observation and assessment centre, a remand centre, or a prison), and the social worker responsible for the child will bring the parents too, so that they can meet staff from the Centre. At that meeting, the parents are told that they will be expected to work closely with the Centre in its attempts to help their child. In particular, they are told that although the Centre is a secure institution, its overall aim is to try to understand and work with factors in the child's disturbance. As a rule, no child is admitted to the Centre until a discussion of this sort has taken place. In accordance with the principles stated above, even where a parent is in prison or in mental hospital, an attempt is made to include them in the admission plans.

As a rule, once a child has been admitted to the Centre, he will not make any visits home for some months. The aim of this initial period is to make the child's environment as simple and as predictable as possible. Children who are referred to St. Charles have usually been through a bewildering barrage of experiences at all stages in their life. None of them have had an experience of parents able to provide an effective filter system to stimuli, screening out potentially overwhelming situations (most of the children have experienced severe parental discord, violence and separations). The initial stage of treatment at St. Charles is therefore directed towards giving the children an experience of consistency. The children's day is ordered almost from minute to minute; in some ways, the children are treated like toddlers: for example, they have an afternoon siesta. The guiding principle here is that of Abraham Maslow's need hierarchy (1976), in which lower-order needs have to be fulfilled before the child can make use of provision for higher order needs. There is little point in trying to provide formal psychotherapy for a child who has not yet learnt to trust the continued existence from day to day of the people who are caring for him.

(2) Regular Parental Contact
As part of the attempt to provide consistency for the child, parental contact is put onto as regular a basis as possible. With a few of the St. Charles families, this is relatively easily done. The great majority, however, fall into two main categories: the disengaged and the enmeshed. Mrs W's relationship to her son was an example of a disengaged family system at work. It was obvious that in many ways she cared very greatly about her son, but because of her own childhood in children's homes, and in approved school, she was utterly unable to sustain consistent contact with him. Having promised to turn up on a particular day, she would disappear for months; at other times she would arrive unannounced. From time to time she would disappear completely from where she was living. During these periods, her son would become utterly distraught and would attack staff and other children. Staff initially adopted a policy of trying to help Mrs W's son to come to terms with his mother's inconsistency. This however resulted in his becoming more rather than less upset, and it was finally decided that the staff and the local authority social worker should make every possible effort at the very least to keep the boy informed about where his mother was living. This involved the local authority social worker in what amounted to private detective work, but it resulted in a considerable alleviation of the boy's distress.

By way of contrast, Mrs M's relationship with her daughter was an example of over-enmeshment (neither she nor Mrs W were living with one man for any length of time). Mrs M could never accept that her daughter was in the least responsible for the difficulties that had brought her to St. Charles. Continuing problems while in the Centre resulted in Mrs M's complaining to the DHSS and her own solicitor that the child was being victimized. Mrs M's attitude clearly had a very disturbing effect on her daughter, and matters came to a head when the daughter, while on a gardening expedition, threw a pair of shears at another child's back. There was a considerable amelioration of the situation once Mrs M had been issued with a timetable regulating contact with her daughter.

B. The Use of the Geneogram

(1) Initial Construction of the Geneogram

During the first weeks of a child's stay in St. Charles, a family geneogram is set out using information from the parents and the local authority social worker. Very frequently with the St. Charles children, these geneograms are complicated, and include a large number of people who have had brief but, from the child's point of view, unsatisfactory contact with the St. Charles child.

In the initial meeting between the St. Charles staff and the family social worker, a family tree is set out using all the information available to the social worker who will also say what she knows of the St. Charles child's contact with the people in the family tree. A decision is then made as to whom to invite to the first family meeting. Unfortunately, it is the rule rather than the exception that various members of the family system are so much at daggers drawn that they absolutely refuse to meet all together. Usually, therefore, they have to be met piecemeal. In addition, as the family work proceeds, it is common to find that people have been left out who have been very significant in the child's development.

(2) Clinical Example: the Mott Family

As an example of this sort of process I have chosen the Mott family. John Mott came to the centre at the age of fourteen because he had been uncontrollable in an adolescent psychiatric unit. He was felt to be potentially a very dangerous boy, and on one occasion tried to poison his brother. Initially, work was done with John and his brother (who is older) together with John's father and John's stepmother. John's host worker was included in all the family meetings. It soon became clear, however, that the main power in the family lay in the hands of John's great aunt (a woman of eighty) who held sway over the family because of relative wealth. Because of the sickliness of his own mother, Mr Mott had been brought up by the aunt. He had in many ways been quite unable to separate from her, and in both his marriages had been unable to exert any real authority. Both his wives had felt quite unsupported by him, and his childishness was indulged by his aunt. At one time, she had also had the care of John during the break up of Mr Mott's first marriage. As a result of the aunt's having been included in the family work, Mr Mott was better able to assert himself and to disengage from his aunt. It was at this stage that we felt able to turn back the family clock and look at Mr Mott's first marriage. Mr Mott's first wife had not seen him or John for a number of years. She had in fact walked out of the house on Christmas day when John was aged three and a half. Her main reason was that John and his older brother had opened some of their Christmas presents before they were supposed to, but behind this lay profound discontentment with the marriage. John's mother had not visited him in St. Charles although she had heard that he was in some sort of children's home. Since her divorce from Mr Mott she had remarried and had another child. She was visited at home on a number of occasions, and her second husband finally agreed that she should meet Mr Mott together with

John and his older brother. This was the first time that the original family members had met for about ten years. One of the main aims of the meeting was to enable John and his brother actually to hear their parents talking about the difficulties that led to the separation, rather than being left in the grip of fantasy about the causes of the family break-up.

(3) The Family Meeting: the Motts
At this family meeting and in subsequent meetings, it soon became very clear that neither member of the couple had really been able to work through their separation. It was as though all their resentments and bitter hatred of each other had become encapsulated in their children. In fact, it was almost as though John's murderous attack on his brother mirrored the still active murderous feeling between his parents. This sort of family archaeology, in which old and apparently buried conflicts may find expression in later generations, has been particularly described by Murray Bowen (1975). As a result of the family work, John's mother has settled down considerably, and although at the time of writing he is in jail for a relatively minor offence, he has become a much less dangerous and sinister boy to live with.

C. What is the Family Boundary?

The St. Charles families seem to have enormous difficulty in forming a stable boundary around themselves: individuals are recruited to the system and expelled from it with bewildering rapidity. This is perhaps a process akin to that described by Rowley (1977) in his paper *Two's Company and three's a Crowd!* Early on (as in the Mott family) a decision has to be made about which people are to be included in the minimal sufficient network. In these families, there is a tendency for members of the network who have been cut off for years to become activated (like moles in an espionage network) when other members have become engaged in family work. An example of this phenomenon, Vanessa, had not met her father for eleven years (she was aged fourteen when admitted to St. Charles). But within months of family work being initiated between Vanessa and her mother, her father reappeared, engineered her absconsion from the Centre, and harboured her for six weeks. Although it never became entirely clear, it is probable that Vanessa contacted him herself. With hindsight, it is obvious that we should have made contact with him at the same time as working with Vanessa's mother.

V. THERAPEUTIC WORK WITH THE FAMILIES:
SETTING AND STRUCTURE

The family therapists at St. Charles were the social worker, the psychiatrist and the psychologist, working either singly or in pairs. Family meetings were set up either throughout the whole of a child's stay in St. Charles, in which case they would be held at intervals of a month or of six weeks or when family meetings were more frequent (this was usually a matter of geography: families living closer to the Centre had more frequent meetings), the family work was arranged in "terms", with a break of a few months between each term of work. As far as possible, for each term a definite focus of work was set.

A. The Use of the Family Maisonette

A particular feature of the St. Charles work is the use of the family maisonette. This is attached to one of the houses and is particularly used for any of the families coming from a long distance. The experience at St. Charles is that any secure institution with a far-flung catchment area needs such accommodation for its families, and that it has to be jealously guarded against administrators who want to use it for such things as staff accommodation. For some of the St. Charles families, a stay in the maisonette is their only chance of having a holiday. While in the maisonette, a programme is organized, somewhat akin to McGregor's (1969) multiple therapy. Families may take part in the daily house meetings in order to reduce their sense of alienation from the work of the house. Their child is also allowed to stay with them in the maisonette, and tensions arising from the re-uniting of the family in this way, and from the whole family going out on trips together, can be examined in daily meetings with the family. For particularly inarticulate families, special techniques such as sculpting may be used. Meetings are also arranged between the family and the director of the Centre to discuss future plans for the child.

VI. SOME EXAMPLES OF FAMILY WORK
AT ST. CHARLES

The following are examples of work done with families at St. Charles, chosen to illustrate both the limitations and the great potential of such work. The first two of these examples are of families in which "cut-offs" had occurred.

A. Families in which the Child
has Experienced a "Cut-off"

(1) Calum
Calum, aged fifteen, was a boy of superior intelligence who had been sent to St. Charles because he had committed a large number of burglaries, some of them involving considerable destruction of property. The burglaries were meticulously planned, and Calum planted a number of clues to mislead the police. For example, he would leave footprints while wearing an army boot on one foot and a carpet slipper on the other. While he was on the job, he usually wore pyjamas so that, if caught, he could claim that he had been sleep walking. He was so successful in misleading the police, that in the end he was reduced to giving himself up. His father was a successful business man who, in court, requested

that his son be taught a lesson. This so enraged Calum that there and then he tried to assault his father. Calum's mother had walked out of the house when Calum was nine years old, and he had not seen her since. Calum was described by the psychiatrist who saw him before his court appearance as being "calculating, cunning and devious". It is noteworthy that Calum's father, in describing his ex-wife, talked of her as being "a devious, cunning woman". It seemed that in many ways Calum was identifying with his father's picture of the missing wife, and that in this way, the family (there were six other children besides Calum) was able to behave as though the mother was still present.

When we started work with Calum's family, there had been little contact between him and his father for about a year. Contact was initiated with a series of home visits to the father's house, followed by meetings at the Centre, in the course of which Calum came to understand his father's difficulties and point of view. From having seen his father as "really awful", he came to see that the split-up in his parent's marriage had as much to do with his mother as his father. Following the reconciliation with his father, however, all Calum's longing for his mother came to the fore, and he began to spin fantasies about how he had contacted her when in fact he was on leave from the Centre to go to football matches. In addition, he developed a passionate attachment to one of the female members of the staff. Calum did very well in the Centre, and was able to be discharged; and at the time of writing he is working for father. Following his discharge, however, he did make contact with his mother, and stayed with her for a short time. In retrospect, as in Vanessa's case (outlined above), Calum's mother should have been contacted at the same time that work started with his father.

(2) Colin

As a contrast to this is the case of Colin, who at the age of thirteen was admitted to the Centre because of violent delinquency and gross cruelty to animals. When work started with his mother, Colin was also put in touch with his father, whom he had not seen since the split-up of the marriage when Colin was about three. Colin's father had remarried, and in addition to one of Colin's full siblings, he had a number of children by his second marriage. This whole branch of the family was completely unknown to Colin, but he was welcomed by them, and said delightedly after the first meeting with them, "I didn't know I had so many relations". In fact, following his discharge from St. Charles, Colin went to stay with his father. In a case like this, we did not insist that the divorced parents should meet together, but on those occasions when this has been possible, by virtue of hearing parents talk about their difficulties at the time of separation, the child is enabled to begin to modify omnipotent fantasies about his own destructiveness.

B. Families which are "unsuitable" for Therapy

The next three examples are of children from families which would not normally be thought of as being good candidates for family work (using, for example,

Bloch and La Perrière's (1973) criteria). Family contact in these cases, however, proved to be very productive for the children.

(1) Tony

A boy, Tony, aged fourteen, was referred to St. Charles because of two attacks on women. He had been in care from the age of eight and was in the middle of three siblings, none of whom were living at home. Tony was preoccupied with violence, and festooned his walls with posters such as that advertising the *Texas Chainsaw Massacre*. His mother had put him into care because she had separated from her husband and had nowhere to live. She herself had a history of violence. She had had very little contact with Tony from the time of his going into care until his admission to St. Charles. She had remarried, had two more children, and had divorced her second husband. Within a month of Tony's admission to the Centre, his mother was invited to stay in the maisonette together with the two children of her second marriage. Tony's younger full sister was living in a local authority hostel and did not want to come to the family meetings. His older full brother was in Borstal. During Tony's stay in the Centre, it was possible for his mother to come to the maisonette on a number of occasions, and in the course of her meetings with Tony, she was able to talk about her own life. She herself had come from a home in which there had been a good deal of violence. At the age of ten, she had had to go into a sanatorium because of tuberculosis. Although she stayed there for about three years, she was not visited once by her family during this time, and shortly after her discharge, her mother died. These insights into his mother's history, enabled Tony to begin to understand and forgive her. His rage with women began to abate, and he was able to begin to use the substitute mothering available to him at the Centre. He was particularly attached to a middle-aged woman with whom he felt especially safe because he felt that she was not frightened of him. Contact was also made with Tony's father, and for a short time after he left the Centre Tony went to live with him.

(2) "Caring" for the Parents

It should be emphasized that in cases like this where one is dealing with very deprived parents, it has been our experience that very great care has to go into making the parents feel welcome and comfortable when they come to the Centre. Usually the child's host worker would be asked to ensure that the maisonette was ready and stocked with basic foodstuffs. As a rule, the programme of family meetings and of social contacts with the staff of the Centre would be very carefully planned before the arrival of the family. As with the programme for the children at St. Charles, their families' lower order needs have to receive as much attention as the higher order needs catered for by formal family therapy. Even with families not staying in the maisonette, it was the custom during family therapy sessions to provide tea and biscuits.

The parents of the children at St. Charles have as a rule been unable in their own childhood to take for granted the basic necessities of life: food, a roof over their heads, parents whose presence can be relied upon. To expect such families to engage in formal family therapy without first going through a phase of helping them to feel secure within the Centre is like giving a starving child a lecture on vitamins.

(3) Susan

The next example is of a girl, Susan, aged sixteen, who had been found guilty of infanticide. Susan was the only child of a schizophrenic mother (her father had died when she was six). Although Susan's mother lived at home, she was capable of only the simplest domestic chores, and had to rely heavily on the local authority social worker when Susan came to St. Charles. In a series of meetings between Susan and her mother, Susan was very greatly helped by our attempt to sort out the extremely convoluted way in which her mother communicated.

The following are brief extracts from two meetings with Susan and her mother, Mrs Mitchell. The extracts are presented in the form of transcripts of the meetings, and these are followed by the transcripts of the meetings (that is, the family therapist's attempt to convey something of the metacommunications that were occurring in the meetings).

Session A: Susan and her Mother

I (Dr B) am talking to Mrs Mitchell about the way in which she never trusts people with her thoughts. She agrees with me. I then turn to Susan and ask whether the sort of picture that I have been getting of Mrs Mitchell (and as I have been describing it to Mrs Mitchell) is a picture that is recognizable to Susan.

Susan: [addressed to Dr B] Well, it's sometimes difficult for me to know what Mum's thinking.

Mrs Mitchell: Has that woman upstairs gone?

Susan: Yes, she's gone.

Mrs Mitchell: Well, that's got rid of that menace then, hasn't it?

Dr B: [to Mrs Mitchell] Hey, just a minute, I was talking to Susan about how she sees you, and then you suddenly ask her about the woman upstairs. What was that about?

Mrs Mitchell: I don't know.

Dr B: Look, I've got an idea that the menace was really that Susan was talking about how she sees you.

Mrs Mitchell: [to Susan] So we won't see her again?

Susan: No.

Dr B: [to Mrs Mitchell] You did it again! And you (to Susan) fitted in with it. You could have said something like "that's not what we're talking about Mum".

Transcript A (The metacommunications or meaning behind the words)

Susan: Yes, I am beginning to get a more objective picture of Mum.

Mrs Mitchell: Don't you dare start to move away from me.

Susan: Oh God, all right, I won't move away from you.

Mrs Mitchell: Thank you, just as long as we've got that straight.

Dr B: I feel lost: what are you two up to?

Mrs Mitchell: Just keep out of this Dr Bruce!

Dr B: Mrs Mitchell, you are furious because Susan is beginning to move away from you.

Mrs Mitchell: You're not moving away from me are you? Please don't do that. Let's show him that he can't split us.

Susan: All right Mum, we'll stick together.

Dr B: O.K., you two win, but it's not going to do either of you any good to carry on in this way. But I've had enough for today; I can't carry on with this much longer.

Session B: Susan and her Mother

(Two months later)

Mrs Mitchell has talked about her boy friends. Susan has tried to butt in on one or two occasions, but has been stopped from doing so; for the past few minutes, however, Susan has been talking about her relations with men.

Susan: [to Dr B] You know the workmen who are working over there?

Dr B: Yes.

Susan: One of them fancies me.

Dr B: What?

Susan: One of them fancies me.

Dr B: Yes?

Susan: I try to ignore him. Cheek, isn't it?

Mrs Mitchell: Can't help it can you? [laughs]

Susan: [to Dr B] I hate him. I don't say a bloody word to him; that's the point. You know I went over to get a light? I rang the door bell, and he's whistling at me.

Mrs Mitchell: Ask him if he wants a kitten.

Susan: Are you still offering for a cat?

Mrs Mitchell: No [laughs] I'm not.

Susan: Do you still want to get rid of one?

Mrs Mitchell: No.

Susan: Yes or No? 'Cause I could find someone easy.

Mrs Mitchell: No.

Susan: You don't, right.

Silence

Mrs Mitchell: [to Dr B] ? Got two kittens at home.

Transcript B: Susan and her Mother

Susan: I can attract men very easily, you included!

Dr B: Yes, you are a pretty girl.

Susan: One of the workmen fancies me.

Dr B: How dare he, without my knowledge or permission!

Susan: I don't have to ask your permission.

Dr B: I suppose not.

Susan: I can't help it, I'm just attractive to men.

Mrs Mitchell: No. You can't help it. You're just attractive to men. Exciting isn't it? But don't leave me out of it. What are you and Dr B up to?

Susan: Ignore her!

Mrs Mitchell: Susan, please listen to me. Don't leave me out. I'll do and say anything to get you back.

Susan: Please be quiet Mum. You're being embarrassing.

Mrs Mitchell: Susan, what do you mean?

Susan: You're embarrassing me Mum. Please be quiet I find it difficult to say, but you've always embarrassed me.

Mrs Mitchell: Dr Bruce, do you see what you've done now? Please help me. Are you going to leave me with only my cats for company?

Repeated attempts to unscramble Mrs Mitchell's communications in a series of sessions lasting over a year gradually helped Susan to disengage from her mother and to become less panic-stricken. Following her discharge from St. Charles, Susan married and had another baby. Four years after the interviews reported above, she and her child remain well and her marriage is relatively stable.

(4) James

The third case concerns a boy, James, aged thirteen. When he was admitted to the Centre, he had been involved in burglary, wilful damage and actual bodily harm. He had also soiled very severely from the age of eight. He came from an intact but extremely disorganized family. His father had done a two-year stretch in prison because of incest with one of James' older sisters. There were five children besides James. James' mother was of low intelligence. A series of family meetings was arranged, some in James' own home, and some in the Centre. James' father managed to come to only one of these meetings, and this was perhaps understandable in view of the history of incest.

The family meetings were extremely painful because although James got some support from his siblings, he was constantly belittled by his mother, who brushed aside his pitiful attempts to gain her approval. For example, an offer to change an electric plug was rewarded with "You can't do anything"; a Christmas present was received with derision. Painful though these episodes were for James, they enabled him to begin to contemplate not returning home after leaving the Centre, and in fact following his discharge, he went to live in a hostel. If we had not worked with his family in this way, James would certainly not have been able to give up his hopeless longing that his mother could turn out to be different, and he would have returned home only to get into further trouble when his longing for his mother's approbation was frustrated.

C. A "Clinic" Family

Following these three cases I have chosen one to illustrate the fact that even in secure institutions, there are children from families whose problems are not very greatly different from those encountered in child-guidance work, where children can be helped by the standard methods of family therapy. Kate, aged fourteen, had been admitted to the Centre because she had kidnapped two babies whom she had cared for very well. The babies had been kidnapped shortly after Kate's younger sister had been killed by a car when Kate was out walking with her. In a letter to her mother about the accident, Kate wrote, "I really hate myself for what I did. Please forgive me this time. I really loved her and will never forget her ever". In spite of the tone of this letter, there was not a shred of evidence that Kate had been at all responsible for her sister's death. She said that she stole the babies because she "felt like looking after someone".

A series of family sessions including mother, father, Kate and her two siblings were organized, and meetings were held over a period of about eighteen months with breaks in between. The crisis point of these meetings occurred after about five months when the family, which had clearly been blocking its mourning of the young sister, began to open up their defences. In their account of this session, the therapists wrote:

> The details of the accident, the little girl's appearance, the rush to hospital and the panic which drove each member of the family to the scene were described with painful clarity, and obviously this was the first occasion in which the details of the day of the death had been brought out. It was clear that each member of the family had erected a defensive isolation to ward off grief and the need to acknowledge the difficulty they experience as a family in sharing and communicating.

Until the family could get in touch with the feelings described in the session, Kate had been the carrier of these feelings, and had stolen the babies in an attempt to make reparation. At the time of writing, Kate has been discharged from the Centre, is working in an office where she is doing well, and is living at home. She recently said of her parents: "They're awful, but they'll do and I love them".

D. Children who have murdered and their Families

Finally, there should be some mention of the families of children who have murdered. Such children can be very depressing for staff to work with, because as a rule most of them will have to go on to other penal establishments after their stay in the Centre. Even so, it is thoroughly worthwhile to work with these children's families because the great majority will eventually return home, and will still be relatively young when they do so. It is of vital importance to keep them in touch with their families, and their families with them. In addition, there is an important area of research here. It is a common experience in secure institutions that children who have murdered are, paradoxically, less difficult to control and less prone to violent outbursts than children who have committed less serious crimes. In addition, some of the child murderers come from families which, on the surface at least, appear to be in no way different from families whose children do perfectly well in life. Where the difference lies remains a mystery.

VII. CONCLUSION

Secure accommodation for children is notoriously expensive in terms both of money and of emotional distress in staff. It is the experience at St. Charles that the systematic involvement of the children's families in treatment can maximize the institution's therapeutic effectiveness and make the task of caring for the children very much easier.

Where possible, provision for family therapy should be made in the planning of a secure institution. It is much more difficult to graft family therapy on to an established institution, especially a secure one in which staff hierarchy and institutional structures have to be relatively rigid. It is the experience in St. Charles that the social work staff in a secure institution are best placed to run a family therapy programme, and that they should be in a ratio of one social worker to about twelve families.

Family therapy is particularly important in closed institutions because of its civilizing effect in keeping such institutions in touch with the outside world, and with the need to re-integrate their inmates with society. But perhaps the most civilizing influence of all is the way in which family therapy cuts across the institutional hierarchies and institutional structures which, although necessary in closed institutions, can become rigid, barren, and at worst, brutal.

REFERENCES

Bloch, D. and La Perrière, K. (1973). Techniques of family therapy: a conceptual framework. *In* "Techniques of Family Psychotherapy", Grune and Stratton, New York.

Bowen, M. (1975). "Family Therapy After twenty years. American Handbook of Psychiatry V", Basic Books, New York.

Colon, F. (1978). Family Ties and Child Placement. *Family Process,* **17,** 289-312.

Ekstein, R., Friedman, S., Caruth, E. and Cooper, B. (1969). Reflections on the need for a working alliance with environmental support systems. *Reiss-Davis Clinic Bulletin,* **6,** 111-120.

Goldstein, J., Freud, A. and Solnit, A. J. (1980). "Beyond the Best Interests of the Child", Burnett Books Ltd., London.

Haley, J. (1975). Why a Mental Health Clinic Should Avoid Family Therapy. *Journal of Marriage & Family counselling,* (January) pp. 3-13.

Maslow, A. (1976). "The Farther Reaches of Human Nature". Penguin Books, Harmondsworth.

MacGregor, R. *et al.* (1964). "Multiple Impact therapy with families", McGraw Hill, New York.

Menzies, I. (1970). "A Case Study in the functioning of Social Systems as a defence against anxiety", Tavistock pamphlet No 3, T.I.H.R., London.

Rowley, J. L. (1972). Two's company — Three's a crowd: some notes on human interaction. *B.J.Med. Psychol.* **45,** 115-126.

Schon, D. A. (1973). "Beyond the Stable State", Penguin Books, Harmondsworth.

Skynner, A. C. R. (1971). The Minimum Sufficient Network. *Social Work Today,* **2,** 3.

Weisfeld, D. and Laser, M. (1977). Divorced Parents in Family Therapy in a residential treatment setting. *Family Process,* **16,** 229-236.

Chapter 27

Family Therapy and General Psychiatry

S. Lieberman and A. Cooklin

I. INTRODUCTION

This chapter touches on one of the least developed areas of the Family Therapy movement. It is sadly ironical that this should be the case since the seminal ideas of Lidz (1949), Bateson (1956), Wynn (1958), and Bowen (1959) all began as attempts to understand the processes involved in adult mental illness, and schizophrenia in particular. That many of these ideas have been more valuable to the generic principles of family treatment than to schizophrenia *per se* in no way belittles the importance of the ideas, or the urgent need to give proper attention to the place of the family model in our psychiatric institutions. The issues raised by the use of family therapy when an adult rather than a child presents as the index patient have been discussed in different ways throughout this volume, and specifically by Dare (Chapter 18). However, a proper look at Family Therapy in relation to General Psychiatry is a mammoth task first because it raises two issues which each require a full volume in their own right:

(*i*) The Ecobiosociopsychological nature of mental illness, and schizophrenia in particular.

(*ii*) The Ecopoliticosocial nature of the institutions in to which patients with such disorders are admitted and treated.

Secondly, such a task requires a detailed study of the interaction between the two fields. Thus in this chapter we shall restrict ourselves to a review of some of the issues and some suggestions for action.

II. THE CARE OF THE MENTALLY ILL

The great humanitarian impetus to improve the lot of the mentally ill (DHSS, 1975) has based its efforts on the improvement of the current standard approaches and their application. This has gone hand in hand with a controversial thrust to change the balance in favour of community-orientated treatments. This latter movement has suffered some reversal recently as the proportion of re-admissions to mental hospital has increased. However, the swinging of this pendulum in either direction has meant "no change" in epistemology, particularly as it concerns the nature of "patienthood".

There has of course been a regular albeit peripheral movement to redefine the

515

"sick" role of patients in psychiatric institutions and their "one down" position (Szasz, 1961; Laing, 1967; Goffman, 1961). In our view, this thrust has been of limited value to the improvement of the treatment of the mentally ill, as it has usually intensified the perception of the patient as victim.

There have been more concerted efforts to change the structure of psychiatric institutions in such a way that the concept of the patient's "illness" should not govern all the interactions in which he or she engages. The work of Jones (1968) and others in the development of the therapeutic community model has had some success to this end. Others have tried to focus on defining the nature of the relationship between patient, illness, relatives, hospital and others (Cooklin, 1973, 1974) in terms of their implied contracts. However, a comprehensive application of these principles, with a focus on the interactional patterns of the family, has in this country been limited to the work of Scott (1980) and others. They have reported a ten year experience of a family-orientated psychiatric service to one London borough. As well as being able to report lowered admission rates and relapse rates, they also argue that they were able to save the Health Service over £400,000 in one year.

This leads us to the nature of the disorder commonly encountered in psychiatric practice. In terms of family studies, this has been almost exclusively in relation to schizophrenia. Therefore, as schizophrenics still make up the bulk of the long-stay population of our psychiatric hospitals, we will limit our discussion to the aetiology of this disorder.

III. THE NATURE OF SCHIZOPHRENIA

Lidz and Lidz (1949) believed that schizophrenic parents had increased marital schism, or one of the parents had a skewed relationship with the identified patient uniting against the other patient. *Bateson et al.* (1956) in a classic report presented their theory regarding the etiology of schizophrenia. They defined double bind as composed of three parts:
(1) a communicational process: not just an interaction,
(2) a communicational bind,
(3) an injunction not to recognize or flee from (1) and (2).
Homeostasis was an earlier concept defined as feedback which occurs like a thermostat; a family strives to maintain the status quo. *Wynne et al.* (1958) developed the concept of pseudomutuality by which schizophrenic families were seen to deny problems and remain united on a superficial level.

Bowen (1965) (Table I) worked by studying the interactions between family members who were all admitted to a special unit. His concepts include: the undifferentiated ego mass (Nuclear Family Emotional System) which describes the cohesive stickiness of certain nuclear families; differentiation which he used as a term to describe the individual's behavioural freedom from his family members; the family projection process in which the parents' project their problems on to a vulnerable child; the emotional cut-off in which conflicts between family members are avoided through physical and/or emotional

Table I.

Concepts	Criticism				
	(a) Retrospective	(b) Highly selective	(c) Controls	(d) Numbers	(e) Diagnostic criteria
Scott (1965) Shadow of ancestor Well-ill axis closure	Yes	No	None	24 consecutive admission	English criteria IPSS
Laing and Esterson (1960) Mystification Parental causation "psychedelic"	Yes	Yes	None	11 private	Unclear
Bowen (1959) Differentiation Family projection Emotional cut-off M.G.T.P.	Yes	Yes	None	5-6 private	American wide criteria
Wynne et al. (1958) Pseudomutuality	Yes	Yes	None	4 families	American wide criteria
Jackson et al. (1956) Double-bind Homeostasis	Yes	Yes	None	8-10 private	American wide criteria
Lidz (1949) Marital schism Marital skew	Yes	Yes	None	17 private	American wide criteria

distance; and the multigenerational transmission process (MGTP) by which Bowen presumed schizophrenia was caused by a family projection process extending over three to five generations.

Laing and Esterson (1964) developed the concepts of: *Mystification,* by which the family mystified the patient and communication was so confused that the victim couldn't retain his sense of identity; *Parental Causation,* in which the family imposed its views on the child to such an extent as to cause illness. They favoured a *Psychedelic Model,* feeling that madness is a growth experience.

Scott (1965) studied the schizophrenic family in England, and developed the idea of "the shadow of the ancestor". He believed that a history of the occurrence of schizophrenia in the family's past cast a shadow on families. He also noted that families with schizophrenic members used a "well-ill" axis as an important dimension of identity. Finally, he recognized a nodal point in the family with a schizophrenic member was the "closure" at which time the patient was cut off forever from the emotional interactions of his family.

As is seen in Table I, all of the above concepts were developed from small, unrepresentative, poorly controlled studies. Their valuable contribution was to focus research on family interaction rather than discovering the cause of schizophrenia. More importantly, they gave rise to an explosion of interest in the treatment of families leading to the birth of the Family Therapy movement. But most of the original workers would agree with Bowen that "Family psychotherapy is effective in families with less serious problems than those of schizophrenia". A more scientific look at family interactions and causation in the schizophrenic syndrome was undertaken, partly stimulated by the early work of the pioneer family investigations.

The International Pilot Study of Schizophrenia established that patients with identical patterns of symptoms could be recognized in nine different cultures. This certainly supports the arguments of those who view schizophrenia as a disease or group of diseases, rather than just a label of social deviancy. Schizophrenic symptoms are recognized to include misinterpretation of sensory stimuli as if due to external agents, delusions of reference, persecution, or being under control of external agents, disorders of thinking and/or disorders of patient's feelings about self.

Hirsch and Leff (1975) surveyed much of the research in the field of family interaction in families of schizophrenics, and reached the following conclusions. They feel that the bulk of the studies reveal that mothers of schizophrenics are overprotective, but they are neither cold, aloof nor rejecting. Schizophrenic families do not show atypical dominances or skew, but there is more conflict between the parents of schizophrenics. This latter finding could be the effect, not the cause, of schizophrenia in the family. It is clear that pre-schizophrenic children can affect their parents adversely. More parents of schizophrenics are psychiatrically disturbed; they show more conflict and disharmony than parents of other psychiatric patients. Pre-schizophrenic children more frequently suffer from physical disability or ill-health in early life; mothers of schizophrenics are overprotective both before and after schizophrenia is diagnosed. Finally, schizophrenics involved in intense relationships with relatives are more likely to relapse than those with less intense relationships. These and other findings have led to a new realism about the nature of family treatment of schizophrenia.

IV. GOALS OF TREATMENT

Recent inpatient work with schizophrenics and their families have provided new goals for the treatment of their family interactions. *Anderson* (1977) devised the following method of dealing with these families (Table II):

Table II.

During Hospitalization	Subacute Goals	Long-Term Goals
(1) Deals with families needs.	(1) Discover those behaviours which prevent family from working together with hospital support.	(1) Adequate aftercare.
(2) Work with families for patient's welfare.		(2) Plan realistically.
(3) Structure staff availability.	(2) Work to change these attitudes and behaviours.	(3) Teach family and patient how to read danger signs.
(4) Facilitate drug treatment.		
(5) Convey hope.		

Boyd (1979) has developed his own goals, some of them based on Bowen's family concepts. He feels that during hospitalization, the staff must limit the family's influence on the patient and vice versa, but keep the family involved while avoiding blame and dispelling guilt. They must then plan reintegration of the patient with the family and decrease family anxiety. After hospitalization, the family therapist should aim to restructure and clarify boundaries, increase differentiation, repair emotional cut-off and help the family grieve and become realistic about the impairment of the schizophrenic member.

Beels (1975) set as his goals those of teaching the family a model which implies retraining, rehabilitation and avoidance of relapse; teaching "tolerance of each other"; and anticipating and preventing crises which might produce acute psychosis.

The most succinct expression of the goals of family therapy of the schizophrenic syndrome are *Goldstein's* (1978). His guiding principle seems to be to help patient and family to use the psychosis rather than seal it over and ignore it. The patient and family are helped to accept that a psychosis occurred. They are helped to identify some of the precipitating stresses that may have created tensions. Future stresses are explored, and plans are made to minimize the effects of future stress.

V. SCHIZOPHRENIA AND THE FAMILY APPROACH

So far we have presented the different goals which have been specified by a number of practitioners. To some extent, these are reflections of the epistemology which has been applied to understanding the process. Sturgeon *et al.* (1981) for example have described in detail a technique for minimizing the noxious effects of high "expressed emotion" parents on the relapse rates of their children. Although their work does not exactly specify "cause or effect", it is nevertheless based on a linear epistemology. They make no hypothesis of circular interaction, nor do they conceive of any techniques to interfere with negative feedback loops.

In addition to this approach, there seem to us to be four main models of family therapy which are most relevant to the general psychiatric setting.

A. Structural/Strategic

Haley (1980) takes the pragmatic view that the schizophrenic child is caught in a paradoxical dilemma with the parents. The pattern is such that the child cannot respond to either the injunction to accept parental control, or the injunction to take control: the latter usually originating at a time when the child's behaviour served a regulatory function in the parent's marriage. In Haley's model, the family is in various ways coached to undercut the child's control, and geared towards the specific goal of him or her leaving home. Although from a very different framework, it is interesting that the practical application of this approach has many similarities with the techniques of Leff and his group (Leff, 1979).

B. Bowen's Model: Increasing Differentiation of Self

This is a didactic approach. Although it is very different from Haley's model, and is not geared to the precipitation of a crisis, it is interesting that it is one in which tensions are kept within the controlled manageable proportions imposed by the therapist. In this respect, it has some similarities to the approach of Leff *et al.*

C. Whitaker's Existential/Experiential Model

Carl Whitaker (1978, 1980) perhaps more than any other family therapist, has devised a whole style of work which has the "craziness" or schizophrenia of the family as its prey. He nearly always works with a co-therapist, works intensively with the family over long periods, and becomes intimately engaged in their process. It is as though he enters the most bizarre elements of the family's life, and by changing the meaning of these, allows them to have a different experience. His work is also the most difficult to describe. He puts it thus:

> Schizophrenia emerges through the baptism of the sacred one. The pattern is insidious, resulting from a biopsychosocial hormone secreted out of the family's living. It colors the family socially, interpersonally and intrapsychically. Treatment involves each of these levels. This complex job is like major surgery and requires more than one surgeon. We work as co-therapists. An important part of our teaming has been our effort to depathologize human experience. Our effort is to get at this through the interpersonal components of schizophrenia. The task

is complicated by the depersonalizing component of schizophrenia. Our first battle is with the depersonalising chain reaction in the family. (Keith and Whitaker, 1980)

D. The Paradoxical Approach of the Milan Group (Palazzoli et al., 1978, 1980)

This group has not become involved in General Psychiatric practice, but has remained outside all institutions. Their work is described elsewhere in this volume (Chapters 3 and 17). They do not refer to the treatment of schizophrenia, but have devised techniques for interaction in what they have called "families in schizophrenic transaction".

VI. THE FAILURES OF SUCCESS: IMPLICATIONS FOR THE INSTITUTION OF APPLYING THESE MODELS

In this chapter we are not concerned to argue that family therapy has a place in the general psychiatric setting. Our epistemology is such that we believe it *has* to have a place, and the work of Leff and others (Leff, 1979; Leff and Vaughn, 1980) we think gives credence to this view. However, in varying degrees, all these models challenge the traditional functioning of the psychiatric institution. It may be of course that this *needs* to be challenged. However that challenge can either be helpful or disastrous to the patient, the institution, or the credibility of the family model.

A. The Shift of Emphasis from the Individual to the Family Group

(1) Issues of Model

Adult in-patient units run smoothly when the staff are harmonious in the work setting. A stable organization and clear hierarchy are usually present. They provide a setting in which to practice skills acquired through years of training, and to teach those skills to students. At this point, we are not concerned with the correctness or otherwise of the goals of such institutions, but with their capacity for survival. Only when organized to ward off some noxious threat to survival can an institution accommodate new in-put. Family Therapy unsettles the hierarchy, and may de-stabilize the organization since it deals with three non-traditional assumptions.

First, causation, the family approach implies that the root of many problems resides in relationships, not in the psyche or soma of individuals.

Secondly, the real world and real people are considered more important to psychiatric illness, than intrapsychic fantasy or biology.

Thirdly, the family therapist views himself as part of the family system rather than as an objective outsider.

Mixing models of individual and family orientation therefore provides conflicts about these issues built into the system from the outset. Other questions must also be answered. Will the identified patient be seen individually, and will he or she receive drugs? If so, how will the therapist resolve the implied contradiction of "patienthood" vs interaction? Many other problems of model arise depending on the family approach used. However, a universal one concerns the shift in role required of the in-patient and other professional staff.

(2) Issues for Staff Roles

The stability of an institution is dependent on the interaction between the internal and external events affecting that institution and the nature of the boundary which separates them.

Internal events are partly controlled by the manner in which internal roles can govern the nature and significance of the internal interactions. Thus the formal relationship between the staff and patient requires that both accept the staffs' "helping" or "custodial" role, and both accept the patient's "patienthood". This is crucial in maintaining an internal steady state. The clear definition of this relationship is also crucial in maintaining the clarity of relationships between different professional groups. For example, if say the nurses agree to socialize with patients outside the hospital, and say the social workers do not, this affects not only the relationship between nurses and patients, but also that between social workers and patients, and nurses and social workers.

When a family model is introduced into an institution, who is to "do the family therapy?" Is it to be an elitist function, high in prestige, or something to suggest to the lowest member of the staff hierarchy when "all else fails"? Is it to be seen as the mark of office of one particular group, say the social workers? The answers to these questions will be different in different institutions, but how they are resolved may be crucial to the success or failure of the family approach.

There is a further and often highly confusing twist to this issue. A nurse is a "patient's person"; often the esteem of the nurse is highly dependent on the belief that he or she can be a helpful and supportive intimate "other" for the patient. If the nurse (and to a lesser extent this applies to other disciplines) works with the whole family, this automatically distances him or her from the patient. This may be challenging the foundations on which his or her role is built; "being close to the patients" and may thus place the patient in the invidious position of having to choose between the nurse and his or her family.

The question of challenging the "patienthood" of the individual can have other consequences. Relatives are often a sensitive issue in all closed or semi-closed institutions. This is partly because their existence challenges the way individuals are defined as members of the institution. They remind the institution that they are also members of another group: the family. When the rules or orderliness of the institution are heavily dependent on a "rule" that patients are clearly defined as patients, then any shift in the definition of patient-hood can severely disrupt the orderly functioning of that institution. This problem may compound the difficulties of solving such practical problems as "How will the administration cope with the family? How many case notes must be made up for a family? How many hospital numbers? Are all family members considered to be patients? How will they be assessed for expenditure by the Health Service?"

(3) Issues of the Relatives' Roles
What part are the relatives really seen to play in these events, and is the stated answer to that question congruent to what is implied by action? Are the relatives seen as family members on the same "level" as the patient? If so, does that disrupt such hierarchical organization as the family has been able to maintain. Are the relatives seen as staff "aides", as patients, or as the "culprits"?

Different institutions have sought often imaginative solutions to these problems. Some have stressed to the patient that he or she must accept medication because the relatives "can only stand him or her" with the help of drugs; thus stressing the interactional rather than the illness framework. Others have asked the relatives to take the same or different drugs from those taken by the patient.

B.   Issues for the Institution

(1) The Definition of the Institution
Since treatment in family therapy is related to the reorganization of relationships, the emphasis of family work has been on strategies which will encourage this reorganization. The diagnosis of individuals is less relevant than is the disequilibrium in the family system. Thus one of the major functions of the institutions is called into question.

(2) The Language of the Institution
Case conferences in which family therapist and individually orientated practitioners take part are often disturbing and unpleasant due to the different languages being spoken. The family therapist seeks to alter relationships, and is concerned with how this is to be done.

In-patient units in which the family therapist works side-by-side with organic and individual dynamic psychiatrists are thus subjected to a curious mixture of models. Staff working on several firms will be subjected to conflicts as they attempt to move from one model to another. They will be asked to retain traditional boundaries on the one hand, and discard those boundaries on the other. They will be concerned with individually based diagnoses on one hand, and relationship strategies on the other. While this dichotomy can be immensely stimulating for a while, the staff, whether nurse, social worker, psychologist or doctor, eventually choose the model with which they are most comfortable. Resistance to the opposing models may then act as an injunction to the patient against using the family experience.

(3) "Intensity" vs "harmony"
Psychiatric institutions were known as asylums. Part of their function was to protect and cushion the patient from the noxious effects of life's pressures. By focussing on the interactional component in the patient's life, the family approach raises the intensity of interactions and revitalizes conflicts which may have been abandoned unresolved. The family therapist must be especially sensitive to this phenomenon and find some way of either preparing the institution for "things getting worse", or ensure that the context of this raised intensity is carefully controlled.

(4) The Failure of Success: Competition
What happens if the therapy is "successful"? Will the therapist be thanked and applauded, or will this "success" raise other conflicts? Does it change the hierarchy of prestige in the situation? If it does, the response may be that "the patient's disorder turned out to be much less severe than we feared", or alternatively an apparently unnecessary new treatment will be instituted. After having survived so many hurdles it may seem "too much" for the therapist to be concerned with this issue, but it may be crucial to the continued development of the family model in the institution.

VII. STRATEGIES FOR INTERVENTION IN THE ILLNESS/INSTITUTION SYSTEM

There are three solutions:

A. Keep Total Control of all Cases

Haley has strongly advocated that the therapist should insist on total control of each case, and only then will he accept patients discharged from or about to leave psychiatric hospitals.

B. Remain "Meta" to the Whole System

The alternative approach is to try and stay "meta", or to maintain a meta-perspective of the patient, family, and institution. The Milan group have particularly adopted this stance. They insist that the therapist must in no way challenge or enter a symmetrical confrontation with the institution. It means that the therapist must remain neutral and cannot accept any "power" over the patient's management. It is a difficult model to employ when working in a statutorily based Health Service, because the roles of psychiatrist, social worker etc. carry with them such powerful expectations in the eyes of other professionals.

However, it is a position which can be taken by family therapists in a teaching role. Thus teaching staff from the Institute have been able to develop the principles of a family model in a teaching hospital by remaining in the role of external consultant.

C. Design your own Unit

The Philadelphia Child Guidance Clinic was developed as an institution which has a family model embedded in its foundations. Thus there is little conflict between the family model and in-patient treatment. The patients there are children or adolescents. We have yet to see so comprehensive a family "hospital" built to provide for cases where an adult is the index patient.

VIII. CONCLUSIONS

We adhere to the need to increase the application of the family model to traditional psychiatric settings. Introducing such a model frequently
  A. challenges the traditional use of the institution,
  B. challenges formal hierarchies and juxtaposes a different hierarchy of competence,
  C. challenges the epistemology of the institution, the basic principles underlying all its thinking,
  D. Thus it offers benefits and dangers.
The benefits are:
  (1) It offers the staff hope for a new competence and effectiveness.
  (2) If offers the staff a model they can apply to improve the functioning of the institution.
The dangers are:
  (1) That polemics develop; the patient versus the "bad family" or "bad hospital".
  (2) It is used as an excuse for "wildness".
Thus (3) The survival of the Institution is threatened, and/or
  (4) The model is discredited.
In our view, whichever approach is used the therapist entering a psychiatric institution *must* make a systemic hypothesis of the whole patient/illness/family/institutional system, and plan interventions on the basis of this.

REFERENCES

Anderson, C. M. (1977). Family intervention with severely disturbed inpatients. *Archives of General Psychiatry*, **34**, 697-702.

Bateson, G., Jackson, D., Haley, J. and Weakland, J. (1956). Toward a Theory of Schizophrenia. *Behavioural Science*. **1**, 251-264.

Beels, C. (1975). Family and Social Management of Schizophrenia. *Schizophrenia Bulletin*, **13**, 97-118.

Boyd, J. (1979). The interaction of Family and Psychodynamic Individual Therapy in an Inpatient Setting. *Psychiatry*, **12**, 99-111.

Bowen, M. (1965). Family Psychotherapy with Schizophrenia in the Hospital and in Private Practice. *Intensive Family Therapy*, (I. Boszormenyi-Nagy and J. Framo, eds), Harper & Row, London.

Cooklin, A. I. (1973). Consideration of the 'contract' between staff and patient and its relationship to current hospital practice. *Br. J. med. Psychol.* **46**, 279-285.

Cooklin, A. I. (1974). "Exploration of the staff-patient 'contract' in an acute female admission ward". *B. J. Med. Psychol.* **47**, 321-335.

Goffman, E. (1961). "Asylums", Anchor Books, New York.

Goldstein, M. J., Rodwick, E. H., Evans, J. R., May P. R. and Steinberg, M. (1978). Drugs and Family Therapy in the aftercare treatment of acute schizophrenia. *Archives of General Psychiatry*, **35**, 10, 1169-1177.

Haley, J. (1980). "Leaving Home", McGraw-Hill, New York.

Hirsh, S. R. and Leff, J. P. (1975). "Abnormalities in Parents of Schizophrenics", Maudsley Monograph No. 22 Oxford University Press, London.

Jackson, D. D. (1957). The question of family homeostasis. Part I. *Psychiatric Quarterly*, **31**, Suppl. 79.

Jones, M. (1968). "Social Psychiatry in Practice", Penguin, London.

Keith, D. V. and Whitaker, C. A. (1980). Add Craziness and Stir: Psychotherapy with a Psychoticogenic Family. *In* "Dimensions of Family Therapy", (M. Andolfi, ed.), Brunner/Mazel, New York.

Laing, R. and Esterson, P. (1964). "Sanity, Madness and the Family", Tavistock, London.

Laing, R. D. (1967). "The Politics of Experience", Penguin, London.

Leff, J. P. (1979). Developments in family treatment of Schizophrenia. *Psychiatric Quarterly*, **51**, 216-32.

Vaughn, C. E. and Leff, J. P. (1980). The interaction of life events and relative's expressed emotion in schizophrenia and depressive neurosis. *British Journal of Psychiatry*, **136**, 146-53.

Lidz, R. and Lidz, T. (1949). The Family Environment of Schizophrenic Patients. *American Journal of Psychiatry*, **106**, 322-345.

Palazzoli, M. S., Cecchin, G., Prata, G. and Boscolo, L. (1978). "Paradox and Counter Paradox", Jason Aronson, New York.

Palazzoli, M. S., Cecchin, G., Prata, G. and Boscolo, L. (1980). Hypothesising—circularity—Neutrality: Three Guidelines for the Conductor of the session. *Family Process* **19**, 3-11.

Scott, R. D. and Ashworth, P. L. (1969). The Shadow of the Ancestor. *British Journal of Medical Psychology*, **42**, 13-32.

Scott, R. D. (1980). A family orientated psychiatric service to the London Borough of Barnet. *Health Trends*, **12**, 65-68.

Sturgeon, D., Kuipers, L., Berkowitz, R., Turpin, G. and Leff, J. (1981). Psychophysiological Responses of Schizophrenic Patients to High and Low Expressed Emotion Relatives. *The British Journal of Psychiatry*, **138**, 40-45.

Szasz, T. S. (1961). "The Myth of Mental Illness", Delta Books, New York.

Whitaker, C. A. (1978). Beyond the Double Blind: Communication and Family Systems, Theories, and Techniques with Schizophrenics. (M. Milton and M. D. Berger, eds), Bruner/Mazel, New York.

Wynne, L., Ryckoff, I., Day, J. and Hirsch, S. (1958). Pseudomutuality in the family relations of schizophrenics. *Psychiatry*, **21**, 205-220.

Chapter 28

A Family Therapy Approach to Making Decisions in Child Care Cases

A. Bentovim

I. INTRODUCTION

This chapter represents a development of an earlier paper (Bentovim and Gilmour, 1981), where we attempted to describe a particular approach adopted when difficult decisions had to be made in cases of child care, access and custody. The approach developed tried to maintain a balance between the needs of the individual child in terms of his future care and the needs of the family unit. Thus it is concerned with providing a therapeutic experience for the family while considering the actual break-up of the family unit if it cannot be helped to become a place in which the child can thrive. Decision-making in this area is vital, given a belief that a family, even if not his family of origin, is the optimal context for a child to grow up in. Currently 120 000 children are in local authority care, 50 000 for more than three years, and 3 out of 4 in care until aged 18. Therefore an assessment using a family therapy frame has to be concerned with how far the family system can stretch and change to meet an individual's needs If that fails, then the task is to both find an alternate family, and to ensure that transitions are successful for all involved despite gains or losses (see Robinson, Chapter 21).

II. REFERRAL SOURCES

The context for the work is a psychiatric department in a post-graduate children's hospital. The team is being asked to assess and give an opinion in situations where decision-making as to a child's future is exceedingly problematic, yet usually there is some urgency that the "best" solution be found as soon as possible. Such decisions may be about whether children at risk should or should not be rehabilitated with their families, about children in care whose present placement is breaking down or is not suitable, about the advisability of placing disturbed older children for adoption, or about infants being removed into care at birth. We are also asked to help over the question of access of children to their natural parents, when termination of access is being considered and, in divorce situations, over custody and access issues where

527

there is a dispute between the parents. Such situations are brought to our notice by Social Services Departments, the Official Solicitor to the High Court, "private advocates" (solicitors acting for the parties), families and parents themselves, or other medical practitioners.

III. EXPLICIT CHILD-CARE VALUES

A. Child Care in a Family Therapy Setting

When trying to put together the basic elements of our approach, we realized that we had an articulated series of child-care values and beliefs which were more or less explicit in our practice. Although our basic orientation was a family systems one in the sense of seeing the logic of the interactional view of behaviour, nevertheless we have found a number of principles of use, particularly in communicating about the needs of the children and families we were seeing. What follows is based on the notion that whatever role children play within the family system, they are basically vulnerable through their developmental immaturity. This means that the family may induct society into its system through its destructive interaction and family breakdown; social agencies may then be forced to intervene to protect the child even though that child may be playing an active part in its own disqualification. A family therapy approach expects that the rigidity of family dysfunction be tested to explore any possibility for change, but the following principles as far as the child is concerned always have to be borne in mind.

B. Least Detrimental Form of Care for the Child

Primarily, we are committed to the importance of the *least detrimental alternative care* principle as described by Goldstein *et al.* (1973). This enunciates the principle of doing least harm when a decision about a child's care has to be made, and also indicates that there is no perfect solution, only the *least detrimental* one. The following factors have to be borne in mind:

(1) Decisions need to be made in relation to the age of the child.
(2) The capacity of the child to become attached to new parent figures must be recognized (see Robinson, Chapter 21).
(3) The time span of child *vs* adult must be recognized.
(4) Good enough parenting and continuity must be supported, whoever is providing it.
(5) Secure psychological parenting may have to be supported over "failed" biological parenting or improved parenting capacity when it is reached "too late".

Although we agree that short-term separations need not be detrimental, longer-term reactions and negative interactional patterns can be triggered or potentiated, and represent a risk in the long-term for the child well-attached to alternative parents if moved. We believe that infants are sensitive to separation from the earliest period of life, and that the notion of a period of invulnerability to separation early on is to be seriously questioned (Bentovim, 1979).

Late fostering and adoption can be successful (Tizard, 1977), and is preferable to "institutional" parenting, but the later the placement, the more problems that are likely to evolve. "Late" return to a parent can be equivalent to a late adoption, yet it can be *more* problematic than placement with a "new" family. Adoption is preferable to long-term fostering because the latter inevitably creates insecurity for all concerned due to the uncertain legal status.

Adopted and fostered children have the right to have some kind of *access to their families of origin,* with information (in the form of a "life book") being the minimum needed to help the child and his new family in their task as a reconstituted group.

In "later" fostering or adoptive situations where attachments to families of origin exist, direct access may be appropriate *provided* that the loss of parent, child and family has been acknowledged, that the new/reconstituted family is a going concern and a "distant relative" role is accepted by the child and natural parents. This is a very major demand, however. Information giving can be a start to the process which needs careful monitoring, and a good deal of work has to be done with all concerned if it is to be successful.

The purpose of access must be clearly defined, access with a view to resume *care* being different to access which provides *information* to the child. This applies to situations of parenting breakdown and divorce, as well as to those of children in care. Children should be able to have direct access channels created before the age of 18.

Access strain which threatens the nurturing capacity of the "good enough" primary caretaker and the security of the child, may be detrimental and may need to be "thinned" and re-negotiated, or changed from direct contact to indirect information only (Bentovim, 1980).

The denial of *access* through information or contact with a "potential" alternative parent (e.g. in divorce) may be against a child's best interests.

Although we see the importance of the custodial parent having some power of controlling access, we favour joint custody, mediation and conciliation in divorce wherever possible, rather than the use of adversarial processes.

We feel "painful" conclusions need direct feedback, and any reports submitted to Court must be available to all parties concerned.

IV. FAMILY THERAPY PRINCIPLES

A. Focal Notions

In the process of developing a brief form of family therapy the notion of *the focus* has been used in an attempt to bring together a large number of disparate and apparently unrelated family phenomena (Kinston and Bentovim, 1981). A model has been described which is well suited to the sorts of cases which we are considering here. A model such as structural family therapy, which is concerned mainly with the family here and now, cannot in our view always encompass the devastating histories that these children and families have experienced and which may be encapsulated in the present (Parkes, 1971). Although structural family therapy methods may be absolutely essential to work with such families as described so powerfully in *Families of the Slums* (Minuchin *et al.*, 1967), in our view, a model is required for *assessment* where historical events can be incorporated from the beginning.

The model described by Kinston and Bentovim (1981) is basically a stress response model. The generally well accepted idea has been reinforced that, for a family to be healthy, there needs to be attempts at acceptance, integration, resolution and working through of the stressful life-events and circumstances which affected the parents of the present-day family, both when they were children and as adults. To say that stressful events have been worked through implies that they have been made sense of by the individuals who have experienced them, and they have an appropriate place in their world of meanings. The reading of meaning and the making sense of the pattern of events is a routine part of family life from the moment of birth, and to be a human being is to experience one's situation in terms of the meanings we give our lives.

B.   Common Meanings and Intersubjective Meanings

(1) Common Meanings
Common meanings were defined as meanings which are rooted in the psychic lives of the individual family member. Each member has his own unique experience, much of which remains unconscious or private and is relevant to the concerns of other family members or the family therapist.

However, there are certain core meanings which are shared at the time of marriage and which develop in common afterwards; when children appear they assimilate and contribute to these. Such common meanings are exchanged and shared unconsciously, by example and instruction, and include beliefs, views, guiding principles, fears and expectations. They are the roots of belonging, loyalty and cohesion within the family. Common meanings are essential for comfortable communication, pleasureable participation in interests, and tolerance of each other's pain. They are the basis for consensus and easy conflict resolution, and a coherent response to the environment. When a member leaves the family he can take these meanings with him without disrupting the family, and use them in the creation of a new family.

(2) Intersubjective Meanings
Intersubjective meanings by contrast are not the property of any single member, but are rooted in the family life, and are part of the self-definition of the family-as-a-whole as a "multi-facetted organism" (Minuchin and Fishman, 1981). Powerful common meanings lead to the development of a web of intersubjective meaning. A number of concepts refer to such notions, such as shared inter-personal reality, family matrix or family identity. The idea of a family myth,

or culture (see Byng-Hall, Chapter 10 and Cooklin, Chapter 4) clearly expresses the notion that the family has its own reality. Such a family reality can of course have an obscuring effect on member's own psychic reality.

C. Healthy Families

In a family functioning healthily, we assume they have a set of common and intersubjective meanings which enable creative responses to occur to life crises and individual needs. When we meet the family, what we see and observe is a healthy *surface action* or family interaction pattern where communications are meaningful and supportive: alliances occur appropriately within generations rather than across generations. A variety of feeling states can be expressed and integrated, parenting and family operations provide for the needs of children and adults in terms of physical protection, stimulation, emotional support, and maintain the integrity of personal and intergenerational boundaries. Individuals are nurtured, socialized and supported (Loader *et al.*, 1981).

D. Unhealthy Families

Unhealthy family functioning, by contrast, presents to the observer a surface action with interactions which are repetitive, destructive, and develop a compulsive circular dominating quality which cannot be stopped on request, despite obvious harmful consequences. In families whose surface action leads to rejection or injury of children, alternative forms of care must be considered. We see a variety of dysfunctional patterns:

(1) Communication being apparently absent, confusing, or full of angry disqualifications, through a lack of mutual listening.

(2) Severe disagreements and lack of resolution of conflict.

(3) A family atmosphere which may be chaotic or panicky and convey a quality of danger and unpleasantness.

(4) Attack, criticism, rejection and denigration or disorganization may overwhelm and a pervading sense of dissatisfaction be present.

(5) Boundaries may be severely intruded upon, such as excessive reaction between individuals, infantilization of parents or parentification of children, or so rigid that there is absence of meaningful interchange.

(6) Family operations and parenting results in lack of sufficient care, accidents or neglect, physical and emotional.

When we examine the salient stressful events and circumstances in the families of origin, or procreation in these families, we find an extraordinary weight of personal and shared experiences of loss and distress. Here, punishing and rejecting attitudes are expected and evoked, and an excess of painful events have occurred. Yet, what to the observer is moving, painful and sad, can be emptied of meaning by the family. Alternately, they appear to share an anticipation that such events will recur endlessly. A belief seems to be held that there is no way of escaping from the loyalty of being the same sort of parent as one's parents, or that children in turn will reject. Professionals in "parenting" relations will be expected and provoked to leave abruptly and cause more of the same pain. Family patterns are recreated, and what was right for the parent will be felt to be right for the child in the face of similar provocative behaviour.

Other families seem perpetually to be attempting to reverse or overturn the meaning of events; deprivation experienced has to be reversed by constantly seeking for objects or new people to be close to, children to be given to so that they can give back in turn. Alternately, someone else has to be found as the cause of all bad things, particularly professionals who are drawn in to try to help, then in turn are seen as the deprivers, the rejectors and the parent who beats. Thus the family homeostasis is maintained and the pathological common and inter-subjective meanings circumscribe the family and prevent creative response.

V. ASSESSMENT MODEL

Ideally, an assessment model will:
(1) define the surface action of the family and the professional system who are attempting to work with that family, and assess the degree of dysfunction of both family and capacity of the therapeutic system;
(2) pinpoint the relevant site of stresses and the way that they have been handled and remain represented in the current family system, influencing surface action;
(3) predict what would be a healthy surface action for this particular family in relationship to the child's needs, and what changes are necessary for that family to become functional, and to assess what therapeutic work might be necessary to achieve this;
(4) make a formulation which connects the events that this particular family has had to accept and integrate, the way in which the family characteristically handles such stresses, the major beliefs and meanings they hold and the surface action which results;
(5) decide what decision needs to be taken in the child's best interests in the light of the formulation of the family.
What is the least detrimental alternative given such factors?

VI. THE ASSESSMENT PROCESS

The assessment process itself requires that we:
(i) hear the individual's, family's, professional's report of self, others, episodes and history;
(ii) elicit and observe characteristic interaction so as to be able to define the family in action.

A. Clinic Team and Setting

We find that a clinic family representing and reflecting the ecosystem of professionals and family who are consulting us is a helpful model in this field.

We need to hold within our own family both the overall interactional view of the ecosystem and the individual needs in that particular context. We find that a psychiatrist or social worker provides the medical and social work backup essential for communication with the professional and legal system. We also find it helpful to have a child psychotherapist on the team who is able to focus on the child's needs and communications *per se*, since the child, as the least physically powerful member of the system, has the quietest voice, yet the whole plan is to do with his needs. Having the whole panoply of one-way screens and video is helpful so that we can maintain a position both "inside" and "outside" the process.

Access to psychologists and paediatricians are also essential in the task of defining both individual needs and capacities, as well as the system as a whole. There are certain advantages of a central hospital or clinic setting which is separate from the localities of those concerned with the case. This enables a clear physical boundary to be established, separating the assessment team from local politicians and media pressures. Having a clearly defined authority role as a supra-regional Hospital clinic helps the clinic team to remain "meta" or at a different level to the system of the professionals and the family. There is a pressure cooker effect in such a consultation which can increase intensity and facilitate decision making. However, there is the disadvantage that family and professionals are having to operate in a strange context, and stress can distort the situation.

B. Who Are Seen?

We see *together* all family members and significant professionals who have "living together" relationships, "responsibility and authority" relationships or access relationships. The "ecosystem" may include parents, foster/adoptive parents, grandparents, new co-habitees, other children, social workers, solicitors, or other professionals.

We also see family or system members in a variety of combinations, depending on the natural, recreated, therapeutic, decision making or significant past systems, but we do not bring together those who have no contact. Thus we would not see children with a parent where there is no current access, unless as part of the therapeutic plan. We would, on occasions, see older children alone, but would try to make it clear that we did not expect loyalty to be breached, and also that we would respect issues of confidentiality. Children must not feel they have *adult* powers of decision making. Seeing everybody in one session or sequentially gives multiple impact on the therapist. This can take several hours and is often very stressful! Tensions are often high and feelings fraught.

C. What Techniques are Used?

(1) *Exploring and elaborating the Surface Action*
In order to see the system as a whole and also the various subsystems, we need to foster interactions. All members of the group are asked to describe to the others

"the problem" as they see it, and to define the decision which needs to be made. On my part, I use techniques of joining by connoting destructive behaviour as "helpful", allowing individuals to negatively connote their own behaviour rather than having others do it. In many situations, there is considerable conflict between social workers and natural parents, and the latter feel judged and blamed, a state compounded by the fact that Court cases are often pending. In this way I attempt to keep myself "meta" to the system rather than creating alliances, i.e. I attempt to maintain a neutral position (e.g. Palazzoli *et al.*, 1980).

(2) Interactional Tasks
To prevent myself from being bombarded by a family who often feel they need to attempt to convince me of their view, I find interactional tasks helpful.
   (a) With infants, I ask the caretakers or potential caretakers to demonstrate their parenting skills, e.g. feeding, changing, comforting, stimulating, etc.
   (b) With toddlers, we provide and encourage care and play situations, setting of limits, separations, reunions, stranger reactions, etc.
   (c) With older children, I ask the various adults involved to talk to the children about the situation and about their life history as well as establishing them (the children) to express their wishes and opinions.
Throughout all, I am keen to assess attachment behaviour (Bentovim, 1979), the nature of relationships, as well as parental competence and insight.

(3) Observations of non-verbal Behaviour-play
While the adults are involved in their communications to each other or to us, the children are often involved in a range of play therapy material, and one or other of the interviewers is usually giving attention to this. If there is more than one child, then as well as noting their separate behaviours, it is important to observe their interaction with each other. The other non-verbal communications between all members of the system are readily enacted before us during the process of the interview so that we can assess the atmosphere, mood and operations of the group.

(4) Exploring the Surface Action of the Whole System
The interviewer needs to take note of the patterns of *dyadic* and *triadic* relationships, to observe circularities of interactions, the repetitive interacion patterns leading back on themselves. I may use structural approaches, e.g. "discuss this with him/her and we'll listen", or "change places" etc., or triangular questions: "which of the children would say they most want to be with you, which with a foster parent" etc. In these various ways, the surface action mapped.

(5) Depth Structure Exploration
The longitudinal process is very important, and through listening to the history of events in the families of origin and procreation, and through observing the *ways* of telling and the *meanings* attached thereto, it is possible to identify the meanings held in *common* and also the *lack* of common meanings which result in conflict (e.g. the role of biological parents as seen by substitute families and

vice versa). Therefore, the variation of meanings in the different subsystems can be endless, but are fundamental, and can be seen to be repeated continuously.

(6)   Use of Geneograms, etc.
Compiling geneograms can be a useful addition to ways of gathering and conveying information, but, being so time consuming, are only of value in a few situations. However, we frequently advocate the need for a *life book* for any child who has a complicated life history involving separations and changes of caretaker. Such a book gives a year by year account of the child's life, with all important events and details recorded. It includes photos of the child, and of the people who have or have had an important role in his life, as well as photos of significant places where he may have lived. Details of a child's early life before he came into care are, sadly, often not available for the older child, and of course frequent changes of personnel during a child's life in care may also result in a lamentable lack of information for that period too. Where natural parents, with help, are able to relinquish their hold on the fantasy that their child ought to return home (e.g. in situations where a child has been in a substitute home for some years and may well be adopted eventually, and whose natural parents have been on the periphery), the compiling of a life book of the period when the child lived at home with them can be a therapeutic task. It can be seen as a gift to the child and therefore as a reparative gesture by the parents who are able to absolve themselves of some of the awful burden of guilt which most of these parents feel.

Parents have asked to present these books directly to the foster/adoptive parents so that they can explain the details face to face with the people who will be interpreting them to the child when the time comes for him to want to know about his real parents. It is conceivable that this could be a helpful occasion to all concerned, but implies that work has to be done with both the natural and the substitute parents. The life book can provide information for the child which can act as background context to give meaning to bewildering life events, and a secure base to explore from.

(7)   Use of Family Doll Figures to convey History
In our assessment interview, we use doll family figures, small pipe-cleaner clothed dolls, to represent parents, grandparents, children, babies and any other significant people in the child's life. These can be used by the adults and the child as aids to the telling of the story. These figures help the older child (over three) to be an active participant in the process, and to demonstrate his attachments often in quite a remarkable way, and can be recreated with the "real" people in the room by seeing whose lap the child would sit on to watch T.V. or whose arms to be comforted in if he falls.

VI.   CASE ILLUSTRATION

The following case illustration demonstrates the application in practice of these principles. The P family have been described briefly in Bentovim (1980), but the issues are so clear that it seems an excellent example to describe in more detail here.

Angelina P was referred as a 2½-year-old by a social services department, having been in care since 3 months of age with an experienced foster-family following a severe abusive episode. Her parents had been of considerable concern even before her birth because of poor marital relationships, marital violence, very poor financial and social coping. Loretta, the mother, had been at a school for slow learning children, and had met her husband when he was ill in the hospital where she was working as a ward orderly.

Angelina had recovered quite remarkably from the abuse, and there was no permanent injury. Her parents had separated when the father was imprisoned, and both returned to their families of origin where they did not resume their former relationship. Neither parent visited Angelina. Loretta had a brief relationship with another man, an abortion, and some six months before the consultation (i.e. after a 20-month gap), started to visit Angelina regularly with her parents' encouragement. The issue to be decided was whether it was in Angelina's interest to be rehabilitated with her own mother now that she was "ready", mother having divorced Angelina's father who had no wish for further contact. Alternately, should Angelina remain with the foster-parents who wanted her to stay with them? Angelina saw her mother one day a week, and was confused about who was who. Because of the intensity of pressure on the foster parents to support Angelina's return, the grandparents were stopped from seeing her to create some sort of boundary and space for decision making.

VII. THE PROCESS OF INTERVIEWING

A. Initial Contact

To have any opportunity of remaining being seen as separate from the local agencies involved, it was felt that it would be best to ask Loretta and her parents to come and "give their story" and be heard first. Accusations of being influenced by the social workers could then be avoided, and they would see that their "meanings" to the events would be heard before anyone else's.

The surface action of this particular family (Loretta herself was the youngest of three children) became evident. The step-grandfather, a quiet, placating man soon took a back seat, while his wife spoke for her daughter.

Therapist: What do you understand as the purpose of this meeting?

Step-grandfather: [a quietly spoken diplomatic man] We understand we are meeting together to see whether in your view, my daughter, or our daughter, has the ability to know how to cope with Angelina if consideration is given to her return. We would like to satisfy ourselves.

Loretta: [talks slowly and hesitatingly] To get something sorted out—to have her back.

Grandmother: [an awkward, jerky, angular lady with jerky movements and a rapid flow of talk] She wants her daughter, doctor, that's all she's asking for; it's not right, she's been punished for what her husband did, she should have her daughter, it's only right. We've been month after month fighting the case through the courts. There's been a change of personality. Speaking as a mother I worry about my daughter: what you don't learn with one, you learn with the next. I don't care how much book knowledge you have, it takes 20 years to know . . .

As described previously, we are interested not only in the salient events of the family's experience, but the way they have been "digested" by the family, and the web of meanings that these events have for the family, and therefore how the present decision is viewed.

B. The Telling of the Histories

Loretta clearly had little voice of her own, and in getting her to tell her story a good deal of boundary making was necessary. Her loyalty to her own mother's view of events, and the meaning she attributed was such that there was no independent view expressed. Instead of grandparents and a parent, there was a mother, a peripheral father and a child not of 20 but of about 11 years.

C. Loretta's Story

Therapist: How have things got to a position—how long is it, 2 years, since she was in hospital and has not been in your care. How did it come about?

Step-grandfather and grandmother: Do you want us to speak?

Therapist: I think Loretta should speak.

Loretta: When she first went into hospital . . .

Therapist: Could you take us back further.

Loretta: I don't know. He used to be out of work; he hit me around; I became pregnant, didn't know until 5 months, he hit me around, went to hit me in the stomach, threatened to kill her. I had her for 6 weeks. He was in and out of jobs like a yoyo. He hit her, she went into hospital. He went inside. The main thing I could do was get a job to pay bills he owed—gas bills, electricity—I went to work . . .

Therapist: How did you get involved with your ex-husband?

Loretta: I was working as a domestic assistant; he was a patient.

Therapist: How did you all get on at first?

Grandmother: [interrupting] He was the sort of fellow who could hide; a terrible liar. His grandfather told us to be wary, a fine time to tell us: at the wedding. He was spendthrift, exaggerates. I said he seems alright, a good family, all part of growing up.

Loretta: He had no end of jobs. He was telling everyone else what to do; gave him notice.

Therapist: You've learned the hard way . . .

Grandmother: May I interrupt, she was battered about but she tried to hold her marriage together like any wife; no one wants to be a failure. Like my first marriage, I was battered about; I tried to hold it together. Loretta was loyal to him, but according to his doctor he was a psychopath and "they will lock him away" the doctor said. I said "At least that's something . . ."

A shared agreement immediately emerges as the ex-husband as the source of all bad things. Loretta tells her story impassively, briefly, with little feelings, as if the whole thing has been emptied of any meaning except that there was nothing Loretta could do, nor her parents, except blame the "psychopathic" husband.

D. The Grandmother's Story

Therapist: [pulled in by the grandmother] Did you make the same mistake as your daughter?

Grandmother: [introducing a second belief that being in a foster home leads to pain and long-standing damage] I've gone through what the baby went through; I was brought up by somebody—you can ask my husband—I ask myself to this day, "Did my mother love me?" I wonder if it was a case like Angelina's—we didn't call it fostering—there was no such thing as fostering in those days was there doctor? I remembered children telling me and it left a scar.

Therapist: What happened in your marriage?

Grandmother: I was alone for 10½ years.

Therapist: Loretta was 4 when he left you?

Grandmother: No, older than that, about 6.

Therapist: Would she have known, do you remember?

Loretta: No.

Grandmother: She would have been too young.

Therapist: [pursuing] There would have been quite an atmosphere.

Grandmother: No, I reassured them and said "Daddy's gone away". I kept the photo on the dresser; he loved the children.

Therapist: What about before he went?

Grandmother: [jerking furiously] Oh . . . Yes—I would have to—it was dreadful —there was another woman on the scene—it was dreadful—I never blamed him, he was a weak man to go—I always blame the woman—I always do.

Therapist: But it was a pretty violent time.

Grandmother: I had to shield them, send them into the front room, watch the T.V. Daddy's coming back for dinner. He would start—the only vicious time was when he picked up the T.V. and threw it on the floor. That frightened them—it would. Then he threw a boiling cup of tea at me. I said "He's upset—he doesn't know what he's doing . . ."

Therapist: It sounds very distressing.

Grandmother: No, it never upset them, you can check with my doctor. I reassured them every day—the picture was on the dresser until they learnt for themselves when they grew up.

A pattern is thus revealed that despite trying to empty and deny the significance and meaning of very painful life events, rejection and violence still pervade marital choice and child-rearing. At the same time, fostering is seen as damaging, and once violent men are excluded, satisfactory partners (e.g. step-grandfather) are found; "Natural" mothers are seen as the best and return of the "natural" child the only solution.

E. Meeting with Angelina, Foster-parents and Social Worker

The next section of the interview involved bringing in Angelina, her foster-parents, and their social workers so that Angelina's relationships with the adults could be observed, and the relationship of the professionals to the families enacted, rather than just be talked about.

Angelina stayed very close to her foster-mother, facing ourselves and her own family. Loretta offered her sweets, and we saw the familiar pattern of the well-attached 2½-year-old who went to each person in the room but returned back on each occasion to her foster-mother for "re-fuelling". It was clear that her foster-mother was her primary attachment figure. Although she *knew* and recognized her natural mother and grandparents, her response was as to a group of strangers, and her principal attachment figures, primary and alternatives, were all in the foster-family.

The "pattern", surface action, between the adults was clearly one where two powerful women, the foster-mother and grandmother, were battling for control, both disqualifying each other and "triangling" in Loretta to back each other up. The social worker, a man, was locked into the "ineffective" father role together with step-grandfather and foster-father. The therapist similarly found himself inducted into the system and a response he recognized of talking continuously to try and stay out of the system followed, quite ineffectively.

Therapist: How does she get on when she goes with her mother?

Foster-mother: Well, she used to be irate, but they have been getting better. Yesterday was exceptional, she was very good.

Loretta: She played, got a small nursery book and pulled me down with her, sat on my lap, or she's even taken my hand to play in the garden (of children's home) or go up and down the stairs.

Therapist: Her development.

Foster-mother: [taking over] Talks in sentences and answers questions, draws and recognizes things in books.

Therapist: [following] Is she attached to you and your husband?

Foster-mother: I am afraid so.

Therapist: Why do you say "afraid"?

Foster-mother [holding Angelina in front of her] I feel it's natural; I feel for grandmother; I know she doesn't believe me, but she's living with us as a family member. It clashes when her own family wants to be the same. I try, you can ask Loretta, to understand but I am tied by what the (social work) office says. We are fond of her, had her since she was 14½ weeks, but it is very difficult all round, all the situation—it is difficult.

Therapist: [to grandparents and Loretta] It is difficult: you want Angelina to be truly loved. For her sake, you wouldn't want her to be in a place where she's not loved, and yet you want to love her and it is hard to hold . . .

Grandmother: [disqualifying] We've said to Mrs S many a time, she cries for her baby, she cries all the time.

Foster-mother [disqualifying] This is the difficulty. I've told her many times, doctor, she's been desperately upset in the house, and when she's been like this, I've wanted a social worker to see her. The conversation that came up last week—and I hope you'll bear me out, Loretta—was that I have had her since she was tiny and to be honest I would like to keep her, but I said I know I can't; it's not my position to say what happens to the baby. You said —tell me if I am lying—if you couldn't have her home you wouldn't want her moved from me. Is that how the conversation went?

Loretta: Of course I want her home.

Foster-mother: We were talking about placements elsewhere; I could accept her coming home, but not moved to another foster home.

Grandmother: [breaking in and disqualifying] I think a lot of these children who are fostered, doctor, and I'm speaking of experience again, and a lot of them are mixed up mentally.

Therapist: Can I stop you for a minute. Look, Loretta, you are in a difficult position in this room at the minute: you are trying to relate to the person who is mothering your child and your own mother, and it's hard; she's doing a good job. [Loretta sobbing]

Grandmother: So would Loretta if she was given a chance.

Therapist: [trying to make an alliance with Loretta] May I please? [to silence grandmother] The fact is you have a 2-year-old who was injured at 6 weeks and almost died, and she was in your and your husband's care at the time. You would want her to be cared for, and you want to care for her, and you're clearly caught between the messages you hear from the foster home and your own home; wanting to see her grow up well. The chances were high that she could be mentally handicapped; it's a credit to her foster family that she's not. You are all very attached to her as families and with yourselves, and want her to grow up in the right place; the question is now what are Angelina's needs; she's the main person here, what are her interests?

F. Interview between Loretta and Angelina

We had been informed that to help Loretta separate from her mother, she had regularly attended a woman's refuge, worked with the children for some months, and had developed a reasonable degree of competence. So we tested this by seeing them together and giving Loretta the task of playing with Angelina. What we saw was as follows.

Loretta chose to play with the small miniature railway, circular track, engine and trucks. What was striking was seeing Loretta wheel the train around, making the appropriate noises, with Angelina standing by watching. Angelina fingered and touched the table and reached across to touch the train, to which Loretta said "You'll get your finger caught—yes you will", and proceeded to push the train around herself. "Put the animals in there" [the centre of the track] was Loretta's next suggestion. "What about all the others", and again Loretta proceeded to do it herself—"Put it on the table". When Loretta was distracted by us asking her something, Angelina immediately took up the game of putting objects in the centre of the track and showed more capacity for actual play.

A phone bell rang in the distance. Angelina looked sharply around and said quite distinctly to us "I want my mummy". Loretta's immediate response was "Do you want to go to the toilet, do you want to go to wee?" The therapist tried to interject that maybe she was suddenly aware of foster-mother's absence, but Loretta ignored it, felt her nappies and took her to the lavatory saying she was wet.

What we were seeing was two sisters rather than a mother and child, and although Loretta showed more independence alone, she failed to "facilitate" Angelina's play, and played herself. She failed to pick up the cue that Angelina wanted her mother (her foster-mother), but was acting in the inter-subjective belief that the meaning to be given to her behaviour was that, despite absence and separation, she was still part of *their* family and not the foster family.

G. Our Formulation and Advice

We saw this as a situation where Angelina was clearly well attached and was thriving with her foster family, and that her own family was locked into a repetitive pattern of maintaining powerful infantilizing relationships between mothers and daughters by excluding violent men, and so needed to restore Angelina to the family. Thus, they gave no meaning to her real position in the foster-family which we felt needed formalizing through adoption if necessary. However painful, Loretta's family must accept a shared responsibility for events, and to see that Loretta had a future and potential to be a good mother, but not for Angelina who was now part of the foster-family. Despite improvements on mother's part, they risked major disturbance if she was moved, due to disruption of attachments, and there could be a danger of recreation of rejection and even abuse.

We would advise lessening contact drastically and a life book for information to be created, going to court to dispense with family permission for adoption if necessary, maintenance of occasional contact could continue providing the family had worked through the losses and could take a more distant relative role, thus enriching Angelina's extended family network. *Realities* could then be shared rather than perpetuate the myth of Angelina being a "live" part of their family essential to its operation.

H. Feedback Process

We had a series of meetings with family, foster-family and workers to share this view and to start the process of painful working through. The grandmother's response was predictable, to attempt to label and exclude the therapist who, in making the formulation above, inevitably moved out of a meta position to one in which he was aligned with the perceived best interests of the child. He was seen as "violently" attacking Loretta, the family and Angelina, and she threatened to leave coffins outside the hospital, put a curse on him, and wished every evil on him.

The violence of her response led the social work department to say that they were not going to return Angelina but instead of holding on to Angelina's needs for continuity, they said that Loretta was too much enmeshed in her own family, and had not proved her independence, and therefore rehabilitation could not be considered then. Furthermore, they did not take the action to get adoption through dispensation of parental consent, but used the power of the court order, giving the authorities care and control and parental authority to regulate contact which was reduced to fortnightly. Therefore, Angelina remained without a clear unequivocal family to call her own, and there was sufficient contact, despite lowering its frequency, to create a conflict of loyalties. This maintained the confusion for Angelina over subsequent years, and the lack of a truly *clear* message to say that Angelina would *never* be able to return to her family of origin.

With hindsight, it was clear that there was a "denied" yet powerful alliance between the *biological* family and the *senior* management of the social services department. They shared the common meaning that "biological" families are "true" families, and there can never be a true divorce, unless the family agree to it. This is a common inter-subjective meaning and myth.

I. Follow-up

Two and a half years later there was a further consultation requested — Angelina was now 5 years of age and the question was the same: should rehabilitation with the biological family be considered? The statement made about rehabilitation of Angelina not being possible while *Loretta* was living and enmeshed with her own family was taken, as so often, as a challenge. Although the agency meant it as a "never to return", it was heard and acted as a statement of "You'll never do it". Inevitably, the reversal occurred. Loretta married a childhood sweetheart who agreed absolutely with the maternal grandparents; he married into their family.

They had a baby who was cared for beautifully; Angelina stayed for two weekends every month and was skilfully addressing all by their correct titles and in the right place, was becoming very attached to the new baby, and cried when she had to leave. The foster-mother was withdrawing; Angelina was about to start school, and her family felt that surely this was the right time to return to the family. This situation is one that occurs inevitably, and represents a failure to take decisive action earlier, and our failure to see where "change" had to occur for Angelina to gain a "real" family and not be in a limbo. She is now in danger of detaching herself from the family she lives with and live a "fantasy" life with the family she spends weekends with. This can seem to be truly perfect, and can result in an adolescent with no "real" family and literally living in a family in her head. Fortunately, we had a second chance, and so could ensure that the previous work could be brought to a more successful conclusion: e.g. to change the social services policy to ensure that a "real" family is created no matter how painful.

J. Conclusions

Angelina's story reveals many of the issues outlined in the earlier sections of this chapter: the characteristic surface action and depth structure of a complex ecostructure, and the approach to interviewing and assessment of the total system. Also the issues of the individuals, particularly the dependent child who is a member of so many competing and conflicting systems, and the needs for a view on that child's behalf. But this view needs to be meta to the whole system as well as keeping the families in mind. The relationship with the professional system also has to be carefully assessed, and the point of leverage needs to be discovered if the least detrimental form of care is to be found for the child. Then she can have an opportunity to grow up in a family, and yet know who her extended family are, and who she is.

REFERENCES

Bentovim, A. (1979). Child development research findings and psychoanalytic theory: an integrative critique. *In* "The First Year of Life", (D. Shaffer and J. Dunn, eds.), London, Wiley.

Bentovim, A. (1980). "Psychiatric Aspects in Terminating Parental Contact". *In* BAAF discussion series, no. 2.

Bentovim, A. and Gilmour, L. (1981). A family therapy interactional approach to decision making in child care, access and custody cases. *Journal of Family Therapy*, **3**, 65-78.

Goldstein, J., Freud, A. and Solnit, A. J. (1973). "Beyond the Best Interests of the Child", Free Press, New York.

Kinston, W. and Bentovim, A. (1981). Creating a focus for brief marital and family therapy. *In* "Forms of Brief Therapy", (S. H. Budman, ed.), Guildford Press, New York.

Loader, P., Burck, C., Kinston, W. and Bentovim, A. (1981). Method for Organising the Clinical Description of Family Interaction: The Family Interaction Summary Format. *Aust. J. Fam. Ther.*, **2**, 131-141.

Minuchin, S., Montalvo, B., Guerney, B. G., Rosman, B. L. and Schumer, F. (1967). "Families of the Slums", Basic Books, New York.

Minuchin, S. and Fishman, H. C. (1981). "Techniques of Family Therapy", Harvard University Press, Cambridge, Mass.

Palazzoli, M. S., Boscolo, L., Cecchin, G. and Prata, G. (1980). Hypothesising-circularity-neutrality: three guidelines for the conductor of the session. *Family Process*, **19**, 3-12.

Parkes, C. M. (1971). Psychosocial Transitions: A Field of Study. *Soc. Science & Med.*, **5**, 101-115.

Rowe, J., Hundleby, M., Paul, H. and Keane, A. (1980). Long-term fostering and the Children's Act 1975. *Adoption and Fostering*, **102**, 11-16.

Tizard, B. (1977). "Adoption—A Second Chance", Open Books, London.

INDEX*

---

*This index refers to Volumes 1 and 2, and is duplicated in both volumes.

IIi